Acceptance-Based Emotion Regulation Therapy

A Clinician's Guide to
Treating Emotion Dysregulation & Self-Destructive
Behaviors Using an Evidence-Based Therapy
Drawn from ACT & DBT

KIM L. GRATZ, PHD
MATTHEW T. TULL, PHD

CONTEXT PRESS
An Imprint of New Harbinger Publications, Inc.

Publisher's Note

This publication is designed to provide accurate and authoritative information in regard to the subject matter covered. It is sold with the understanding that the publisher is not engaged in rendering psychological, financial, legal, or other professional services. If expert assistance or counseling is needed, the services of a competent professional should be sought.

NEW HARBINGER PUBLICATIONS is a registered trademark of New Harbinger Publications, Inc.

New Harbinger Publications is an employee-owned company.

Copyright © 2025 by Kim L. Gratz and Matthew T. Tull

Context Press
An imprint of New Harbinger Publications, Inc.
5720 Shattuck Avenue
Oakland, CA 94609
www.newharbinger.com

All Rights Reserved

Cover design by Amy Shoup

Acquired by Jennye Garibaldi

Edited by Brady Kahn

Library of Congress Cataloging-in-Publication Data on file

Printed in the United States of America

27 26 25

10 9 8 7 6 5 4 3 2 1   First Printing

"Kim Gratz and Matthew Tull have synthesized over twenty-five years of research, experience, and wisdom into a beautifully written, practical, and indispensable guide to their highly effective and scalable treatment. Grounded in robust evidence, acceptance-based emotion regulation therapy compassionately, systematically, and transdiagnostically addresses emotion regulation challenges. Readers will immerse themselves in key principles for addressing emotion regulation, reducing suffering, and enhancing self-awareness and acceptance across diverse clientele. This comprehensive resource is essential reading for both novice and seasoned clinicians."

—**Alexander L. Chapman, PhD, RPsych**, professor in Simon Fraser University's department of psychology, president of the DBT Centre of Vancouver, and author of *The Borderline Personality Disorder Survival Guide*

"*Acceptance-Based Emotion Regulation Therapy* is a vital addition to the bookshelves of every therapist and therapist-in-training. Gratz and Tull provide clear, conceptually grounded, practical guidance for flexibly addressing emotion regulation difficulties in therapy. Their vast clinical wisdom and expertise is evident throughout as they guide readers in applying this evidence-based approach with nuance, compassion, and sensitivity. I will be using this book regularly in my clinical courses and supervision."

—**Lizabeth Roemer, PhD**, professor of psychology at the University of Massachusetts Boston, and coauthor *Acceptance-Based Behavioral Therapy*

"This work is a practical, empirically supported, step-by-step masterpiece on addressing self-destructive behaviors. It can be easy to cast stones and judgment at those who struggle with behaviors with which we do not, so the authors' empathic, nonjudgmental approach is as refreshing as it is hopeful. I consistently incorporate their recommendations into my therapy sessions with individuals who self-injure. A must-have treatment manual for anyone who treats self-harming behaviors."

—**Nicholas J. Westers, PsyD, ABPP**, clinical psychologist at Children's Health, associate professor at UT Southwestern Medical Center, and host and producer of *The Psychology of Self-Injury* podcast

"Emotional dysregulation underlies a range of mental health challenges, from mood and anxiety disorders to self-destructive behaviors. In this groundbreaking book, leading experts Kim Gratz and Matthew Tull introduce acceptance-based emotion regulation therapy—an evidence-based, acceptance-focused approach designed to help clients tackle this important *transdiagnostic* process. This guide equips clinicians with practical tools to effectively treat emotion regulation difficulties across diverse populations, making it essential for any therapist's bookshelf."

—**Shannon Sauer-Zavala, PhD**, associate professor of psychology at the University of Kentucky, founder of Personality Compass Mental Health, and coauthor of *Unified Protocol for Transdiagnostic Treatment of Emotional Disorders* and *Neuroticism*

"This groundbreaking guide addresses the core challenge of emotion regulation difficulties, offering a flexible, efficient, and highly effective approach to treatment. *Acceptance-Based Emotion Regulation Therapy* is presented in a clear and accessible format, complete with practical tools, scripts, and strategies that clinicians can readily implement. With its precise, digestible guidance, this resource empowers clinicians to deliver a compelling, impactful treatment for a wide range of emotional difficulties."

—**Katherine Dixon-Gordon, PhD**, associate professor at the University of Massachusetts Amherst

"Clinicians using process-based therapies for people with a wide range of clinical presentations will love this book. Grounded in scientific support and useful for clinicians at all levels, this is an anchoring resource and transdiagnostic light that brilliantly illuminates the many different reasons and ways to use mindfulness when treating people with emotion dysregulation."

—**M. Zachary Rosenthal, PhD**, associate professor and director of the Center for Misophonia and Emotion Regulation at Duke University

"This book is an excellent resource for any therapist looking for more tools they can use with their clients to improve emotion regulation. It provides a comprehensive set of practical strategies, organized by key emotion regulation processes and grounded in established research. Written by leading experts in emotion regulation, this book provides a clear, well-structured guide to acceptance-based emotion regulation therapy."

—**Michael E. Levin, PhD**, professor at Utah State University, and author of *Innovations in Acceptance and Commitment Therapy* and *The Oxford Handbook of Acceptance and Commitment Therapy*

"Gratz and Tull's expertise shines in this book. It will be an asset to anyone struggling with large and difficult emotions as well as self-destructive behaviors. The guidance provided is based on the best existing science."

—**Michael P. Twohig**, professor at Utah State University, and coauthor of *The Anxious Perfectionist*

To all of my clients over the years who struggled with self-injury and difficulties regulating emotions, I wish you peace, acceptance, and self-compassion.

—KLG

To the clients who were enrolled in our trials of emotion regulation group therapy. Your strength, courage, and willingness continue to be an inspiration.

—MTT

Contents

Foreword: The Focus and Clarity of Acceptance-Based Emotion Regulation Therapy		vii
Introduction and User's Guide to This Book		1

Part 1: Foundations

Chapter 1	Theoretical and Empirical Basis of This Therapy	8
Chapter 2	Identifying Symptoms and Target Behaviors Driven by Emotion Dysregulation	16
Chapter 3	Assessing Progress and Outcomes in This Therapy	26
Chapter 4	Therapeutic Stance of This Emotion Regulation Therapy	32

Part 2: Interventions

Chapter 5	Identifying the Emotion-Regulating Function of Target Behaviors	46
Chapter 6	Increasing Emotional Acceptance	53
Chapter 7	Increasing Emotional Awareness	66
Chapter 8	Increasing Emotional Clarity and Understanding	81
Chapter 9	Increasing Emotional Willingness	100
Chapter 10	Increasing Emotion Modulation Effectiveness and Flexibility	118
Chapter 11	Increasing Impulse Control	131
Chapter 12	Clarifying Valued Directions in Life	144
Chapter 13	Increasing Valued Actions	164
Chapter 14	Maintaining Treatment Gains and Preventing Relapse	181
	Acknowledgments	189
	References	191
	Index	197

FOREWORD

The Focus and Clarity of Acceptance-Based Emotion Regulation Therapy

Dialectical behavior therapy (DBT) and acceptance and commitment therapy (ACT) have been fellow travelers from the beginning. They are both drawn from behavioral roots, but they have a firm focus on mindfulness processes and learning how to be open to emotion without either wallowing or dysregulation. DBT moves some of the same processes as ACT, accounting for some of its impact (Berking, Neacsiu, Comtois, & Linehan, 2009). There are historical connections as well. Marsha Linehan, the originator of DBT, collaborated with me and my students in the earliest days of our respective work, when we documented the importance of experiential learning over mere "rule-based" change (Rosenfarb, Hayes, & Linehan, 1989).

At the same time, these two methods and models initially evolved with different primary targets. DBT was developed for borderline personality disorder (BPD), and ACT was more focused on the impact of psychological flexibility outside of *DSM* disorders than within them (Hayes & King, 2024). Kim Gratz and her colleagues were the first professionals to build on these two models and methods as a foundation for an approach that precisely targets emotion dysregulation (Gratz & Gunderson, 2006).

The authors of this volume, Kim Gratz and Matthew Tull, have provided a clear and evidence-based framework for how emotion dysregulation and self-destructive behaviors can be efficiently targeted in acceptance-based emotion regulation therapy (ERT). Several randomized controlled trials, reviewed in this volume, show that this ERT is helpful for a variety of clinical presentations in which the transdiagnostic process of emotion dysregulation is central.

A strength of this volume is the sensitivity to the functions of self-destructive behaviors and the many ways that healthy emotional functioning can be facilitated. Particularly in today's era of process-based approaches to therapy in which the focus is shifting from disorder-specific protocols to targeting core processes of change, it is helpful to broaden one's repertoire while maintaining a process-based focus. A person well-trained in ACT will find new ways of increasing emotional awareness, for example, and will acquire additional sensitivity of how best to observe and describe emotional states and their functional role in guiding behavior. A person well-trained in DBT will appreciate the relative efficiency of this ERT, a feature shown in the very first trial (Gratz & Gunderson, 2006). Persons unfamiliar with ACT or DBT may find value in this combination of focus and efficiency that this ERT represents, and they can then extend their repertoire from this foundation.

Another strength of this book is its emphasis on process over technique and its clear writing and clinical sophistication. Gratz and Tull have walked the walk, which shows up in the gentle and nuanced approach the book reveals. In a process-based framework—the goal is not to rigidly adhere to any one set of techniques but rather to focus on the core therapeutic processes that foster meaningful change within a coherent model and meta-model. In this volume, the authors focus on the key processes that are at the heart of effective emotion regulation: emotional acceptance, awareness, clarity, willingness, improving impulse control, and facilitating valued action. In broad terms, these processes are familiar to many forms of intervention, including ACT and DBT, but its clarity of focus has value.

As we move further into the era of process-based therapy, in which the emphasis is on understanding and targeting core psychological processes rather than fitting clients into diagnostic categories, mental health professionals are called to broaden skill sets while seeking theoretical coherence. I think the natural evolution of psychotherapy is to become more integrative and process focused. This not only advances our understanding of how to treat emotion dysregulation, but it also provides a roadmap for the future of psychotherapy, one that is flexible, process-oriented, and deeply compassionate.

—Steven C. Hayes, PhD
Originator of acceptance and commitment therapy (ACT),
and Foundation Professor Emeritus, University of Nevada, Reno

Introduction and User's Guide to This Book

Emotion regulation difficulties are among the most common presenting problems encountered by clinicians. One reason for the ubiquity of emotion regulation difficulties in clinical settings is that problems with emotion regulation underlie numerous psychological difficulties, from psychological disorders like mood, anxiety, trauma-related, substance use, and personality disorders to a variety of health-risk behaviors including self-injury, substance use, and disordered eating behaviors, to name a few. For this reason, most clinicians will treat clients with emotion regulation difficulties throughout their careers, making it even more important that you have the tools you need to effectively treat these difficulties.

This book was designed to assist you with this by providing an evidence-based treatment for improving emotion regulation difficulties and related symptoms and behaviors among a wide range of clients. The treatment reviewed in this book, acceptance-based emotion regulation therapy (referred to from this point forward as ERT for short), was developed by the first author (KLG) in 2004 to target emotion dysregulation directly and efficiently. This treatment was originally developed to treat self-injury among women with borderline personality pathology by directly targeting the primary mechanism theorized to underlie this behavior—emotion regulation difficulties—and was provided in the form of a group therapy, called emotion regulation group therapy (ERGT). The idea behind this treatment was that teaching clients more adaptive (nonavoidant) ways of responding to their emotions would both decrease the need for maladaptive behaviors that function to escape or avoid unwanted emotions (such as self-injury, substance use, or bingeing or purging behaviors, among others) and improve symptoms that are driven by emotion regulation difficulties. For this reason, the primary focus of this treatment is to teach clients more adaptive ways of responding to their emotions by systematically targeting multiple dimensions of emotion dysregulation.

This ERT is an acceptance-based behavioral therapy, which is a form of cognitive behavioral therapy that focuses on the acceptance of internal experiences such as emotions and thoughts, in addition to identifying the functions of problem behaviors and changing ineffective behavioral patterns. As such, it is similar to other acceptance-based behavioral therapies like dialectical behavior therapy (DBT; Linehan, 1993a) and acceptance and commitment therapy (ACT; Hayes, Strosahl, & Wilson, 1999). In fact, this ERT draws heavily from both DBT and ACT, integrating the most relevant skills for improving emotion regulation from each of these treatments to more efficiently and effectively target all emotion regulation difficulties experienced by clients.

Although this treatment was originally developed to treat self-injury among women with borderline personality pathology, research provides support for the efficacy of this therapy in the treatment of emotion dysregulation, psychiatric symptoms, and risky behaviors in general across a number of different client populations. This research will be reviewed in greater detail in chapter 1. What's most important for you to know for now is that the utility of this treatment for emotion dysregulation and related clinical difficulties has been examined in seven separate clinical trials to date (Bjureberg et al., 2017; Bjureberg et al., 2018; Bjureberg et al., 2023; Gratz & Gunderson, 2006; Gratz & Tull, 2011; Gratz, Tull, & Levy, 2014; Sahlin et al., 2017), all of which provide support for the benefits of this emotion regulation therapy across adolescents and adults. That's why we wanted to write a book to teach clinicians how to deliver this treatment effectively: so that more clients can have access to a comprehensive empirically-supported treatment for emotion regulation difficulties.

How This Book Works

This book is organized into two parts. The first part (chapters 1 through 4) presents an overview of and orientation to this treatment, providing you with a solid foundation for learning the specifics of this treatment in the second part of the book. Chapter 1 reviews the conceptual and empirical underpinnings of this ERT, as well as the current empirical support for this treatment. We also discuss the benefits of using an acceptance-based approach to target emotion regulation in therapy. Chapter 2 focuses on the various mental and physical health symptoms and self-destructive behaviors that may be driven by emotion regulation difficulties and, thus, may warrant monitoring in the context of this treatment. In addition to highlighting the numerous clinical difficulties that may be effectively targeted with this treatment, this chapter will teach you how to select the most relevant target behaviors or symptoms for your client to track throughout treatment to monitor their progress. Chapter 3 focuses on the role of assessment in this ERT, including techniques and tools for assessing your client's baseline levels of emotion regulation difficulties and strengths at the onset of treatment, as well as specific measures and forms you can use to assess your client's emotion regulation difficulties, psychological symptoms, and self-destructive behaviors throughout treatment. This chapter also reviews best practices for monitoring treatment progress and outcomes in the context of an evidence-based therapy. Finally, chapter 4 reviews the therapeutic stance that is necessary for the effective delivery of this treatment (consistent with the stance used in DBT and ACT).

The second part of this book (chapters 5 through 14) walks you through specific strategies for targeting emotion regulation within this therapy. The first nine chapters in this section focus on strategies for helping clients learn key emotion regulation skills, including: (1) identifying the emotion-regulating function of self-destructive behaviors; (2) increasing emotional acceptance; (3) increasing emotional awareness; (4) increasing emotional clarity and understanding; (5) increasing emotional willingness; (6) increasing emotion modulation flexibility and effectiveness; (7) increasing impulse control; (8) identifying valued directions; and (9) increasing valued actions, whereas the last chapter focuses on strategies for preventing relapse and maintaining treatment gains following treatment.

Chapter 5 discusses how to help clients identify the functions of their self-destructive behaviors and reviews psychoeducation on the common functions of these behaviors, including emotion regulation. This chapter includes exercises aimed at assisting clients in identifying the ways in which their self-destructive behaviors may function to avoid or escape emotions, as well as clarifying the positive and negative, short- and long-term consequences of these behaviors. One of the primary goals of the strategies described in this chapter is to assist clients in identifying the paradoxical emotional consequences of their self-destructive behaviors; specifically, that although these behaviors may provide relief from emotional distress in the short term, they tend to increase distress in the long term, intensifying the original emotions and resulting in other negative emotions like shame or guilt.

Chapter 6 focuses on strategies for increasing clients' emotional acceptance, including helping them identify their judgments about emotions and providing them with psychoeducation on the function and utility of emotions. In particular, this psychoeducation emphasizes that emotions are evolutionarily adaptive and provide important information about the environment that can be used to guide behavior and inform an adaptive course of action. This chapter also reviews skills for taking a step back from judgments about emotions that may arise, rather than buying into or attaching to these judgments.

Chapter 7 discusses how to help clients increase their emotional awareness by improving their ability to identify, label, and differentiate between emotional states. Specifically, both the in-session and outside-of-session exercises discussed in this chapter assist clients in identifying the cognitive, physical/bodily, and behavioral components of a variety of specific emotional responses, as well as labeling their emotions in the moment. This chapter also discusses how to help clients identify both the information provided by their emotions and effective ways of acting on this information and expressing their emotions (depending on the situation and the information provided by their emotions). Chapter 8 builds on these skills by discussing how to help clients improve their emotional clarity and understanding by learning to distinguish between primary emotions (initial emotional responses to a situation) and secondary emotions (emotional reactions to these primary emotional responses), as well as between clear emotions (emotions that are directly tied to and proportionate to the immediate stimulus/situation) and cloudy emotions (emotions that are not a direct response to the immediate stimulus/situation, but rather influenced by other emotional responses). This chapter also reviews skills for identifying both the information provided by primary and clear emotions and adaptive ways of acting on this information.

Chapter 9 discusses how to help clients increase emotional willingness and decrease emotional unwillingness through both psychoeducation and a series of experiential exercises. The strategies in this chapter help clients learn about the experiential benefits and emotion-regulating consequences of emotional willingness (an active process of being open to emotional experiences as they arise), as well as the ways in which emotional avoidance and unwillingness can paradoxically amplify emotional distress over time. A distinction is drawn between emotional pain (which is a necessary part of life) and emotional suffering (which includes secondary emotions and failed attempts at emotional control/avoidance). Clients also learn that emotional willingness results in less suffering than emotional avoidance, as it prevents the amplification of emotional arousal (despite not necessarily reducing the primary emotional response). Finally, a variety of both in-session and outside-of-session exercises discussed in this chapter help clients actively monitor and assess the different experiential consequences of emotional willingness versus emotional unwillingness.

Chapter 10 focuses on how to teach clients healthy, nonavoidant strategies that may be used to modulate the intensity and/or duration of their emotions (with a distinction drawn between distraction and avoidance). This chapter includes exercises aimed at assisting clients in identifying a variety of adaptive emotion modulation strategies they can use, as well as the contexts in which these strategies are most likely to be effective. The goal is to help clients match different emotion-modulation strategies to different contexts, identifying the strategies that may be most helpful for different emotions, at different times of the day and night, when alone versus with others, and when at home or not. Chapter 11 focuses on how to help clients improve their ability to control impulsive behaviors when distressed by using four basic behavioral impulse control strategies: distraction/delay; behavioral substitution (i.e., replacing the impulsive behavior with a more effective and less harmful behavior that serves the same function as the impulsive behavior); increasing awareness of the negative consequences of impulsive behaviors; and consequence modification (i.e., having clients reward themselves for resisting urges to engage in these behaviors and remove the positive consequences typically associated with these behaviors). The in-session handouts included in this chapter provide clients with information on all four of these skills and the outside-of-session exercises give clients the opportunity to practice these skills when they experience urges to engage in impulsive behaviors.

Chapters 12 and 13 focus on strategies for helping clients identify and clarify valued directions (those things in life that matter or are meaningful to the individual) and engage in actions consistent with these directions. An emphasis is placed on moment-to-moment choices in everyday living and on process rather than outcome. Specifically, these strategies help clients learn that valued directions require a present-moment focus and are distinguished from goals, which are future-oriented, static outcomes. These chapters also review how to assist clients in identifying a variety of concrete actions that are consistent with their valued directions and can be performed immediately in the moment. For example, a client who values learning would be encouraged to identify and engage in a variety of different actions consistent with the valued direction of learning, such as going to the library and reading a book of interest, researching things of interest on the internet, or joining a group for people with similar interests. Chapter 13 also reviews strategies for helping clients overcome both internal and external barriers to valued actions, with an emphasis on emotional willingness, problem solving, and commitment.

Finally, chapter 14 focuses on strategies for helping clients maintain treatment gains and prevent relapse, including approaching the clarification of valued directions and commitment to valued actions as a lifelong process, focusing on the process versus outcome, planning ahead for how to cope with high-risk situations, and introducing clients to the concept of the rule violation effect and differences between a lapse and a relapse.

Each of the chapters in part 2 of this book provides detailed information on effective strategies for teaching clients the respective skills, reviewing both key concepts and specific techniques for introducing these skills to clients. Many of these chapters also include discussion of common sticking points or challenges that can arise when teaching clients these skills, as well as tips for addressing these and teaching the skills in a treatment-consistent manner. Finally, handouts for psychoeducation and both in-session and outside-of-session exercises are included in each of the chapters and are available for download at http://www.newharbinger.com/53622.

Indeed, as a behavior therapy, this treatment consists primarily of skills training and instruction, psychoeducation, and both in-session and outside-of-session exercises. The importance of skill generalization and daily practice is emphasized, and regular outside-of-session practice exercises and monitoring are considered essential to treatment success. Throughout the treatment, clients are asked to complete daily monitoring forms on the emotional precipitants of their urges to engage in self-destructive behaviors, as well as the consequences of their behavioral choice (among other factors). All versions of these self-destructive behaviors monitoring forms are available for download at http://www.newharbinger.com/53622. Additional daily monitoring forms are tailored to the particular session content, and include identifying emotions and the information provided by these emotions, distinguishing between primary and secondary emotions, identifying the consequences of emotional unwillingness versus willingness, and engaging in actions consistent with valued directions, among others. All of these session-specific monitoring forms can be found at the end of the corresponding chapter and are available for download at http://www.newharbinger.com/53622.

Moving Forward

We hope that this book will give you the skills you need to effectively target emotion regulation difficulties in your work with clients. The therapy described in this book has been scientifically evaluated in multiple studies and found to be effective in improving client emotion regulation. We expect that the resources presented here will be helpful in your work with clients who struggle with emotion regulation difficulties and provide the tools you need to assist clients in learning valuable emotion regulation skills.

As you begin to delve into the material presented here, we wanted to note that although this treatment was designed to progress as outlined here, with certain foundational emotion regulation skills taught in the earlier weeks of this treatment and other skills building on material covered previously in the treatment, it is also possible to present some of the skills selectively to individual clients, depending on their needs. For example, if you are working with someone who is experiencing difficulties in only certain domains of emotion regulation, or who has some emotion regulation skills but could benefit from learning new skills in other areas, the skills in each chapter can be presented individually as stand-alone skills, and the treatment can be customized to meet the needs of that client.

Foundations

Part 1

CHAPTER 1

Theoretical and Empirical Basis of This Therapy

As we mentioned in the introduction, this treatment was originally developed to treat self-injury among women with borderline personality pathology by directly targeting both self-injury and its proposed underlying mechanism of emotion dysregulation. Specifically, based on the theory that self-injury stems from emotion dysregulation (Gratz, 2003; 2007), this ERT was developed with the expectation that teaching self-injuring women more adaptive ways of responding to and regulating their emotions would reduce the frequency of their self-injury.

Theoretical Basis of This ERT

The first step in developing this therapy was to define *emotion dysregulation*, as it was only by determining a precise definition of emotion dysregulation and what it does and does not encompass that we could target it efficiently and effectively in treatment. At the time this treatment was developed, there were several conceptualizations of emotion regulation in the literature that varied in both their understanding of the role of emotions in functioning and their approach to emotion regulation. One of the main differences between these conceptualizations of emotion regulation was how emotions, particularly negative emotions, were viewed. Whereas some conceptualizations viewed emotions as potentially disruptive to the pursuit of goals and in need of control or modification, others focused on the functionality of all emotions and their utility in guiding behaviors and valued actions.

As you can probably imagine, these differences in how emotions were viewed had a direct impact on how emotion regulation was conceptualized and what the goal of emotion regulation was thought to be. Specifically, when emotions were viewed as potentially disruptive and in need of control, conceptualizations of emotion regulation emphasized the down-regulation of negative emotions, reduction of negative emotional arousal, and modification of the experience or expression of emotions in some way. Conversely, when emotions were viewed as functional and adaptive, corresponding conceptualizations of emotion regulation focused on adaptive ways of responding to emotions that facilitate the functional use of emotions as information to guide behavior.

Given evidence that many self-destructive behaviors function to avoid or escape emotional distress (Chapman, Gratz, & Brown, 2006; Garke et al., 2021; Prefit, Candea, & Szentagotai-Tătar, 2019), as well as extensive literature indicating that efforts to control, suppress, or avoid emotions may have paradoxical consequences, increasing the frequency and severity of those emotions (Hayes, Luoma, Bond, Masuda, & Lillis, 2006; Salters-Pedneault, Tull, & Roemer, 2004), we questioned the clinical utility of conceptualizations of emotion regulation that emphasized the control or reduction of negative emotions. These approaches seemed to confound processes that undermine effective emotion regulation with those that promote adaptive emotion regulation (potentially interfering with effective treatment or even having iatrogenic effects). Instead, we decided that approaches to emotion regulation that emphasized the functionality of emotions and problems associated with deficits in the capacity to experience the full range of emotions would be most clinically useful and helpful in guiding treatment development.

Therefore, we decided to ground this treatment in one particular acceptance-based model of emotion regulation developed by the first author (KLG). This model conceptualizes emotion regulation as adaptive ways of responding to emotions (regardless of their valence, intensity, or reactivity), including the understanding, acceptance, and effective use and modulation of emotions (Gratz & Roemer, 2004; Gratz & Tull, 2022). According to this model, adaptive responses to emotions are those that facilitate both the functional use of emotions as information and the pursuit of valued actions, whereas maladaptive responses are those that interfere with accessing, using, or learning from the information provided by emotions. As such, acceptance and understanding of emotions are considered foundational emotion regulation abilities that are necessary for adaptive emotion regulation. Moreover, although the effective modulation of emotions is considered one aspect of adaptive emotion regulation within this model, it is not necessary for adaptive regulation to occur; instead, identifying and labeling emotions and being willing to experience emotions are theorized to be regulating in their own right. Likewise, although specific modulation strategies are not considered inherently adaptive or maladaptive within this model (as the effectiveness of any strategy can only be evaluated in the context of the individual's goals and situational demands), strategies that facilitate access to the information provided by emotions and application of that information in a functional way are considered more adaptive than strategies that interfere with understanding emotions and the information they provide.

Specifically, this ERT was developed to systematically target each of the dimensions of emotion regulation identified in Gratz and Roemer (2004)'s multi-dimensional conceptualization of emotion regulation, including the awareness, understanding, and acceptance of emotions; the ability to control impulsive behaviors and engage in goal-directed behaviors when experiencing negative emotions; the flexible use of nonavoidant, situationally appropriate strategies to modulate the intensity and duration of emotional responses in order to meet individual goals and situational demands; and the willingness to experience negative emotions in the pursuit of desired goals and meaningful activities in life. Given its grounding in an acceptance-based model of emotion regulation and its emphasis on emotional acceptance, this treatment draws heavily from both DBT (Linehan, 1993a) and ACT (Hayes et al., 1999), and emphasizes the following themes: (1) the potentially paradoxical effects of emotional avoidance; (2) the emotion-regulating consequences of emotional acceptance and willingness; and (3) the importance of controlling behaviors when emotions are present rather than controlling emotions themselves.

It is also important to note that the focus of this ERT is not on changing the nature or quality of a client's emotions but on changing a client's relationship to their emotions. In other words, the goal of this therapy is not to decrease or otherwise change a client's emotional intensity or sensitivity. These are considered aspects of a client's temperament that are both less amenable to change and also less in need of change (as they are not problematic in and of themselves). Instead, this treatment focuses on helping clients respond more adaptively to their emotions when they arise, regardless of their intensity or reactivity.

Empirically-Supported Versions of This ERT

Since this therapy was first developed to treat self-injury among adult women with borderline personality pathology in a group format, it has been delivered as an individual therapy to numerous adult clients (men and women) and adapted to be an individual therapy for adolescents (which has been examined in both a traditional face-to-face format and as an online treatment). Thus, this ERT can be offered to clients as both a group therapy and an individual therapy, depending on their needs.

The group therapy version of this ERT is a fourteen-session treatment, with two sessions each allocated to teaching clients skills for improving emotional awareness (chapter 7 of this book), increasing emotional clarity and understanding (chapter 8), increasing emotional willingness (chapter 9), identifying and clarifying valued directions (chapter 12), and increasing valued actions (chapter 13). Thus, we recommend dedicating at least two weeks to each of these particular skills when providing this therapy to adults in either a group or individual format. The material covered in these chapters is sufficiently comprehensive to require multiple sessions to ensure sufficient understanding and integration of the skills. Table 1.1 outlines the specific content of this group therapy across the fourteen sessions, as well as the chapters in which the content of each of these sessions is reviewed.

The individual therapy version of this ERT for adolescents was originally examined as a twelve-session face-to-face treatment that included a final session on relapse prevention. It was shortened from the original fourteen-session group therapy format to ensure that it could be provided to adolescents over the course of a single school semester. In order to add the session on relapse prevention at the end of the treatment and reduce the therapy to twelve sessions in total, the two sessions focused on increasing emotional clarity and understanding were combined into one session and the four sessions focused on clarifying valued directions and increasing valued actions were reduced to two sessions. Other adaptations to the original version of this ERT included simplifying the homework sheets and incorporating a youth-friendly design and format and age-appropriate examples. Finally, in an effort to increase access to this therapy among adolescents, the individual therapy version of this ERT has also been adapted to be offered as a twelve-week internet-delivered treatment.

TABLE 1.1. Content of the Fourteen-Session Group Therapy Version of This Emotion Regulation Therapy

Session 1	Identifying the function of self-destructive behaviors (chapter 5)
Session 2	Increasing emotional acceptance (chapter 6)
Sessions 3-4	Increasing emotional awareness (chapter 7)
Session 5	Increasing emotional clarity and understanding (part 1): primary versus secondary emotions (chapter 8)
Session 6	Increasing emotional clarity and understanding (part 2): clear versus cloudy emotions (chapter 8)
Sessions 7-8	Increasing emotional willingness (chapter 9)
Session 9	Increasing emotion modulation flexibility and effectiveness (chapter 10)
Session 10	Increasing impulse control (chapter 11)
Session 11	Identifying valued directions in life (chapter 12)
Session 12	Clarifying valued directions and identifying valued actions (chapters 12 and 13)
Sessions 13	Increasing valued actions (identifying and overcoming barriers to valued actions) (chapter 13)
Session 14	Increasing valued actions (committing to valued actions) (chapter 13)

Empirical Support for This ERT

Treatment Outcomes

To date, seven separate clinical trials have provided support for the utility of this ERT among adults and adolescents. Four of these studies examined the original group version of this treatment among adult women with borderline personality pathology, including two open trials (Gratz & Tull, 2011; Sahlin et al., 2017) and two randomized controlled trials (RCTs; Gratz & Gunderson, 2006; Gratz, Tull, & Levy, 2014). The first, a small RCT, found that the addition of this ERT to participants' ongoing outpatient therapy had positive effects on self-injury, emotion dysregulation, experiential avoidance, borderline personality disorder (BPD) symptoms, and symptoms of depression, anxiety, and stress (Gratz & Gunderson, 2006). Moreover, participants who received this ERT evidenced significant changes over time on all outcome measures and reached normative levels of functioning on most. The second, an open trial examining the utility of this ERT within a more diverse and underserved setting, found significant improvements from pre- to post-treatment in self-injury and other self-destructive behaviors, emotion dysregulation, experiential avoidance, BPD, depression, anxiety, and stress symptoms, and social and vocational impairment (Gratz & Tull, 2011).

The third, a larger RCT and uncontrolled nine-month follow-up, provided further evidence for the efficacy of this ERT (relative to a treatment-as-usual only waitlist condition), revealing positive effects of this treatment on self-injury and other self-destructive behaviors (including substance abuse, disordered eating behaviors, risky sexual behavior, and suicidal behaviors), emotion dysregulation, BPD symptoms, depression and stress symptoms, and overall quality of life within a conservative intent-to-treat sample (Gratz, Tull, & Levy, 2014). Moreover, findings from the nine-month follow-up period provide preliminary support for the durability of treatment gains, as all improvements observed from pre- to post-treatment were maintained or further improved upon at follow-up, including additional significant improvements from post-treatment through nine-month follow-up for self-injury, emotion dysregulation, experiential avoidance, BPD symptoms, and quality of life (Gratz, Tull, & Levy, 2014). Finally, the most recent study of the group version of this ERT, a nationwide, multi-center, open trial of the utility of this treatment in routine clinical care in Sweden, revealed significant improvements from pre- to post-treatment in self-injury and other self-destructive behaviors, emotion dysregulation, and depression and stress symptoms (Sahlin et al., 2017). Moreover, these improvements were maintained or further improved upon at six-month follow-up (Sahlin et al., 2017).

The next three studies focused on the individual therapy version of this ERT for adolescents with self-injury. The first of these was an open trial of the face-to-face version of this treatment among adolescent girls with nonsuicidal self-injury disorder (Bjureberg et al., 2017). Consistent with the findings for the group therapy version of this ERT, results of this study provided support for the feasibility, acceptability, and utility of this therapy in the treatment of emotion dysregulation, self-injury, and other self-destructive behaviors among adolescents (Bjureberg et al., 2017). Specifically, this study found significant improvements in self-injury, emotion dysregulation, self-destructive behaviors, and global functioning from pre- to post-treatment. Moreover, all of these improvements were either maintained or further improved upon at six-month follow-up (Bjureberg et al., 2017).

The second of these studies was an open trial of the internet-delivered version of this individual ERT for adolescents with nonsuicidal self-injury disorder (Bjureberg et al., 2018). This study produced comparable results to the study examining the face-to-face version of this treatment, providing initial support for the utility of the online version. Specifically, this study found significant improvements from pre- to post-treatment in self-injury, emotion dysregulation, experiential avoidance, and global functioning (Bjureberg et al., 2018). Moreover, all of these improvements were either maintained or further improved upon at three- and six-month follow-ups (Bjureberg et al., 2018). Finally, the most recent study of the individual therapy version of this ERT was a large RCT of the online version of this treatment among adolescents with nonsuicidal self-injury disorder (Bjureberg et al., 2023). This study provided support for the efficacy of this individual ERT (relative to a treatment-as-usual only condition), revealing positive effects of this treatment on self-injury and other self-destructive behaviors, emotion dysregulation, and global functioning within a conservative intent-to-treat sample (Bjureberg et al., 2023). Once again, all of these treatment effects were maintained at the three-month follow-up (Bjureberg et al., 2023).

Mechanism of Change

As we described previously, this ERT was developed specifically to target the transdiagnostic mechanism of emotion dysregulation (as targeting the underlying mechanism of symptoms and behaviors is considered the most efficient and effective way of treating those difficulties). In particular, we expected that teaching clients more adaptive ways of responding to and regulating their emotions would reduce any symptoms or behaviors stemming from emotion dysregulation. In this way, emotion regulation is considered the mechanism of change in this therapy—that is, the process through which this therapy works and how it results in positive outcomes. Although findings that this therapy consistently leads to improvements in emotion regulation for clients provide suggestive support that this treatment may be working as we had expected, it is important that the role of emotion regulation as the mechanism of change in this ERT be examined empirically to ensure that it is the improvements in emotion regulation over the course of this treatment that account for the observed improvements in psychiatric symptoms and self-destructive behaviors.

Importantly, five different studies have provided support for emotion regulation as a mechanism of change in this therapy (Bjureberg et al., 2017; Bjureberg et al., 2018; Bjureberg et al., 2023; Gratz, Levy, & Tull, 2012; Gratz, Bardeen, Levy, Dixon-Gordon, & Tull, 2015). Specifically, across both the initial RCT and open trial samples of the group version of this treatment, changes in overall emotion dysregulation over the course of this ERT were found to mediate, or explain, the observed reductions in self-injury from pre- to post-treatment (Gratz et al., 2012). Additionally, findings from the most recent RCT of the group version of this treatment revealed that improvements in overall emotion dysregulation over the course of treatment mediated the observed reductions in BPD cognitive and affective symptoms during treatment and predicted further improvements in self-injury during the nine-month follow-up (Gratz et al., 2015).

Finally, all three studies examining the individual therapy version of this ERT among adolescents with self-injury provide further support for emotion regulation as a mechanism of change in this ERT, finding that changes in emotion dysregulation mediated improvements in self-injury over the course of both the face-to-face and online versions of this individual ERT (Bjureberg et al., 2017; Bjureberg et al., 2018; Bjureberg et al., 2023). Specifically, the open trial of the face-to-face version of this treatment revealed a significant indirect relation of time in treatment to improvements in self-injury through improvements in emotion dysregulation, suggesting that improvements in emotion regulation over the course of the treatment account for the observed improvements in self-injury (Bjureberg et al., 2017). Likewise, the open trial of the online version of this treatment revealed that improvements in emotion regulation over the course of this treatment mediated improvements in both self-injury and other self-destructive behaviors during treatment (Bjureberg et al., 2018). Finally, results of the RCT of the online version of this treatment revealed that week-to-week improvements in emotion dysregulation mediated week-to-week reductions in self-injury throughout the course of this treatment (Bjureberg et al., 2023).

Predictors of Treatment Response

Two studies have also examined client characteristics that may predict response to this ERT to see if this treatment is more helpful for certain clients than others. The results of these studies provide support for the utility of this therapy for emotion dysregulation across a wide range of clients with varying diagnoses and therapy experiences, revealing few significant predictors of treatment response to the group therapy version of this ERT (Gratz, Dixon-Gordon, & Tull, 2014; Sahlin et al., 2019). Of particular importance, both studies revealed minimal impact of client demographics or characteristics of their ongoing therapy in the community on treatment response to this ERT (Gratz, Dixon-Gordon, & Tull, 2014; Sahlin et al., 2019).

Using This ERT Flexibly in Treatment

As we mentioned previously, although this therapy was developed to target multiple dimensions of emotion regulation systematically, progressing from more foundational emotion regulation skills to more advanced or nuanced skills that build off of the previous skills clients have learned, it is also possible to select only those skills most relevant to the client you're treating, in order to personalize and streamline the treatment. That said, we do recommend ensuring that clients have the foundational skills they need to effectively understand and practice the skills covered in later chapters in this book, to ensure that the treatment is as effective as possible. This is particularly relevant to certain skills that require specific prerequisite skills or training to be practiced most effectively.

For example, we have found that an initial focus on emotional acceptance facilitates client willingness to experience, reflect on, and label their emotions and, thus, is imperative for much of the work done later in the treatment. Likewise, before clients can work on improving their emotional clarity, they need fundamental emotional awareness skills to facilitate getting in touch with and labeling their basic emotions. In addition, we have found it incredibly important for clients to have a solid foundation in and firm understanding of emotional acceptance and willingness before moving into teaching them skills for modulating their emotions and distinguishing between distraction and avoidance modulation strategies. If clients do not have sufficient experience with emotional acceptance and willingness, it is easy for them to use distraction strategies to avoid emotions, decreasing the effectiveness of these strategies and interfering with the development of more adaptive emotion regulation strategies. Finally, it isn't possible for clients to work on increasing valued actions until they have identified at least some valued directions that are meaningful to them.

Thus, if you are interested in using only select skills from this book with certain clients, we strongly recommend conducting a thorough assessment of your client's current emotion regulation abilities to ensure that they have the foundational emotion regulation skills necessary to learn the skills you are interested in teaching them. One way to do this is to have your client complete the Difficulties in Emotion Regulation Scale (DERS; Gratz & Roemer, 2004), a thirty-six item self-report measure of emotion regulation difficulties that was developed specifically to assess the acceptance-based model of emotion regulation in which this ERT is grounded. We will provide more information on this measure and how to use it in chapter 3. For now, we just want you to know that this measure assesses all of the specific aspects of emotion dysregulation targeted in this treatment and, thus, can provide a helpful tool for assessing your client's baseline emotion regulation abilities and difficulties and informing treatment planning.

As we've discussed, it is also possible to use this therapy as both an individual and a group therapy, depending on the needs of your clients and the nature of your practice. If you choose to provide this treatment in the form of a group therapy, we would recommend using the fourteen-session format described above. This format has been found to improve emotion regulation and related difficulties effectively, and yet is a brief and targeted treatment that allows clients to make gains in a relatively short period of time. It is also the format that has been found to be helpful across a wide range of clients with varying characteristics and levels of severity.

If you choose to provide this ERT as an individual therapy (which we expect will often be the case), then you have a bit more flexibility in terms of the duration of the treatment and how many sessions you spend on each skill. Indeed, the benefit of offering this ERT as an individual therapy is that it allows you to customize the treatment to meet the unique needs of your particular client. For example, if your client already has some basic emotional awareness skills, they may not need to spend two sessions learning those skills. Likewise, if a client resonates with the idea of valued directions or has previous experience with ACT, they may be able to learn the skills covered in chapter 12 in one session versus two. Conversely, if a client is struggling with emotional acceptance and having a difficult time taking a step back from their judgments about emotions, or presents to treatment with multiple impulsive self-destructive behaviors, they may benefit from some additional time covering the skills in chapters 6 or 11, respectively. Although we do recommend adhering to the original intention of this treatment, which was to treat emotion regulation difficulties in a targeted and efficient way, the flexibility accorded when providing this ERT as an individual therapy to clients allows for tailoring of this treatment and the time spent on each skill to the individual needs of your client.

CHAPTER 2

Identifying Symptoms and Target Behaviors Driven by Emotion Dysregulation

Over the past three decades, the field of psychology has seen tremendous growth in research on both emotion regulation in general and its specific influence on diverse symptom presentations and behaviors. This research has provided strong evidence that emotion regulation difficulties are a transdiagnostic mechanism underlying multiple maladaptive behaviors and diverse forms of psychopathology (Sloan et al., 2017). In other words, although specific maladaptive behaviors (such as self-injury, substance misuse, or disordered eating) and psychiatric disorders may look very different on the surface (involving a different constellation of symptoms or pattern of behaviors), they may be functionally similar in that they are driven by the same underlying difficulties in emotion regulation.

The identification of transdiagnostic mechanisms underlying diverse forms of psychopathology, such as emotion regulation difficulties, has immense clinical benefits, paving the way for the development and use of more efficient and targeted interventions that can treat multiple co-occurring difficulties simultaneously. This is a particularly important advancement in the treatment of psychopathology, given just how common it is for various psychological disorders and self-destructive behaviors to co-occur (Buckholdt et al., 2015; Kessler, Chiu, Demler, & Walters, 2005). Specifically, having access to a single treatment that targets a shared underlying cause of many of the difficulties clients experience is far more efficient and effective than having to treat each of their difficulties separately with disorder- or behavior-specific treatments.

This chapter provides an overview of the research on the role of emotion regulation difficulties in the development and maintenance of numerous clinical difficulties, including both mental and physical health problems. The goal of this chapter is to highlight the various clinical difficulties that may be effectively treated with this ERT, as well as the specific client behaviors or symptoms that may be helpful to monitor over the course of this treatment.

Self-Destructive and Other Maladaptive Behaviors

Research has shown that many self-destructive and maladaptive behaviors (including all of the behaviors listed in table 2.1) are motivated by the desire to obtain relief from emotional pain and function to avoid, escape, or control unwanted emotions (Weiss, Sullivan, & Tull, 2015). These behaviors can provide powerful (albeit temporary) relief from emotional distress by distracting attention away from painful emotions, releasing emotional tension, expressing emotions, externalizing or concretizing emotional pain, or, in the case of some behaviors like substance use or risky sexual behavior, generating positive emotions that can counter an unpleasant emotional state.

Studies have shown that people who engage in the maladaptive behaviors listed in table 2.1 are more likely than those who don't engage in these behaviors to report a variety of emotion regulation difficulties, including difficulties distinguishing between emotional states, controlling impulsive behaviors when distressed, engaging in goal-directed behaviors when distressed, accepting their emotions, and modulating their emotions effectively (Brockmeyer et al., 2014; Garke et al., 2021; Garofalo, Velotti, & Zavattini, 2018; Gratz & Tull, 2010; Messman-Moore et al., 2010). Research has also found that people are more likely to rely on these behaviors when they don't have confidence in their ability to modulate their emotions (Spitzen, Tull, & Gratz, 2022), when they struggle with tolerating intense emotional states (Akbari, Seydavi, Hosseini, Krafft, & Levin, 2022), or when they are unwilling to experience emotions (Chapman et al., 2006).

TABLE 2.1. Self-Destructive and Maladaptive Behaviors Driven by Emotion Regulation Difficulties

The following behaviors are associated with emotion regulation difficulties:

- Nonsuicidal self-injury (Gratz & Tull, 2010)
- Suicidal behaviors (Law, Khazem, & Anestis, 2015)
- Substance use (Garke et al., 2021)
- Disordered eating behaviors, including bingeing, purging, and restricting behaviors (Brockmeyer et al., 2014)
- Risky sexual behavior (Messman-Moore, Walsh, & DiLillo, 2010)
- Pathological gambling (Williams, Grisham, Erskine, & Cassedy, 2012)
- Problematic smartphone and internet use (Gioia, Rega, & Boursier, 2021; Squires, Hollett, Hesson, & Harris, 2021)
- Illegal behaviors, such as theft (Moore, Clemens, Gratz, & Tull, 2022)
- Aggressive behaviors (Garofalo & Velotti, 2017)

Borderline Personality Disorder

At its core, borderline personality disorder is considered a disorder of emotion regulation. Specifically, emotion regulation difficulties are theorized to underlie the development and maintenance of this disorder, as well as many of the most concerning symptoms and maladaptive behaviors associated with this disorder (Gratz, Moore, & Tull, 2016; Linehan, 1993a). For example, there is extensive research showing a strong association between borderline personality disorder and numerous emotion regulation difficulties, including difficulties identifying and understanding emotions, controlling impulsive behaviors and engaging in goal-directed behaviors when distressed, accepting emotions, and accessing effective emotion regulation strategies (Gratz et al., 2016). Difficulties in emotion regulation have also been linked to many of the emotional, interpersonal, cognitive, and behavioral difficulties observed among people with borderline personality disorder (Gratz et al., 2016), including rapid shifts in emotional states, relationship difficulties, impulsive behaviors, and identity problems (Stepp et al., 2014). Indeed, it is because emotion regulation difficulties play such a key role in borderline personality disorder and its associated difficulties that the original version of this ERT was developed specifically for clients with borderline personality pathology.

Anxiety Disorders

People with anxiety disorders tend to react negatively to experiences of anxiety and fear and engage in behaviors to escape or avoid those experiences. For this reason, it is probably not surprising that studies have shown that emotion regulation difficulties play a key role in the development and maintenance of a variety of anxiety disorders (Cisler & Olatunji, 2012).

Generalized Anxiety Disorder

Studies show that people with generalized anxiety disorder are more likely than those without this disorder to view their emotions as aversive and experience difficulties with emotional willingness and understanding—all of which increase their reliance on worry to avoid their emotions (Mennin, Heimberg, Turk, & Fresco, 2002; Roemer, Salters, Raffa, & Orsillo, 2005). Indeed, people with generalized anxiety disorder report using worry to distract themselves from more emotionally upsetting events or experiences (Borkovec & Roemer, 1995). The problem with this, though, is that these efforts to avoid emotions through worry paradoxically increase the frequency and intensity of those emotions, fueling an even greater reliance on worry and contributing to a vicious cycle of emotional unwillingness, worry, increased distress, increased worry, and so on (Mennin et al., 2002).

Panic Disorder

Studies show that people who experience panic attacks have greater difficulties understanding their emotions and are both less willing to experience emotions and less accepting of their emotions than people who don't experience panic attacks (Tull & Roemer, 2007). Notably, this nonacceptance and avoidance of emotions has been found to apply to both negative and positive emotions (Tull, Rodman, & Roemer, 2008), presumably because the physical sensations associated with some positive emotions (e.g., excitement, joy) are the same as those associated with fear and anxiety (i.e., increases in arousal and heart rate) and, thus, feared by individuals with panic attacks due to their associations with impending panic (Chambless & Gracely, 1989).

Social Anxiety Disorder

People with social anxiety disorder have also been found to experience broad difficulties in emotion regulation (Helbig-Lang, Rusch, & Lincoln, 2015), primarily driven by negative beliefs about emotions that prompt the avoidance and control of emotions (Goodman, Kashdan, & İmamoğlu, 2021). For example, research has found that people with social anxiety disorder tend to endorse beliefs that emotions are a sign of weakness and need to be controlled, and that expressing emotions is not appropriate in social situations and may lead to rejection (Goodman et al., 2021). This, in turn, is expected to result in ineffective attempts to directly control and avoid emotions (Kashdan et al., 2014), paradoxically increasing emotional distress and contributing to further difficulties accessing and understanding emotions (Vine & Aldao, 2014).

Obsessive-Compulsive Disorder

Finally, people with obsessive-compulsive disorder have also been found to exhibit a number of emotion regulation difficulties, including difficulties identifying, understanding, and accepting emotions, difficulties engaging in goal-directed behaviors and controlling impulsive behaviors when distressed, and difficulties accessing effective emotion regulation strategies (Fergus & Bardeen, 2014). Moreover, difficulties with emotion regulation can increase reliance on compulsive behaviors in an attempt to avoid, control, or escape emotions perceived as unpleasant (Stern, Nota, Heimberg, Holaway, & Coles, 2014).

Mood Disorders

Similar to the anxiety disorders, research has found that people with mood disorders experience extensive emotion regulation difficulties.

Major Depressive Disorder

Both depressive symptoms and major depressive disorder per se are associated with emotion regulation difficulties targeted directly within this ERT, including difficulties identifying, understanding, and accepting emotions, accessing and applying effective emotion regulation strategies, and engaging in goal-directed behaviors when distressed (Brockmeyer et al., 2012; Tull & Gratz, 2008). There is also support for the role of specific emotion regulation strategies in the onset and maintenance of major depressive disorder. Specifically, whereas the use of adaptive emotion regulation strategies is theorized to prevent or attenuate depressive states, the use of maladaptive strategies (common among people with major depression) is thought to exacerbate depressive symptoms (Aldao, Nolen-Hoeksema, & Schweizer, 2010). In particular, longitudinal studies have found that rumination, one of the most common emotion regulation strategies among individuals with major depression, predicts both the development of depression (Abela & Hankin, 2011) and increases in depression over a year (Arnarson et al., 2016).

Bipolar Disorder

Individuals with bipolar disorder also report difficulties with emotion regulation. For example, Miola and colleagues (2022) found that, compared to people without bipolar disorder, individuals with bipolar disorder report greater difficulties controlling impulsive behaviors and engaging in goal-directed behaviors when distressed, accessing effective emotion regulation strategies, accepting their emotions, and distinguishing between emotional states. Researchers have also suggested that the extreme fluctuation between positive and negative emotional states seen among individuals with bipolar disorder may tax their ability to regulate their emotions, leading to inflexible or otherwise ineffective attempts to regulate emotions (Dodd, Lockwood, Mansell, & Palmier-Claus, 2019).

Posttraumatic Stress Disorder

Posttraumatic stress disorder is associated with a number of intense, painful, and often overwhelming emotions, including fear, anxiety, shame, guilt, and sadness, as well as extreme fluctuations in emotions (Horowitz, 1986). For these reasons, it can be incredibly difficult for people with posttraumatic stress disorder to understand, tolerate, and regulate their emotions, resulting in chronic efforts to escape or avoid these emotions. Indeed, studies of emotion regulation difficulties in posttraumatic stress disorder have consistently found that people with posttraumatic stress disorder have difficulties distinguishing between emotional states, controlling impulsive behaviors and engaging in goal-directed behaviors when experiencing negative emotions, accessing effective emotion regulation strategies, and accepting their emotions (Tull, Vidaña, & Betts, 2020). They have also been found to avoid their emotions to a greater extent than people without posttraumatic stress disorder (Tull et al., 2020). For example, research has shown that posttraumatic stress disorder is associated with greater risk for a number of maladaptive or self-destructive behaviors that function to avoid emotions, including disordered eating behaviors, self-injury, substance use, and risky behaviors (Tull et al., 2020).

Eating Disorders

Emotion regulation difficulties are also thought to play an important role in the development and maintenance of eating disorders, including binge-eating disorder, anorexia nervosa, and bulimia nervosa (Brockmeyer et al., 2014; Prefit et al., 2019). Studies show that people with eating disorders exhibit a number of emotion regulation difficulties, including difficulties identifying, understanding, and accepting emotions, accessing effective emotion regulation strategies, and controlling impulsive behaviors when experiencing emotional distress. Research has also found that people with eating disorders tend to rely on more maladaptive emotion regulation strategies, such as avoidance or rumination (Prefit et al., 2019). Specific emotion regulation difficulties have also been linked to particular disordered eating behaviors, with research finding that difficulties engaging in goal-directed behavior when distressed are uniquely associated with purging and compensatory exercise (Lavender et al., 2014) and difficulties controlling impulsive behaviors when distressed are uniquely associated with binge-eating and purging behaviors among patients with anorexia nervosa (Racine & Wildes, 2013).

Substance Use Disorders

Current models of substance use suggest that this behavior may be driven by efforts to avoid or escape unpleasant emotions (Baker, Piper, McCarthy, Majeskie, & Fiore, 2004), with people who do not have access to more adaptive emotion regulation strategies being more likely to rely on substances as a way of obtaining fast relief from unpleasant emotions. Indeed, one of the most prominent theories of substance use among people with mental health problems, the self-medication hypothesis (Khantzian, 1997), posits that individuals with mental health difficulties use substances to obtain relief from mental health symptoms and related distress.

Research supports these theories, finding that emotion regulation difficulties are associated with greater substance use frequency (Garke et al., 2021) and a greater reliance on substances to cope with negative emotions (Paulus, Heggeness, Raines, & Zvolensky, 2021). Studies also support the self-medication hypothesis of substance use among individuals with psychological disorders, finding that people with posttraumatic stress disorder are more likely to use substances in response to unpleasant emotions (Waldrop, Back, Verduin, & Brady, 2007), social anxiety disorder is associated with stronger motivations to drink to cope with negative emotions (Goodman et al., 2022), and people with more severe symptoms of depression are more likely to seek out alcohol in response to a negative mood (Hogarth, Hardy, Mathew, & Hitsman, 2018).

Physical Health Problems

Although less research has examined the role of emotion regulation in physical health (relative to the mental health difficulties reviewed above), a growing body of research implicates emotion regulation difficulties in a number of physical health problems. For example, maladaptive emotion regulation has been found to be associated with elevated levels of C-reactive protein (a biomarker of inflammation associated with the development of coronary heart disease) (Appleton, Buka, Loucks, Gilman, & Kubzansky, 2013). Studies have also found that adults with a chronic illness are more likely to have difficulties regulating emotions and that these emotion regulation difficulties are associated with worse health indicators (Wierenga, Lehto, & Given, 2017). Likewise, among adults with type 2 diabetes, maladaptive emotion regulation strategies have been linked to greater diabetes-related distress and physical symptom burden (Kane, Hoogendoorn, Tanenbaum, & Gonzalez, 2018), and emotion regulation difficulties have been linked to poorer diabetes self-management and greater medication nonadherence (Kollin, Gratz, & Lee, 2024). Emotion regulation difficulties have also been found to be associated with greater pain-related disability and severity among individuals with chronic pain (Yuan et al., 2024). Finally, emotion regulation difficulties have been linked to later physical health problems among women with symptoms of borderline personality disorder (Gratz et al., 2017).

Identifying Target Behaviors for This ERT

Given the number of maladaptive, self-destructive, and/or otherwise unhealthy behaviors linked to emotion regulation difficulties, it may be challenging at times to determine the specific client behaviors to focus on within this ERT, especially if the extent to which these behaviors are driven by emotion regulation difficulties isn't clear. Although some clients will be able to identify why they engage in certain problem behaviors and the emotion-regulating function of those behaviors, others may struggle to identify the function of their behavior during the initial session. In these situations, as well as times when your client engages in a number of behaviors that may be driven by emotion regulation difficulties, it can be helpful to conduct a functional analysis of these possible target behaviors.

A functional analysis is an assessment technique that can assist you in understanding the conditions that are most likely going to give rise to a particular behavior, as well as the consequences that may maintain the behavior over time. A functional analysis essentially helps you and your client understand why a behavior occurs and may continue to occur over time. As such, it can be a particularly helpful tool when clients are unaware of the factors that give rise to or maintain their behaviors, or when their behaviors could be driven by or reinforced by a number of different factors.

There are four components of a functional analysis: (1) identifying the target behavior; (2) identifying the factors that precede the behavior; (3) identifying vulnerability factors or characteristics that may increase risk for the behavior in certain contexts; and (4) identifying consequences of the behavior (Farmer & Chapman, 2008). Table 2.2 provides an overview of each of these components, as well as some example questions that you can ask your client to assess these components.

Target Behavior

The first step in conducting a functional analysis is to clearly identify the behavior that is being assessed. If your client is engaging in multiple maladaptive behaviors, it can be helpful to conduct a functional analysis for each behavior. This will assist you in identifying similarities and differences with regard to the factors that motivate these behaviors and their consequences. When identifying the target behavior(s), it is important to be as specific as possible in the description of each behavior. For example, instead of identifying "self-injury" as a target behavior, it is more helpful to describe exactly what that behavior typically looks like for your client, such as "Nonsuicidal self-injury in the form of cutting with a paring knife. Cuts are typically about two to three inches long and only deep enough to cause some minor bleeding." If your client engages in a sequence of behaviors (for example, excessively drinking alcohol and misusing prescription medication followed by engaging in risky sexual behavior), you can treat the entire sequence of events as a single target behavior.

TABLE 2.2. Components of a Functional Analysis	
Component	Example Questions
Target behavior	• What do you tend to do when you feel overwhelmed by your emotions? • Are there any behaviors you are particularly concerned about, or that seem to be interfering with your life or health?
Preceding events	• In what kinds of situations is this behavior most likely to occur? • How do you typically feel right before you choose to engage in this behavior? • What thoughts give rise to urges to engage in this behavior? • How do you feel in your body when you notice urges to engage in this behavior?
Vulnerability factors	• Are there times when it seems harder to resist urges to engage in this behavior? • Are there any factors that make it harder to resist engaging in this behavior, such as being tired, hungry, ill, or stressed? • Are there any aspects of your personality that you think make it harder to cope with certain types of situations?
Consequences of the target behavior	• What happens right after the behavior occurs? How do you feel? What thoughts do you have? • How do you feel hours after the behavior occurs? How about the next day? • Do you notice changes in how you feel from right before to right after engaging in the behavior? • Does this behavior have any downsides?

Preceding Events

The next step in conducting a functional analysis is to assist your client in identifying the myriad factors (for example, thoughts, emotions, physical sensations) that typically precede the target behavior. In this part of the functional analysis, it may be helpful to ask your client to think of a recent time when the target behavior occurred and the situation that prompted the behavior (for example, an argument with their partner). Next, assist your client in identifying the specific sequence of events that led from the prompting event to the target behavior, as if they were identifying links in a chain connecting the prompting event to the target behavior. Each of these links can take the form of thoughts, emotions, physical sensations, behaviors, or other external events (for example, reactions of a loved one). The goal is to assist your client in identifying the chain of internal and external events that ultimately led to the target behavior. In addition to helping your client increase awareness of the function of their behaviors, this information can help you better understand your client's specific emotion regulation difficulties. For example, if a functional analysis revealed a prominent role of judgments about emotions and shame in a client's self-injury, this could highlight that your client may be especially likely to struggle with secondary emotions (i.e., emotional reactions to primary emotional responses that are driven by judgments; we will go into more detail about secondary emotions and how to manage these emotions in chapter 8).

When assisting your client in identifying the factors that precede their target behavior, it can also be helpful to gather information on the contexts in which the cascade of events they identified is particularly likely (versus not likely) to lead to the target behavior. For example, there may be some contexts in which the same sequence of events that often prompts a target behavior when your client is alone does not prompt the behavior, such as when your client is around other people or doesn't have privacy. Knowing the specific contexts in which your client is more or less likely to engage in a target behavior will be helpful in tailoring the skills in this ERT to be most applicable to these high-risk contexts.

Vulnerability Factors

There may be times when your client finds it more challenging to resist urges to engage in a target behavior, or when their emotional reactions to a prompting event are stronger or more distressing. This may be due to the presence of vulnerability factors, which are any factors (e.g., individual difference characteristics, experiences, situations, self-care actions, or symptoms) that increase the risk for a target behavior or explain why such behavior may be more likely to occur in certain contexts. For example, a client may be more likely to experience shame in response to rejection by a friend if they had a history of neglect or rejection by their parents as a child. Or, your client may notice that they are less likely to resist urges to binge-eat when they are experiencing symptoms of depression or have not gotten enough sleep.

Consequences of the Target Behavior

The final step in conducting a functional analysis is to assist your client in identifying the short- and long-term positive and negative consequences of the target behavior. This component of the functional analysis provides you with the opportunity to assist your client in identifying both the reinforcing consequences of their behavior (i.e., the desired consequences that maintain the behavior, such as relief from distress) and the punishing consequences of the behavior (i.e., consequences that decrease the likelihood of the behavior occurring in the future, such as an increase in distress). It is important to recognize that even behaviors that are harmful to clients in the long term tend to be associated with positive consequences in the short term, which is why these behaviors persist. For that reason, it's important to be as comprehensive as possible when identifying the consequences of a target behavior. Identifying the positive consequences of the behavior will help your client understand why they engage in the behavior and the important functions it serves, whereas identifying the negative consequences of the behavior can help increase your client's motivation to work on stopping the behavior and replacing it with a more adaptive behavior that serves a similar function.

Tracking Target Behaviors Throughout This ERT

Because this ERT focuses on teaching clients more adaptive ways of responding to their emotions, particular attention should be placed on client target behaviors that function to avoid, escape, distract from, or express unwanted emotions. Alternatively, if your client engages in unhealthy behaviors that stem from emotion regulation difficulties (even if those behaviors don't serve an emotion-regulating function), those could also be a helpful target of this treatment. For example, a client with a chronic illness may identify not taking medications regularly as a target behavior. Even though this behavior is not serving an emotion-regulating function (i.e., they are not actively skipping medication in order to avoid or escape their emotions), it may be driven by their emotion regulation difficulties (as these may make it more challenging for them to adhere to their medication regimen). In this scenario, this client could benefit from tracking medication adherence in this ERT, as we would expect nonadherence to decrease as they learn more adaptive emotion regulation skills.

Finally, if your client reports multiple problem behaviors, work with your client to determine which behaviors are of the highest priority. These may be the most severe behaviors, the most frequent behaviors, or the behaviors that have the most serious negative consequences for your client. Alternatively, if all of the problem behaviors exhibited by your client share the same emotion-regulating function, you could instruct your client to monitor all of these in the overarching category of maladaptive emotion regulation behaviors and just indicate on their monitoring forms which specific behavior occurred.

CHAPTER 3

Assessing Progress and Outcomes in This Therapy

One benefit of this ERT is that many of the modules can stand on their own. Although some of the skills presented in this treatment build on material covered in previous sessions, it isn't necessary to teach clients all of the skills included in this ERT if some are not applicable to them. In this way, the treatment can be delivered flexibly and modified based on your client's needs. For example, some clients may not experience difficulties controlling impulsive behaviors when distressed. If that's the case, you could exclude the skills presented in that session (reviewed in chapter 11). Such an approach personalizes this treatment for your clients, increasing its efficiency.

If you are interested in tailoring this treatment for some of your clients by focusing on only the select skills that are most relevant to them, you will need to determine their baseline emotion regulation abilities and the particular domains of emotion regulation in which they are experiencing difficulties. The best way to do this is to have them complete the Difficulties in Emotion Regulation Scale (DERS; Gratz & Roemer, 2004), which was developed specifically to assess the acceptance-based model of emotion regulation in which this ERT is grounded and has extensive empirical support (Gratz & Roemer, 2004; Gratz & Tull, 2010; 2022). This thirty-six item measure assesses individuals' typical levels of emotion regulation difficulties across six domains targeted within this ERT: (1) difficulties with emotional acceptance; (2) difficulties with emotional awareness; (3) difficulties with emotional clarity; (4) difficulties accessing effective emotion regulation strategies; (5) difficulties controlling impulsive behaviors when distressed; and (6) difficulties engaging in goal-directed behaviors when distressed. Total scores on this measure range from 36 to 180 and reflect your client's overall emotion regulation difficulties. Because the specific emotion regulation difficulties assessed by the DERS map closely onto the skills taught in this ERT, the DERS is a particularly helpful tool for assessing your clients' baseline emotion regulation abilities and difficulties and personalizing this ERT. Both the full version of the DERS and instructions for scoring this measure are available for download at http://www.newharbinger.com/53622. For reference, the average DERS scores found among clients with different clinical difficulties, as well as nonclinical samples of adults in the community, are presented in table 3.1 (see Brockmeyer et al., 2012; Gratz & Tull, 2010).

TABLE 3.1. Average DERS Scores Among Different Clinical and Nonclinical Populations	
Borderline personality disorder	120–125
Major depressive disorder	115
Posttraumatic stress disorder	100–105
Generalized anxiety disorder	95–100
Panic attacks	90–95
Nonsuicidal self-injury	85–90
Substance use disorders	85–90
Nonclinical samples of adults in the community	75–80

Assessing Treatment Progress

When conducting any evidence-based psychological treatment, it is important to periodically assess clients' progress on the primary targets of that treatment, as well as relevant symptoms and behaviors. In the case of this ERT, we recommend tracking your clients' progress on both emotion regulation difficulties (by administering the DERS regularly throughout treatment) and the primary behaviors and symptoms being driven by these difficulties for them (suggested measures to capture these are reviewed below). Assessing client progress regularly throughout treatment allows you to determine if the treatment is working for your client and, if not, to modify the treatment approach as needed. For example, if the data suggest that your client is not improving on emotion regulation or specific target behaviors or symptoms, you can share this information with your client, identify potential barriers to skill acquisition or application, and revisit relevant ERT modules as needed.

Specific measures that may be useful for assessing relevant target behaviors and symptoms at baseline and throughout this ERT are described below. Although this is not an exhaustive list of measures and there are numerous others you could use depending on the specific presenting problems and needs of your client, we chose to highlight these measures because they are publicly available, frequently used, relatively brief, and have strong evidence in support of their reliability and validity.

Self-Destructive and Other Maladaptive Behaviors

Table 3.2 includes a list of self-report measures that assess a variety of maladaptive behaviors that have been found to serve an emotion-regulating function.

TABLE 3.2. Checklists and Self-Report Measures of Self-Destructive and Other Maladaptive Behaviors

Measure	Length	What it assesses	How to access the measure
Deliberate Self-Harm Inventory (Gratz, 2001)	16 items	Frequency, severity, age of onset, and last occurrence of sixteen different forms of nonsuicidal self-injury	Available in Gratz (2001)
Eating Pathology Symptoms Inventory (Forbush et al., 2013)	45 items	Eight different forms of disordered eating behaviors, including muscle building, excessive exercise, binge-eating, purging, and restricting	https://tinyurl.com/bdp298hf
Sexual Risk Survey (Turchik & Garske, 2009)	23 items	Risky sexual behaviors	Available in Turchik and Garske (2009)
Aggression Questionnaire (Bryant & Smith, 2001)	12 items	Anger, hostility, verbal aggression, and physical aggression	Available in Bryant and Smith (2001)
Alcohol Use Disorder Identification Test (Babor, Higgins-Biddle, Saunders, & Monteiro, 2001)	10 items	Frequency of alcohol use, as well as features of risky or harmful alcohol consumption	https://tinyurl.com/2nahvata
Drug Use Disorder Identification Test (Berman, Bergman, Palmstierna, & Schlyter, 2007)	11 items	Frequency and severity of drug use	https://tinyurl.com/yx5wt5fd
Gambling Symptom Assessment Scale (Kim, Grant, Potenza, Blanco, & Hollander, 2009)	12 items	Severity of gambling symptoms	Available in Kim et al. (2009)
Smartphone Addiction Scale (Kwon et al., 2013)	33 items	Features and consequences of excessive smartphone use	Available in Kwon et al. (2013)
Internet Disorder Scale—Short Form (Pontes & Griffiths, 2016)	9 items	Excessive and problematic internet use	Available in Pontes and Griffiths (2016)

Measure	Length	What it assesses	How to access the measure
Depression Symptom Index–Suicide Subscale (Metalsky & Joiner, 1997)	4 items	Frequency and intensity of suicidal thoughts, plans, and impulses	Available in Metalsky and Joiner (1997)
Suicidal Behaviors Questionnaire—Revised (Osman et al., 2001)	4 items	Suicidal thoughts and behaviors	Available in Osman et al. (2001)
Illegal Behavior Checklist (McCoy et al., 2006)	22 items	Presence or absence of illegal behaviors	Available in McCoy et al. (2006)

Psychological Disorder Symptoms

Table 3.3 provides a list of measures of various symptoms of psychological disorders that have been linked to emotion regulation difficulties.

TABLE 3.3. Self-Report Measures of Psychological Symptoms

Measure	Length	What it assesses	How to access the measure
Depression Anxiety Stress Scales (Lovibond & Lovibond, 1995)	21 items	Severity of core symptoms of depression, anxiety, and stress	https://tinyurl.com/54ka3zrx
Obsessive Compulsive Inventory—Revised (Foa et al., 2002)	18 items	Severity of obsessive and compulsive symptoms	Available in Foa et al. (2002)
Social Phobia Scale (Mattick & Clarke, 1998)	20 items	Symptoms and behaviors characteristic of social anxiety disorder	https://tinyurl.com/3uxf85jn
Panic Disorder Severity Scale (Shear et al., 1997)	7 items	Panic attack frequency, panic-related distress, and panic-related life interference	https://tinyurl.com/ycdbtzwa
Generalized Anxiety Disorder—7 (Spitzer, Kroenke, Williams, & Löwe, 2006)	7 items	Generalized anxiety disorder symptom severity	https://tinyurl.com/3xm5dak9

Assessing Progress and Outcomes in This Therapy

Measure	Length	What it assesses	How to access the measure
Altman Self-Rating Mania Scale (Altman Hedeker, Peterson, & Davis, 1997)	4 items	Mania symptoms	Available in Altman et al. (1997)
PTSD Checklist for the DSM-5 (Weathers et al., 2013)	20 items	Posttraumatic stress disorder symptom severity	https://tinyurl.com/bdj29swe
Borderline Evaluation of Severity over Time (Pfohl et al., 2009)	15 items	Severity of borderline personality disorder symptoms and related thoughts, emotions, and behaviors	Available in Pfohl et al. (2009)

Physical Health Symptoms and Quality of Life

As we described in chapter 2, growing evidence suggests that emotion regulation difficulties may play an important role in physical health as well, contributing to poorer physical health outcomes and exacerbating physical health problems. If your client struggles with co-occurring physical health difficulties, you may want to consider assessing these throughout the treatment as well. A large number of self-report measures assessing a variety of physical health symptoms are available at https://www.healthmeasures.net/search-view-measures. In addition, given the focus on valued actions within this ERT, as well as the emphasis on assisting clients in building a meaningful life, it is important to remember that treatment success is not defined solely by a reduction in symptoms or self-destructive behaviors. Instead, it is important to consider if your client is making progress in building a meaningful life. Therefore, we also recommend considering measures that assess the pursuit of values, such as the ten-item Valuing Questionnaire (Smout, Davies, Burns, & Christie, 2014), or quality of life (a number of measures assessing quality of life are available at https://www.healthmeasures.net/search-view-measures).

Best Practices for Assessing Progress

The first step in systematically tracking your client's progress throughout this ERT is to determine the precise behaviors and symptoms that will be most important to assess. As important as it is to collect data on your client's progress during treatment, it is equally important to remain mindful of the burden associated with completing these measures. Although the measures presented in this chapter are relatively brief, having clients complete several of them could take some time. Administering too many measures may cause clients to lose focus or attention, negatively affecting the accuracy of their data. The time needed to complete a long assessment battery could also interfere with clients completing the outside-of-session exercises and monitoring forms that are central to this treatment. Therefore, when choosing measures to administer, consider those that are most relevant to your client's primary presenting problems and the focus of this ERT.

The next step is to consider when to administer these measures, balancing the importance of regular assessments with minimizing client burden. Keep in mind that it isn't necessary to administer most measures on a weekly basis, as some of the measures assess the past two weeks (for example, Depression Anxiety Stress Scales) and others would not be expected to change on a weekly basis (for example, DERS). Instead, we recommend administering measures biweekly or monthly depending on your client's needs and the specific measures you choose. Whatever assessment schedule you choose, just make sure that the time frame in between assessments is consistent (for example, every two weeks or every four weeks).

Once your client has completed the measures, it is important to put aside some time to review their responses and discuss them with your client. Data from these measures can provide important information on whether and to what extent the treatment is working for your client. It is also helpful to ask your client if the data are consistent with their experiences and assessment of their own progress. Indeed, one downside of self-report measures is that they don't always capture the nuance of a client's experience or the context in which symptoms are occurring. Thus, it can be most helpful to use the data as a starting point for a conversation with your client about their symptoms and experiences in the treatment. This conversation may highlight stuck points for your client, or areas where they need additional instruction or support in implementing a skill in their daily lives or within a particular context.

Finally, it is important to consider these data in the context of all the other data you have on your client, including behavioral changes you have observed throughout the treatment, your client's perceptions of their own behavioral changes and improvements, and the observations of others in your client's life. Although data from self-report measures provide an important piece of the puzzle, they do not capture a client's entire experience. Therefore, considering all sources of data you have on your client will provide you with a more complete picture of how your client is responding to the treatment.

CHAPTER 4

Therapeutic Stance of This Emotion Regulation Therapy

One of the most important elements of this ERT and a key component to its successful delivery is the therapeutic stance taken by clinicians when delivering this treatment. Because this therapy focuses on teaching clients more adaptive ways of responding to their emotions, it is essential that clinicians model this approach to emotions in all of their interactions with clients. Infusing all interventions delivered in the context of this treatment with this particular ERT-consistent therapeutic stance helps reinforce this new approach to emotions, ensuring that clients are continuously exposed to this novel way of approaching their emotions and providing repeated modeling of and training in this approach to emotions throughout all elements of the treatment.

In particular, as an acceptance-based behavioral treatment that draws heavily from DBT and ACT, this therapy is most effectively delivered when clinicians take an acceptance-based stance toward emotions and other internal experiences, approaching their clients' (and their own) emotions with acceptance, validation, and willingness. The goal across all sessions of this ERT is for clinicians to model this stance for clients.

Modeling an Acceptance-Based Stance Toward Emotions

To this end, we encourage clinicians to be on the lookout for any emotional expressions by clients that can be used to model and further reinforce this acceptance-based approach to emotions. Throughout each of your sessions with a client, pay attention to how they talk about and express their emotions, with the goal of validating their emotions and acknowledging the function those emotions are serving. The goal is to infuse this stance toward emotions throughout the treatment so that approaching emotions with acceptance becomes the expected and standard response.

This stance also necessitates that you directly address any negative judgments about themselves or their emotions that clients express in a gentle and compassionate way. Most clients who struggle with emotion regulation also struggle with accepting their emotions, judging both their emotions and themselves for experiencing certain emotions. Therefore, it is reasonable to expect that most clients who would benefit from this therapy will regularly express negative judgments about their emotions. Most often, this will take the form of referring to their emotions as bad, stupid, wrong, or unimportant, or beating themselves up and judging themselves for experiencing certain emotions (e.g., judging themselves as bad, evil, weak, or flawed for having certain emotions).

When you're delivering this ERT, it is incredibly important to call attention to these judgments whenever they arise and encourage clients to approach their emotions in a more accepting way. This could involve asking clients to acknowledge and take a step back from their judgments of their emotions, label the judgment as a judgment (e.g., "You are having the judgment that your emotion is bad"), or use nonjudgmental language when discussing their emotions. The goal is to increase clients' awareness of these judgments over the course of the treatment and encourage them to apply the skills they learn in this ERT to approach their emotions in a more accepting way. Table 4.1 provides some examples of effective, ERT-consistent responses to different judgments about emotions that clients may express in session.

TABLE 4.1. Effective Responses to Clients' Judgments About Emotions

Judgment Expressed by Client in Session	ERT-Consistent Responses
This emotion is so stupid.	Okay, so you're having the judgment that your emotion is stupid. How might you describe this emotion nonjudgmentally? Given the downsides of judging our emotions, can you take a step back from that judgment of your emotion?
I'm sorry for crying. I don't know why I get like this.	You have absolutely no need to apologize for crying. That's a natural and valid response to feeling sad. It sounds like you're judging yourself for crying. Can you take a step back from that judgment? How might you approach yourself in a different way? There is absolutely nothing wrong with crying when you're sad. That seems like a very reasonable response to me.
Why do I always have to feel this way? It's so ridiculous.	That sounds like a judgment to me. It seems incredibly reasonable that you'd feel this way in response to what happened. Ahem (clears throat). That sounds like a judgment! Can you reframe this nonjudgmentally? It sounds like you are getting frustrated with yourself for experiencing this emotion, which is a secondary emotional response.

Judgment Expressed by Client in Session	ERT-Consistent Responses
Anger is a dangerous emotion.	The term "dangerous" sounds like a judgment. Do you know where this judgment may have come from? Were you taught this by someone? Or did you have experiences where people expressed anger in an ineffective way? As we discussed previously, anger is a natural human emotion and has some very important functions.
	I'm trying to figure out how this aligns with what we know about the function of emotions, including anger. Given that all emotions serve an important purpose, do you believe the emotion of anger is truly problematic? Or could it be that the way in which some people express anger is ineffective or harmful? Can you think of times when anger would be helpful? What functions does anger serve for people?
I'm such a loser for feeling anxious all the time.	It sounds like you're judging yourself for experiencing anxiety—which is a natural human emotion. I'm guessing that beating yourself up for feeling this way is actually making you feel worse. This is one of those secondary emotional responses we discussed previously that just adds to emotional suffering. I'm wondering if it would be helpful to use the skills you learned to take a step back from these judgments and approach your anxiety in a more helpful way. Even though anxiety can be uncomfortable or unpleasant to experience, it provides you with important information about your environment. Let's see what happens if you make space for that experience and connect with the information the emotion provides.
My emotions are too intense.	It sounds to me like you're judging your emotions. Any time we say that an emotion is "too" something, that is a judgment. See if you can take a step back from that judgment and describe your emotions objectively.
	Well, that's a judgment! This suggests that there is something wrong with having intense emotions, which is not the case. People differ in how intensely they experience emotions, with some people experiencing strong emotions and others experiencing less intense emotions. Neither of these is inherently better or worse than the other; it's just the way someone is hardwired. What matters is not how intensely someone experiences their emotions but how they respond to those emotions when they arise.

Although emotional nonacceptance is targeted directly in this ERT in the second session, it is also discussed as part of the orientation to this treatment in the first session. Therefore, even before you teach clients skills for increasing emotional acceptance directly, clients are aware that this treatment will teach them an alternative (and arguably more helpful!) way of approaching and responding to their emotions, with an emphasis on emotional acceptance. It is a central tenet of this treatment introduced to clients from day one.

Given how entrenched emotional nonacceptance is for most clients who struggle with emotion regulation difficulties, it is also important that you remain mindful of your own emotional responses and the ways in which you speak about these experiences in session, modeling nonjudgmental awareness of your emotions and practicing emotional acceptance and willingness in session with clients. Modeling this approach to your own emotions further reinforces the skills you will be teaching your clients and provides in the moment training in how to practice these skills. A key element of modeling this approach involves actively refraining from sending clients the message that emotions need to be controlled or down-regulated, or that emotional distress needs to be avoided. Such messages, even if subtle, can inadvertently reinforce emotional nonacceptance and make it more challenging for clients to learn the acceptance-based stance toward emotions that is so central to this ERT.

Indeed, although it's easy when thinking about this aspect of the ERT therapeutic stance to focus on the direct statements you make about emotions when you're giving examples in session or teaching clients the skills, it is equally (if not more) important to remain mindful of any indirect messages about emotions that you may be sending without even realizing it. It is the pervasiveness and ubiquity of these more indirect messages about emotions that can make them particularly powerful and influential in clients' lives. It is for this reason that we encourage clinicians to remain mindful of any judgments or negative beliefs about emotions they may hold that run counter to this therapy and could be communicated to clients indirectly. Exercise 4.1 will assist you in identifying any negative beliefs about emotions you may have that could be unintentionally communicated to your clients. Identifying these beliefs is the first step in ensuring that you don't inadvertently send clients negative messages about their emotions or reinforce their judgments about emotions.

EXERCISE 4.1. Identifying Your Own Negative Beliefs About Emotions That Could Be Indirectly Communicated to Clients in Session

This exercise will assist you in identifying any negative beliefs about emotions you may hold that could influence your responses to clients' emotions in therapy or how you deliver this ERT. Take some time to reflect on the following lists of beliefs and behaviors that could influence how a clinician delivers this ERT. Then, consider the questions below each of the lists.

The following are negative beliefs about emotions that many individuals hold and that could influence responses to clients' emotions in therapy.

- Some emotions need to be controlled.
- Some emotions are dangerous or disruptive to people's lives.
- Having intense emotions is a sign of emotion dysregulation.

- It is emotionally healthy to be able to control one's emotions.
- The goal of effective therapy is for clients to control their emotions.
- Anger is unhealthy.
- Anger is always a secondary emotional response.
- When emotions are very intense, it can be impossible for someone to control their behaviors.
- In order to change their emotions, people just need to change the way they think.
- Decreasing negative emotions and increasing positive emotions is the key to psychological health.

Do any of these beliefs stand out as relevant to you? How do you think these beliefs could influence how you respond to your clients' emotions in treatment? How might they influence how you deliver this ERT?

The following are behaviors that people may engage in when they are not completely accepting of their emotions, or that may signify the presence of some judgments about emotions. When you are experiencing painful emotions, do you engage in any of these behaviors? Take a moment to identify any behaviors that stand out as relevant to you.

- Apologizing for crying
- Apologizing for becoming upset or expressing certain emotions (even if these are expressed in healthy and effective ways)
- Looking down or away from others when expressing certain emotions
- Saying "I'm fine" to abruptly change the topic after expressing a certain emotion
- Avoiding eye contact when expressing your emotions to someone else
- Expressing judgments about your emotions (e.g., "It's ridiculous that I'm this anxious about this!")
- Avoiding certain emotions or making choices to prevent certain emotions from arising

How might these behaviors come up for you in the context of delivering this ERT? How might they affect your clients or your delivery of this treatment? What could you do to modify how you approach or discuss your emotions to be more consistent with the therapeutic stance encouraged within this ERT?

The following are ways of responding to others' expressions of emotions that may indicate beliefs that emotions need to be controlled or down-regulated, or that may send the message to others that they need to dampen the intensity of their emotions or control their expression of their emotions.

- Telling them to calm down

- Changing the subject
- Distracting the person by talking about something else
- Telling them to take a breath
- Telling them to lower their voice
- Providing excessive reassurance (e.g., "Don't worry about it!")
- Expressing discomfort (verbally or nonverbally) with the expression of intense emotions

Do you respond in any of these ways when others express emotions to you? How about when clients express emotions to you in session? What messages do you think these responses could send to clients about their emotions? Are there other ways you could respond to clients' expressions of emotion to be more consistent with the therapeutic stance emphasized within this ERT?

Modeling Mindfulness- and Acceptance-Based Language in Session

Another key element of the therapeutic stance that is so central to this ERT involves the language you use throughout the treatment, when teaching your clients the skills, discussing their outside-of-session practice exercises, or discussing their experiences in general. Specifically, it is important to model language consistent with the therapeutic concepts of willingness, defusion, nonjudgmental awareness, and mindfulness in all interactions with clients. This includes nonjudgmentally describing emotions and other internal experiences, distinguishing thoughts from facts, objectively labeling judgments as judgments and thoughts as thoughts, distinguishing emotions and action urges from behaviors, and acknowledging dialectics.

With regard to the last of these, we believe it is important to both encourage clients to approach their emotions *and* acknowledge how challenging it can be to do so and how human it is to want to avoid emotional pain. Likewise, we believe it is helpful for clinicians to acknowledge the function of risky or self-destructive behaviors that serve to avoid or escape emotions even as they encourage clients to refrain from engaging in these behaviors. This type of language helps model and reinforce the concepts being taught to clients in this ERT on an ongoing basis. Both of these examples are also consistent with another language convention emphasized within ERT. Specifically, and similar to DBT, we ask clinicians to use the word "and" in place of "but" when discussing aspects of the client's experience or the treatment itself in session. Such language reinforces the idea that seemingly conflicting experiences can occur together and need not be in conflict. For example, rather than saying to a client who engages in self-injury, "Cutting yourself may make you feel better in the moment, but it is causing problems for you in the long run," we recommend saying, "Cutting yourself makes you feel better in the moment *and* it has a number of negative consequences in the long term." Whereas the use of the term "but" in the first statement implies that the negative consequences of self-injury cancel out its positive consequences, the second statement acknowledges that both can be true and doesn't invalidate the positive short-term consequences of the behavior. Finally, in the event that you inadvertently express any judgments in session, these should be explicitly acknowledged as such and reframed in a nonjudgmental way.

Sharing Your Struggles with Emotion Regulation

Consistent with our recommendation that clinicians model an acceptance-based approach to emotions throughout this treatment, we also encourage clinicians to selectively share relevant examples from their own lives in order to model for clients that the struggles they're experiencing with emotion regulation and their desire to avoid painful emotions are human struggles. Well-placed and well-timed examples of times when you didn't choose to practice emotional willingness, weren't sure how you were feeling, experienced cloudy emotions, or tried to avoid your emotions can be a very powerful technique for normalizing these experiences and countering clients' shame and self-judgment related to their struggles with emotion regulation. Sharing these examples with clients can also help reinforce one of the key themes of this treatment: that emotional acceptance and willingness are a process versus an outcome and, thus, clients are not expected to reach an end point of choosing willingness or acceptance at all times. Although this focus on process versus outcome is a key element of this ERT, it can be a particularly challenging concept for clients to grasp, as many clients enter treatment with a focus on a desired outcome and achieving perfection with regard to treatment goals. Therefore, using strategic examples from your own life to demonstrate to clients that no one *achieves* an outcome of persistent and stable emotion regulation or chooses emotional willingness at all times can be a helpful way of further reinforcing the emphasis on process versus outcome in this treatment. For these reasons, we encourage you to remain mindful of possible examples of emotion regulation-related struggles that arise in your daily life and consider bringing those that are relatively benign (i.e., examples that you've fully processed and that are not too emotionally charged) to sessions with your clients.

The importance of this form of modeling with your clients cannot be overemphasized. Clients will be more inclined to nonjudgmentally acknowledge their own struggles and work toward changing their relationship to their emotions if they do not evaluate themselves as flawed or inadequate for fighting their emotions or choosing emotional unwillingness. Seeing that you also struggle with your emotions at times and do not always choose emotional willingness can help reduce clients' shame for experiencing these difficulties and free them up for changing their relationship to their emotions. Indeed, clients who've received this ERT in the past have frequently commented on the fact that the emotional openness and willingness of the clinicians delivering this treatment, including their acknowledgment of their own struggles and their need to recommit to the process of emotional willingness again and again, made it possible to connect with the material (and, ultimately, to change their relationship to their emotions) in a way that would not have been possible had their clinicians not shared their own struggles with emotions.

Emphasizing Key Acceptance-Based Themes Throughout Treatment

In addition to asking clinicians to model the acceptance-based approach to emotions that is so central to this ERT, we find that it is most helpful if certain key themes related to this acceptance-based approach are emphasized and reinforced throughout the treatment, across all sessions with a client. In addition to reinforcing the key messages and skills of this therapy, keeping these themes in mind can be helpful in determining how best to intervene in any given session. Specifically, because it is not possible to predict the exact examples that may come up in session or how a client may react to any of the skills, it can be helpful to have key themes to fall back on if you aren't sure how to respond to a client in an ERT-consistent manner. The main themes that can be emphasized throughout the treatment are summarized in table 4.2 and reviewed below.

TABLE 4.2. Key Themes to Emphasize Throughout Treatment
• Emotions are functional.
• Emotional avoidance and unwillingness have paradoxical emotional consequences.
• Emotion regulation involves the control of behaviors when emotions are present and not the control of emotion themselves.
• Emotional willingness is a choice that is possible in every moment.
• Emphasis on process versus outcome.

Emotions Are Functional

As we discussed in chapter 1, the conceptualization of emotion regulation on which this ERT is based emphasizes the functionality of emotions and their usefulness in guiding behaviors and valued actions. As such, adaptive responses to emotions are those that facilitate the functional use of emotions as information to guide behavior and the pursuit of valued actions. This means that it is important for clients to be able to identify their emotions and the information these emotions are providing them, and to use this information to guide their behaviors and inform their choices. When clients are able to identify and label their emotions and to access and use the information provided by their emotions in an adaptive way, they are likely to respond more effectively to their environment.

Avoiding Emotions Has Paradoxical Consequences

Another theme that's important to emphasize throughout this ERT centers on the paradoxical emotional consequences of emotional nonacceptance, avoidance, and unwillingness. Although it is completely understandable (and human) to want to avoid emotional pain, persistent efforts to avoid emotions can paradoxically intensify those emotions and contribute to the experience of those emotions as undesirable and intolerable. This is one of several themes where you can see the emphasis on dialectics within this treatment. Emotional unwillingness is both understandable *and* not effective. Emotional avoidance may provide some relief from emotional pain in the moment *and* will often increase suffering and emotional distress in the long term. Thus, as challenging as it can be to consider approaching and experiencing one's emotions, this is necessary for overcoming emotional suffering.

We'll go into more detail about the differences between emotional pain (which is a necessary part of life) and emotional suffering (which arises from emotional nonacceptance and unwillingness) in chapters 8 and 9. For now, though, the key point to remember is that efforts to avoid emotions are generally not effective in the long run, and can actually intensify those emotions and the pain associated with them. There will be numerous opportunities in every session to emphasize this theme and encourage clients to practice emotional acceptance and willingness instead. The more you can reinforce the message that emotional acceptance and willingness (although painful and challenging) result in less *suffering* than emotional avoidance (as they prevent the intensification of emotional arousal and the exacerbation of emotional pain that go along with avoidance), the more likely your clients will be to practice this new stance toward their emotions.

Emotion Regulation Doesn't Mean Controlling Emotions

As you may remember from chapter 1, there are a number of different conceptualizations of emotion regulation in the literature. Although some of these conceptualizations view emotions (especially negative emotions) as something in need of control or modification, the conceptualization of emotion regulation on which this ERT is based views emotions as functional and in need of acknowledgment and acceptance. Likewise, although some efforts to modify emotions can take the form of adaptive distraction strategies aimed at redirecting one's attention toward something else for a while in an effort to take the edge off of an emotion, most efforts to control emotions directly will backfire and have paradoxical consequences. We'll discuss this in further detail in chapters 9 and 10 when we discuss the paradoxical consequences of emotional unwillingness and the differences between distraction and avoidance emotion modulation strategies. The key point to keep in mind for now is that most attempts to control emotions directly in the moment, especially in the context of emotional nonacceptance and avoidance, are not effective and can prompt engagement in self-destructive or otherwise maladaptive emotion regulatory behaviors.

Nonetheless, although emotions, like all internal experiences, are not directly controllable, it is possible for clients to learn to control their behaviors in response to their emotions (both the ways in which they express their emotions and the ways in which they act on the information provided by their emotions). Thus, focusing on the control of behaviors when emotions are present rather than the control of emotions themselves promotes an active stance toward the aspect of clients' experience that is actually controllable: their behavior. In addition, clients are likely to experience their emotions as less overwhelming and out of control if they can both learn skills to control their behaviors in response to emotions and reduce efforts to control emotions directly.

Emotional Willingness Is a Choice

As we discussed earlier in this chapter, this ERT conceptualizes emotional willingness as a process and a choice that can be made (or not) in any given moment. Thus, there is no expectation that clients can ever achieve a state of persistent emotional willingness or that they will choose emotional willingness at all times. Instead, clients are taught to view emotional willingness as a choice they can make at any time, which greatly increases flexibility in responding and the willingness to take this new stance toward emotions. Approaching emotional willingness as an all-or-nothing stance that needs to be chosen in every moment would be incredibly overwhelming for most clients (and most clinicians for that matter!), and would likely interfere with progress or a willingness to consider this stance. Instead, framing this as a non-static choice makes the prospect of choosing willingness at times less overwhelming and more achievable.

This is another theme in which a dialectic is present: emotional willingness decreases emotional suffering and increases effectiveness *and* we do not expect clients to make this choice all the time. Instead, clients are told that the first goal of treatment is simply to become more aware of these choice points, even if unwillingness is the option chosen in the moment. Because the choice of willingness can be made in every moment, however, clients never lose the chance to make this choice. If your client chooses unwillingness in one moment, the very next moment provides them with the opportunity to choose willingness. Thus, the goal of treatment is for clients to choose willingness more often now than in the past, and to work toward actively practicing willingness in their daily lives.

Emphasis on Process vs. Outcome

As we discussed earlier, a key element of this ERT is the focus on process versus outcome. This theme shows up in all sessions of this treatment when discussing any of the emotion regulation skills. The main point to emphasize with clients is that changing their relationship to their emotions and their old patterns of behavior is a process. These changes are not expected to occur overnight. Initially, progress is made simply by increasing awareness of old patterns of behaviors, the consequences of some of these behaviors (such as emotional avoidance or self-destructive behaviors), and the possibility of alternative responses.

As such, the first goal of this ERT is to increase clients' awareness of moment-to-moment choices they make throughout the day and the possibility of approaching emotions and other internal experiences in a different way. In this way, clients are initially encouraged simply to identify the emotions that precede self-destructive behaviors (or urges to engage in these behaviors), increasing their awareness of the connections between their emotions and responses to these emotions and engagement in self-destructive behaviors. Although eventually clients are encouraged to replace these self-destructive behaviors with more effective behaviors, identifying how difficulties with emotions and emotion regulation may drive self-destructive behaviors is the early goal in treatment.

Likewise, when the concepts of emotional unwillingness and willingness are first introduced, clients are encouraged simply to reflect on (and increase awareness of) the experiential consequences of their choice(s). Clients are not expected to embrace the idea of willingness immediately; rather, the expectation is that clients will struggle with the material and attempt to make sense of it on the basis of their experiences. This process of struggling with the skills and grappling with what it would be like to take a new stance toward their emotions is where many of the benefits of this treatment are expected to occur.

Table 4.3 provides some examples of therapeutic statements and behaviors that are and are not ERT-consistent, in order to further illustrate the therapeutic stance that is critical to delivering this ERT effectively. This table lists a variety of therapeutic statements, interventions, and behaviors that are and are not consistent with the acceptance-based therapeutic stance recommended in this ERT, along with a detailed explanation of why each statement or behavior is or is not encouraged when delivering this ERT.

TABLE 4.3. Examples of ERT-Consistent and ERT-Inconsistent Therapeutic Statements and Behaviors

Therapeutic Statements and Behaviors	Explanation
ERT-Consistent Statements and Behaviors	
Assisting a client in reframing a judgment about emotions in a nonjudgmental way	This is a key component of this ERT and considered vital to the effective delivery of this treatment.
Sharing an example of a time when you experienced difficulties regulating emotions	This is considered a helpful strategy within this ERT for normalizing struggles with emotions and reinforcing the idea that no one ever achieves emotion regulation as an end point. This reinforces the theme that emotion regulation is a process versus an outcome.
Sharing an example of a time when you chose to avoid your emotions for a moment	This is a helpful strategy for reinforcing the message that emotional willingness is a choice and that no one is expected to choose emotional willingness all the time. This helps normalize the desire to avoid emotional pain and demonstrate the humanness of choosing avoidance at times.
Helping clients identify the function of their emotion	This is one of the key skills in this ERT and a helpful strategy for increasing emotional acceptance and understanding.
Assisting clients in labeling their emotions	This is one of the key skills in this ERT and a helpful strategy for increasing emotional understanding and clarity.
Saying to a client that you understand why they are having urges to self-harm *and* you need them to commit to working on reducing this behavior	This statement is consistent with the emphasis on dialectics within this ERT. Specifically, the use of the word "and" validates the desire to avoid emotional pain and the function of self-destructive behaviors while also acknowledging the downsides of these behaviors and their paradoxical consequences.

Therapeutic Statements and Behaviors	Explanation
ERT-Inconsistent Statements and Behaviors	
Telling a client to calm down when they experience intense distress in session	This statement suggests that there is something wrong with experiencing intense emotions and that such emotions require down-regulation. It also sends the message that clients must down-regulate their emotions in order to be acceptable.
Telling a client that they should have chosen emotional willingness	In addition to the fact that the word "should" is a judgment, this statement is counter to the stance within this ERT that emotional willingness is a choice that clients can make (or not) in any given moment (as telling someone they should have done something removes their choice in the matter). It is also counter to one of the key themes in this treatment: that no one is expected to choose emotional willingness all the time.
Telling a client that the goal of treatment is to be emotionally willing	Although subtle, this suggests that clients can reach an end point of ongoing emotional willingness, and that this is an outcome of treatment versus an ongoing choice and process. It would be more effective to tell clients that the goal of treatment is to increase emotional willingness and to choose willingness more often than they've done in the past.
Asking a client to tell you about the bad emotions they felt that week	Labeling emotions as "bad" is a judgment of those emotions. It would be more effective to ask your client to tell you about a painful or overwhelming emotion they experienced.
Avoiding bringing attention to a client's judgments about emotions so as not to make them feel ashamed	Although we appreciate the desire to not contribute to a client's shame about themselves, it is important within this ERT to assist clients in increasing their awareness of their judgments about emotions so that they can approach their emotions in a different and more effective (nonjudgmental) way. To this end, it is important to bring their attention to judgments about emotions when they occur in session. The key to ensuring that this does not increase their shame is to do this in a nonjudgmental way and emphasize how natural judgments about emotions are.
Telling clients that anger is not a helpful emotion	This reinforces judgments about anger and is counter to the conceptualization of emotion regulation on which this treatment is based, which emphasizes the utility and functionality of all emotions, including anger.
Telling a client not to talk about their emotions so that they don't become more upset	This suggests that there is something dangerous or threatening about emotions and/or their expression. It also suggests that becoming upset is problematic and, thus, reinforces judgment and avoidance of emotions.

Therapeutic Statements and Behaviors	Explanation
Telling clients that their intense emotion is a sign of emotion dysregulation	This suggests that there is something wrong with experiencing intense emotions and implies that in order to be emotionally regulated, your client must dampen their experience of their emotions.
Requiring that clients stop engaging in self-destructive behaviors and emotional avoidance immediately	Requiring clients to immediately stop engaging in behaviors that serve an important function (particularly before they've learned skills for regulating their emotions in more adaptive ways) is ineffective and likely to have paradoxical consequences, increasing the risk for these very behaviors. This type of requirement is also counter to the focus on process versus outcome within this ERT and could be interpreted as invalidating the function of these behaviors. It would be more effective to acknowledge both the function of these behaviors and their significant downsides and then encourage clients to begin replacing these behaviors with more adaptive emotion regulation strategies and to choose emotional willingness more often than they have in the past.

Interventions

Part 2

CHAPTER 5

Identifying the Emotion-Regulating Function of Target Behaviors

As we've discussed previously, this ERT was originally developed to treat self-injury by directly targeting its proposed underlying mechanism of emotion dysregulation. The idea behind this treatment was that improving emotion regulation among individuals with self-injury would decrease their need for self-injury as an emotion regulation strategy.

Since this treatment was first developed, however, it's been used with clients with a wide variety of self-destructive behaviors in addition to self-injury, including disordered eating behaviors, risky sexual behaviors, substance use, and suicidal behaviors, and found to be efficacious in the treatment of these behaviors (Bjureberg et al., 2023; Gratz, Tull, & Levy, 2014). The utility of this treatment for a range of self-destructive behaviors beyond self-injury makes sense, as all of these behaviors have also been found to serve an emotion-regulating function. Specifically, as we discussed in chapter 2, there is strong evidence supporting the role of emotion dysregulation in numerous self-destructive behaviors, including those listed above. Therefore, although self-injury was the original behavioral target of this treatment, any behavior that serves an emotion-regulating function would be expected to improve as a result of this ERT.

This is a particularly relevant consideration given how often these types of self-destructive behaviors co-occur. Indeed, one reason we started monitoring the effects of this therapy on other types of self-destructive behaviors was that so many of the clients receiving this treatment in our studies endorsed numerous self-destructive behaviors in addition to their self-injury—behaviors that seemed to serve a similar emotion-regulating function to their self-injury. Therefore, to ensure that this therapy would be as helpful as possible for these clients, we had them monitor these other behaviors in the same way that they monitored their self-injury throughout the treatment, and encouraged them to use the skills they were learning in this treatment to assist them in reducing these other self-destructive behaviors as well. In so doing, we found that the same skills that were helpful in reducing clients' self-injury were also helpful in reducing their other self-destructive behaviors.

For these reasons, we recommend this ERT for clients struggling with any self-destructive behaviors that serve an emotion-regulating function. If these behaviors are being used to avoid or escape negative emotions, then improving a client's emotion regulation skills and teaching them more adaptive ways of responding to their emotions should reduce their need for all of these behaviors. Therefore, for any clients presenting with self-destructive behaviors that may serve an emotion-regulating function, we recommend beginning this therapy with the skills covered in this chapter and orienting your client to the ways in which this treatment will help them reduce their self-destructive behaviors.

That said, it is important to note that this particular session of ERT is optional, and relevant to only clients who struggle with self-destructive behaviors. Thus, if you are using this treatment with any clients who do not engage in self-destructive behaviors, we recommend skipping this session and beginning this ERT with the session focused on increasing emotional acceptance (described in chapter 6). Emotional acceptance is the first dimension of emotion regulation targeted in this treatment and a foundational emotion regulation skill on which many of the other skills are based.

For clients who do present to treatment with self-destructive behaviors, however, there are two main components of this first session. The first is an exercise aimed at helping clients identify the functions of their self-destructive behaviors and increase their awareness of the positive and negative consequences of these behaviors. The second involves psychoeducation on the emotion-regulating function and paradoxical consequences of many self-destructive behaviors. We will review each of these in turn.

Identifying the Functions of Self-Destructive Behaviors

When clients present to treatment with self-destructive behaviors in addition to emotion regulation difficulties, the first step in targeting these behaviors is to help them increase their awareness of the functions of these behaviors and their positive and negative consequences. In this ERT, this is first done in the context of an in-session exercise aimed at helping clients identify the positive and negative consequences of their self-destructive behaviors. The worksheet for this exercise, Target Behavior Functions: In-Session Exercise 1 (Consequences of Self-Destructive Behaviors), can be found at the end of this chapter and is available for download at http://www.newharbinger.com/53622.

When leading your client through this exercise, we recommend having them start by identifying the positive, short-term consequences of their behavior. This is the quadrant that will likely be easiest for your client to complete, as it captures why they engage in this behavior and the functions it serves. Focusing on this quadrant first provides you with the opportunity to validate the functions of your client's self-destructive behavior and demonstrate that you will not judge them for engaging in these behaviors. As such, it can help reduce the shame that clients often experience for engaging in self-destructive behaviors, particularly when other people in their lives have judged them for these behaviors or sent the message that there is something wrong with them for engaging in these behaviors. Throughout this part of the exercise, it is important to highlight the functionality of their behavior and the important needs this behavior meets.

Once you have assisted your client in generating as many positive short-term consequences of their behavior as possible, ask your client to reflect on all of the important needs met by their behavior and highlight how valid these needs are. Next, emphasize that the goal of this treatment is not to simply get them to stop engaging in self-destructive behaviors so that these important needs go unmet. Instead, the goal of this ERT is to help them get their needs met in other ways, without having to engage in self-destructive behaviors. This will help increase the perceived credibility of the treatment for your client and alleviate any concerns they may have that giving up their self-destructive behaviors will mean that they need to resign themselves to a lifetime of suffering and misery.

Next, move on to the quadrant corresponding to the positive long-term consequences of their behavior. Although it is important that you assist your client in identifying at least a couple of these consequences, a key point to emphasize during this part of the exercise is how few positive long-term consequences their behavior has (especially relative to its positive short-term consequences).

Finally, move on to discussing the two quadrants of the exercise that correspond to the negative consequences of their behavior. During this part of the exercise, it can be helpful to highlight the fact that self-destructive behaviors generally have more negative consequences in the long term than in the short term, which is one of the reasons why it can be so difficult to stop these behaviors. Assist your client in generating a comprehensive list of the negative consequences of their behavior, in both the short term and the long term.

Once your client has identified as many negative consequences of their behavior as possible, highlight the paradoxical emotional consequences of the behavior in the long term by pointing out how the upper-left and lower-right quadrants of the worksheet are mirror images of one another. The key point to emphasize in this discussion is that the long-term negative consequences of their behavior are almost the opposite of its short-term positive consequences. Therefore, if your client is engaging in this behavior to help themselves feel better in some way or to alleviate distress in the moment, they may actually end up feeling worse in the long run than they did initially. The hope is that by highlighting the paradoxical emotional consequences of this behavior, clients will be more motivated to stop the behavior and engage in this ERT.

Tips for Assisting Clients with This Exercise

As you lead your client through this exercise, it is important to ensure that they identify consequences of their behaviors in each of the four quadrants on the worksheet. Although some sets of consequences will be more difficult to identify than others, it is rare that a behavior does not have at least a couple of consequences that are positive and negative in both the short term and long term. The goal of this exercise is to assist your client in identifying as many consequences of their behavior as possible so that they have a complete understanding of the impact of their behavior on their lives and the ways in which this behavior both is and isn't working for them. Therefore, even if your client isn't able to identify any consequences in one of the quadrants immediately, we strongly recommend not moving on from the exercise until all of the quadrants have at least some information within them.

Psychoeducation on the Functions of Self-Destructive Behaviors

Once your client has identified the positive and negative consequences of their self-destructive behavior, the next step is to provide your client with psychoeducation on the functions of self-destructive behaviors in general. This information is summarized in a handout, Target Behavior Functions: In-Session Handout 1 (Functions of Self-Destructive Behaviors), that can be given to your client during the session and used to guide this discussion. This handout can be found at the end of this chapter and is available for download at http://www.newharbinger.com/53622. The goal of this part of the session is to highlight for clients how the functions of self-destructive behaviors identified by research correspond to the positive short-term consequences they identified for their behavior during the in-session exercise. Not only does this validate your client's experience, it can increase their confidence in the treatment.

As you review this handout with your client, there are three additional key points to emphasize. The first is that many of the functions of self-destructive behaviors listed on the handout can be conceptualized as a form of emotion regulation, or an attempt to help people feel better in some way. And, in fact, this is one of the reasons why these behaviors can be so difficult to stop: anything that provides someone with immediate relief from emotional distress is incredibly reinforcing.

The second point to emphasize is that even though these behaviors can provide relief from emotional distress in the short term, they tend to backfire in the long term and paradoxically increase clients' distress. Specifically, it is important to highlight for clients that the very behaviors they are engaging in to feel better are actually making them feel worse in the long term. The goal is to increase your client's motivation to stop engaging in self-destructive behaviors by having them connect with the ways in which these behaviors are not effective and actually increase their distress. It can also be helpful during this discussion to highlight the long-term negative consequences of chronic efforts to avoid emotional distress, particularly with regard to a client's ability to tolerate distress. In particular, the more your client avoids distress, the less distress they will be able to tolerate, until they eventually lose their tolerance for any distress at all. Basically, by not allowing themselves to experience distress on a regular basis, and by shutting down their feelings whenever they reach a certain intolerable level, clients can gradually lose their tolerance for emotional distress until even small amounts of distress feel incredibly overwhelming.

The final point to emphasize during this discussion is that it is the qualitative differences in the short-term and long-term consequences of self-destructive behaviors that make them so difficult to stop (despite their harmful long-term consequences). Human beings are more strongly influenced by the short-term consequences of behaviors than by their long-term consequences. Therefore, when a behavior has positive short-term consequences and negative long-term consequences, the consequences that become most strongly associated with this behavior are its positive consequences. This, in turn, reinforces the behavior and makes it more likely to persist in the future. The goal of this part of the discussion is to validate how challenging it can be to stop engaging in self-destructive behaviors even if clients are aware of the ways in which these behaviors are not working for them.

Orienting Clients to This Treatment

Once you've finished reviewing the in-session handout with your client, it is important to orient them to the premise of this ERT, tying the purpose and goals of this treatment back to the material you've reviewed with them during the session. The key points to emphasize during this discussion are the following:

- Self-destructive behaviors often serve an emotion-regulating function.

- Although these behaviors may be effective in the short term, they are much less effective in the long term and may paradoxically increase emotional suffering.

- If clients can learn more adaptive ways of responding to their emotions (i.e., ways that do not exacerbate emotional distress), emotion regulation will increase and the need for self-destructive behaviors will decrease.

- That's why this treatment was developed and why you believe it will be helpful in treating their self-destructive behaviors.

It can then be helpful to end this session by giving clients a brief overview of the skills you will be teaching them in this treatment. You can use the overview provided in the introduction to this book to guide this discussion.

Monitoring the Precipitants and Consequences of Target Behaviors

The outside-of-session exercise for this session focuses on helping clients increase their awareness of the emotional precipitants of their urges to engage in self-destructive behaviors, as well as the consequences of these behaviors if they occur. The worksheet for this exercise is a monitoring form that asks clients to track the following on a daily basis throughout the week: their urges to engage in self-destructive behaviors, the emotions preceding these urges, and the consequences of resisting their urges or engaging in the behaviors, along with any protective factors that may have been prevented these urges or behaviors. This form, Target Behavior Functions: Outside-of-Session Monitoring Form 1 (Self-Destructive Behaviors Monitoring Form), is available for download at http://www.newharbinger.com/53622. The goal of this form is to increase clients' awareness of the role of negative emotions in urges to engage in self-destructive behaviors, as well as more adaptive alternatives to these behaviors that they are already using at times.

Target Behavior Functions: In-Session Exercise 1

Consequences of Self-Destructive Behaviors

	Positive	Negative
Short-term consequences		
Long-term consequences		

Identifying the Emotion-Regulating Function of Target Behaviors

Target Behavior Functions: In-Session Handout 1

Functions of Self-Destructive Behaviors

Many self-destructive behaviors are considered emotion regulation strategies

- These behaviors may function to:
  - Alleviate distress
  - Relieve tension and unpleasant/intolerable feelings
  - Release emotions
  - Externalize emotional pain (i.e., transform intolerable emotional pain into more tolerable physical pain)
  - Escape emotional pain
  - Self-soothe
  - Communicate emotional pain
  - Express emotions
  - Validate emotional pain
  - Self-punish (and therefore alleviate guilt)
  - Provide sense of control
  - Divert attention away from painful internal experiences
  - Decrease dissociative symptoms (e.g., depersonalization)

Many of these functions can be conceptualized as emotion regulation

- Attempts to control, avoid, or escape intolerable emotions

Self-destructive behaviors may have paradoxical emotional consequences

- In the short term, these behaviors have positive emotional consequences
  - Appear to regulate emotions
- In the long term, these behaviors have negative emotional consequences
  - Increase emotional distress and dysregulation in the long term
    - Intolerance of distress leads to greater intolerance of distress

Behaviors are naturally more strongly influenced by short-term consequences than long-term consequences

- Many self-destructive behaviors are reinforced by their positive short-term consequences and yet interfere with emotion regulation in the long term

CHAPTER 6

Increasing Emotional Acceptance

One of the most important foundational emotion regulation skills is emotional acceptance. Not accepting one's emotions and, thus, judging those emotions or judging oneself for experiencing emotions is thought to drive many of the other emotion regulation difficulties with which clients tend to struggle. Clients who are not accepting of their emotions are far more likely to be unwilling to experience their emotions, or to try to avoid or escape their emotions by engaging in risky or self-destructive behaviors. They also tend to have greater difficulties connecting with and understanding their emotions, and are far more likely to experience intense emotional suffering when dealing with painful emotions (suffering that is driven by their judgments of their emotions). Thus, increasing clients' emotional acceptance is considered a key target for this ERT.

In ERT, emotional acceptance is targeted in three primary ways. First, clients are taught to identify their judgments about emotions, as well as the experiences they had that likely contributed to the development of these judgments. Second, clients are provided with psychoeducation on the function and utility of emotions and the reasons why emotions are important. Finally, clients are taught skills for taking a step back from judgments about emotions when they arise (rather than buying into these judgments). We will cover each of these here.

Identifying Judgments About Emotions and Their Origins

Before clients can learn how to respond to judgments about emotions in a more effective way, they need to recognize the judgments that they hold. For many clients who struggle with emotion regulation difficulties, judgments about emotions are long-standing, entrenched, and relatively automatic. Thus, these judgments often operate outside of their awareness.

Identifying Negative Beliefs About Emotions

One helpful strategy for increasing clients' awareness of their judgments about emotions is to present them with a list of common judgments or negative beliefs about emotions and ask them to select the judgments that stand out as relevant to them. We've developed a list of common negative beliefs about emotions that many clients who struggle with emotion regulation difficulties endorse, and present these to clients in Emotional Acceptance: In-Session Exercise 1 (Beliefs About Emotions), found at the end of this chapter and available for download at http://www.newharbinger.com/53622. If you're familiar with DBT, this handout will probably remind you of "Emotion Regulation Handout 2" in the *Skills Training Manual for*

Treating Borderline Personality Disorder (Linehan, 1993b) and "Emotion Regulation Handout 4A" of the *DBT Skills Training Manual, Second Edition* (Linehan, 2015). Give your clients some time to review this list and make note of the negative beliefs about emotions that stand out to them.

Identifying the Origins of These Beliefs

Once your client has identified the specific negative beliefs about emotions that stand out as most relevant to them, the next step is to have a brief discussion with your client about how these beliefs may have developed. We find it particularly helpful to share with clients that beliefs such as these are not present from birth; they are always learned, often due to experiences people have had or things others have told them.

The goal of this discussion is to help clients connect with the fact that these beliefs were learned over time and, thus, may not reflect facts. Oftentimes, these negative beliefs about emotions are so overlearned that clients experience them as facts and don't see that there may be alternative approaches to their emotions that are available to them and more effective. Helping clients connect to the fact that these beliefs were learned, either directly or indirectly, from loved ones, friends, or society as a whole can help them see that other beliefs may also be possible.

Identifying where these beliefs stem from and how they were learned can also help counteract any shame clients may experience when they connect to the fact that some of these beliefs are not helpful and don't fit the facts. It can help normalize the development of unhelpful beliefs so that clients don't judge themselves for having them in the first place.

As you have this discussion with your client, focus on exploring with them where they learned these beliefs and the experiences they had that may have contributed to these beliefs. Table 6.1 contains a list of questions that may be helpful to ask your client during this discussion.

It is common at the start of this discussion for clients to focus on aspects of their upbringing and specific experiences they had with their parents or other members of their family. Although this is very useful and pertinent information, it can also be helpful to focus on larger contextual factors, such as aspects of their culture or society as a whole. As clients discuss the possible origins of their beliefs, make sure you validate their experience, especially with regard to how much sense it makes that these beliefs would have developed given their past or current contexts.

Identifying the Consequences of These Beliefs

Next, assist your client in identifying the ways in which these beliefs influence how they respond to their emotions and how they behave when they feel certain ways. Help them to identify how these beliefs influence how they feel about themselves when they experience certain emotions. The goal is to help clients connect with the fact that these judgments about emotions are not effective and are actually causing further problems in their lives.

TABLE 6.1. Questions for Guiding the Discussion About the Origin and Development of Negative Beliefs About Emotions

Where did these beliefs come from?

Were you told any of these directly?

Did you have experiences as a child that taught you that emotions were bad, unacceptable, or scary?

Were you ever punished for expressing certain emotions?

Did you observe others getting punished for expressing certain emotions?

Were you told that certain emotions are not okay, or that it is not okay to express them?

Did you observe anyone express anger in an unhealthy way?

Were you ever told you were wrong for feeling a certain way?

Were you ever ridiculed or mocked for your feelings?

Did people judge you for expressing certain feelings?

Once you've had this discussion with your client, it can be helpful to introduce the concept of rule-governed behavior, or behavior that is driven by certain beliefs that someone holds. This can be distinguished from behavior that is driven by current contingencies in the environment, where one would expect that adaptive behavior is reinforced and maladaptive or ineffective behavior is not reinforced. When it comes to negative beliefs about emotions, it is often the case that there was a time when it was helpful for clients to act in accordance with those beliefs. For example, if your client was taught that feelings like anger or sadness were bad or that the expression of these would result in punishment, then it would have been adaptive at the time to avoid the experience or expression of those emotions. This behavior was the most effective for that context and could have helped your client avoid punishment or other unwanted consequences of expressing these emotions.

However, once these circumstances changed and the client left that environment, the hope is that they would learn that all emotions are functional and that experiencing them is both acceptable and useful. The problem with rule-governed behavior is that rules are, by their very nature, inflexible and insensitive to changes in contingencies. Thus, even when the context and current contingencies change, it isn't these changed contingencies that guide behavior but the beliefs or rules clients developed based on their previous experiences and previous environment. For this reason, clients miss out on the opportunity to learn that their negative beliefs about emotions may no longer be helpful or effective.

Having this discussion with your client can help highlight the fact that although their negative beliefs about emotions may once have been helpful or adaptive, this likely isn't the case anymore. Rather, not having access to their emotions or the information provided by these emotions due to buying into their negative beliefs about emotions is likely ineffective at best and harmful at worst. This discussion can also help clients understand why these beliefs may have persisted even if they are no longer effective, and lessen the shame that may come up once they realize these beliefs are not helpful.

Psychoeducation on the Function and Utility of Emotions

Once your client has identified the negative beliefs about emotions that are most relevant to them, as well as the origins and consequences of these beliefs, the next step is to provide your client with psychoeducation on the function and utility of emotions. Helping clients connect with the functions of their emotions and the important purposes that their emotions serve can be a useful first step in helping them take a step back from their judgments and respond to their emotions in more adaptive ways.

The purpose of this part of the session is to provide clients with information on all of the ways in which their emotions are adaptive and helpful to them. The goal is to provide clients with the facts they need to stop buying into their negative beliefs about emotions and to start responding to these beliefs, and their emotions, in more adaptive ways.

We have developed a handout that summarizes this information and can be given to clients during the session, Emotional Acceptance: In-Session Handout 1 (Facts About Emotions). This handout can be found at the end of this chapter and is available for download at http://www.newharbinger.com/53622. When reviewing this handout with your client, there are several key points that are important to emphasize. These are summarized below, along with additional information that may be helpful to incorporate into this discussion with your client (to ensure that they understand and connect with the information you are providing them).

Emotions Are Universal and Evolutionarily Adaptive

From the moment of birth, all human beings around the world have the capacity to experience six basic emotions: sadness, anger, fear, disgust, surprise, and joy. The fact that emotions are programmed into all human beings from birth means that they must exist for a reason and serve a purpose. Otherwise, emotions would have been phased out as humans evolved, just as tails were. Emotions have persisted throughout evolution because they are adaptive.

Emotions Serve Multiple Important Functions

Emotions play an important role in people's lives and serve several very important functions. Even emotions that aren't present from birth and that people learn to experience as they grow up, like guilt, embarrassment, and pride, serve important purposes. There are five specific functions of emotions that are highlighted in ERT, in order to promote emotional acceptance. These are reviewed below.

1. EMOTIONS PROVIDE IMPORTANT INFORMATION ABOUT THE ENVIRONMENT

Emotions do not arise out of the blue or randomly. They are always cued by something (even if one is not aware of the cue). For this reason, emotions provide important information about a client's environment and their relationship to their environment. Emotions are their body's way of communicating with them. Thus, knowing the emotion they're experiencing and the information this emotion is providing is imperative for effective functioning. If clients are missing out on this important information, they won't be able to respond as effectively.

Much of the information provided by emotions has its roots in information that was evolutionarily adaptive and allowed our species to survive. At its core, this information would have allowed human beings to protect themselves from danger and threat and maintain needed social connections. Although the information emotions provide now, in this day and age, is far more complex and nuanced, the basic function of emotions remains the same and the general themes of the information provided by emotions can still be seen.

To ensure that clients understand this function of their emotions and have a basic understanding of the information provided by different emotions, it can be helpful to walk them through several examples. We recommend starting with hypothetical examples (for example, "Imagine that you are walking through the forest, and all of a sudden you see a bear in front of you. What emotion would you experience?"), as these are often less provocative and emotionally intense than real-world examples from the client's life and, thus, may be easier for clients to discuss and tolerate. Remember that the purpose of this discussion is to help clients understand that emotions serve a function and provide information about the environment; at this time, it's okay if clients are not yet applying this information to their own experiences. Table 6.2 can help guide this discussion, as it outlines the basic information provided by a number of different emotions.

TABLE 6.2. Types of Information Provided by Different Specific Emotions

Emotion	Information Provided
Sadness	You have experienced a loss.
Anger	Something you need or want has been blocked in some way; you have experienced a violation; you perceive things as out of control.
Fear	A threat is present; you are in danger.
Disgust	You have encountered something unpleasant; there's risk of contamination.
Surprise	You have encountered something that is unexpected but pleasant.
Joy/Happiness	You're doing something that is rewarding or meaningful; keep doing more of this.

Emotion	Information Provided
Guilt	You've done something that goes against your values or isn't consistent with the type of person you want to be in the world.
Embarrassment	You've done something that others may find unacceptable or judge in some way.
Pride	You've done something consistent with your values and how you want to be in this world.

2. EMOTIONS PREPARE PEOPLE FOR ACTION

One of the functions of emotions is to organize a person's behavior and help prepare them for action. All emotions are accompanied by *action urges*, or urges to behave or respond in a certain way. This is actually one component of an emotional response, and the body's way of preparing a person for action and motivating them to respond to a situation or stimulus in a certain way. As with the previous discussion of the information provided by different emotions, it can be very helpful to walk clients through examples of the general action urges associated with a range of emotions, so they understand the concept. Table 6.3 can assist you in this discussion.

TABLE 6.3. Action Urges Associated with Different Specific Emotions

Emotion	Action Urge
Sadness	Seek out what you are missing or obtain support
Anger	Fight or establish dominance and control; stand up for yourself or someone else
Fear	Avoid or escape a situation
Disgust	Avoid or expel whatever you've encountered that is unpleasant
Surprise	Prepare to engage and approach, bring attention to something
Joy	Increase or maintain contact with whatever is rewarding
Guilt	Make amends for what you did
Embarrassment	Hide, escape, or retreat
Pride	Share or show a part of yourself with others

3. EMOTIONS HELP PEOPLE RESPOND QUICKLY

One reason emotions are so functional is that they prepare people to respond quickly. Every emotion is accompanied by a variety of instantaneous biological changes that prepare people to act quickly without thinking. This, in turn, allows them to respond more quickly to threats or other information in their environment that require an immediate response. This is another reason that emotions are evolutionarily adaptive: they increased people's chances for survival when threats in the environment necessitated an immediate response to ensure safety.

4. EMOTIONS COMMUNICATE TO OTHERS

Emotions can be a powerful form of communication. Not only can emotions communicate more quickly than words, they can often be more persuasive than words. It can be helpful when discussing this function of emotions to assist clients in reflecting on experiences they've had where someone's emotions communicated more powerfully than their words—for example, a time when one of their friends looked really sad, with a downturned mouth, quivering lower lip, and eyes welling with tears, but then said that they were fine. For an example like this, it can be helpful to ask clients if they believed their friend's words, or if their friend's facial expression and the message being sent by their friend's emotion were more believable and compelling to them. The goal is to help clients connect with the fact that when people's body language or facial expressions contradict how they say they feel, their words are usually far less powerful than the message their emotion is communicating.

5. EMOTIONS DEEPEN PEOPLE'S EXPERIENCE OF LIFE

All emotions, both pleasant and unpleasant, deepen a person's experience of life. Emotions make us human, and having emotions can connect a person with what they care about in life. It can also be helpful to remind clients that it is negative emotions that deepen their experience of positive emotions, and it isn't possible to have one without the other.

Taking a Step Back from Judgments About Emotions

Once clients have been provided with psychoeducation on the function and utility of emotions, the final step for improving a client's emotional acceptance within this ERT is to teach them more adaptive ways of responding to the negative beliefs about emotions they identified earlier. The expectation is that providing clients with the facts about emotions will put them in a better position to take a step back from their judgments about emotions when they arise.

Now, because ERT is an acceptance-based behavioral therapy, we do not recommend having clients use cognitive restructuring techniques to try to modify their negative beliefs about emotions directly. Instead, the approach taken to addressing ineffective or nonhelpful thoughts within ERT is an acceptance-based approach that focuses on changing a client's relationship to their thoughts rather than changing the content of these thoughts directly. Specifically, there are three recommended strategies for helping clients revisit their negative beliefs about emotions and begin the process of changing their relationship to these beliefs within ERT, all of which are drawn from DBT and ACT. These three strategies are reviewed in detail below. As you discuss these strategies with your client, it can be helpful for them to return to the in-session exercise on beliefs about emotions that they reviewed earlier in the session (Emotional Acceptance: In-Session Exercise 1) and take notes on possible alternative approaches to the beliefs they identified based on the skills you are teaching them.

Check the Facts

The first strategy you can teach your client to help them respond more adaptively to their judgments about emotions is to use the information they learned from this session to consider whether their negative beliefs about emotions actually fit the facts. This is called *check the facts* in DBT (Linehan, 2015) and is one of the most helpful skills for responding to ineffective thoughts or beliefs. In this case, you can encourage your client to use the information they learned about emotions during the session to assess whether their negative beliefs about emotions fit the facts, and, if not, to consider alternatives that may be more consistent with the facts. For example, your client can remind themselves why humans have emotions, or mentally list off what they learned in the session about the function of emotions.

Mindfully Observing the Negative Belief

One of the most helpful strategies for taking a step back from unhelpful or ineffective beliefs is to practice mindfully observing the belief, without reacting to it or buying into it. Helping your client take a step back from their negative beliefs about emotions by mindfully observing these beliefs rather than buying into these beliefs as facts can minimize the impact of these beliefs on how they respond to their emotions. Thus, teaching your client basic mindfulness skills for observing their thoughts can reduce the influence that their negative beliefs about emotions have on their lives and their responses to emotions.

Cognitive Defusion

The final strategy for changing a client's relationship to their negative beliefs about emotions within ERT is *cognitive defusion*. This is a particularly useful strategy for helping clients take a step back from their negative beliefs and recognize that these beliefs are simply thoughts generated by their mind that may or may not be accurate, rather than something they need to buy into as the truth. There are multiple variations of this strategy within ACT (Hayes et al., 1999), all of which focus on helping clients take a step back from and reduce attachment to unhelpful thoughts. The two that we find most useful in the context of this ERT are discussed in greater detail here.

The first involves having your client choose one of their negative beliefs about emotions and break it down into a few words, such as "Emotions are bad." Next, have your client repeat this phrase over and over again as quickly as they can in session. The more they repeat this phrase, the more likely it is to lose meaning and begin to sound like gibberish. Saying the words over and over again helps clients defuse from the meaning of the words and reduce the power of the belief when it arises.

The second strategy involves teaching your client to label their thoughts as just a thought. This mindfulness skill can be a particularly useful strategy for helping clients take a step back from their negative beliefs about emotions and recognize these beliefs as just thoughts their mind has generated, rather than an accurate reflection of how things are. Specifically, have your client label any negative beliefs about emotions that arise as just a thought their mind has generated. For example, if they notice themselves thinking, *I shouldn't be feeling this way* or *Emotions are bad*, teach them to say to themselves something like *I am having the thought that I shouldn't be feeling this way* or *I am having the thought that emotions are bad*. Approaching their negative beliefs about emotions in this way and clearly labeling them as thoughts will help them take a step back from these beliefs and not buy into them as if they were literally true.

Skill Consolidation and Generalization

By the time you reach the end of the session, your client should have a much better understanding of their negative beliefs about emotions (including how these beliefs influence their responses to their emotions), the function and utility of emotions, and helpful strategies for taking a step back from negative beliefs about emotions when they arise (rather than buying into these beliefs). The outside-of-session exercises for this session focus on helping clients further integrate the information they learned in this session and increase their awareness of their negative beliefs about emotions and how these beliefs influence their emotions and behaviors.

The first outside-of-session exercise, Emotional Acceptance: Outside-of-Session Exercise 1 (Exploring Your Negative Beliefs About Emotions), asks clients to reflect on the times and contexts when their personal negative beliefs about emotions are more or less present and believable. This exercise can be found at the end of this chapter and is available for download at http://www.newharbinger.com/53622. The aim of this exercise is to help clients identify times when they are most likely to buy into their negative beliefs about emotions, and, therefore, the times when these beliefs may have the strongest influence on how they respond to their emotions. Connecting with the fact that their attachment to these beliefs can vary and that these beliefs don't always have the same influence over their emotions and behaviors can also be helpful in reinforcing the idea that it is possible to change their relationship to these beliefs and reduce the impact they have on their lives.

It can also be helpful to encourage your client to return to the worksheet for the in-session exercise on beliefs about emotions (Emotional Acceptance: In-Session Exercise 1) over the course of the next week to continue to generate alternative approaches to their negative beliefs about emotions and strategies they can use to respond more effectively to these beliefs when they arise.

Finally, the outside-of-session self-destructive behaviors monitoring form for this session, Emotional Acceptance: Outside-of-Session Monitoring Form 1 (available for download at http://www.newharbinger.com/53622), expands upon the monitoring of emotions and urges to engage in self-destructive behaviors that clients started in the previous session by incorporating a column on negative beliefs about emotions that may have arisen in response to emotions and prompted engagement in self-destructive behaviors. The goal of this form is to increase clients' awareness of the role of negative beliefs about emotions in self-destructive behaviors and the ways in which these beliefs may serve as an intermediary step between the presence of emotions and urges to engage in self-destructive behaviors.

Tips for Teaching Clients These Skills

It's important when covering the material in this session not to suggest that the continued presence of negative beliefs about emotions is problematic in and of itself, or that the goal of the treatment is to get rid of negative beliefs about emotions entirely. When clients have been struggling with negative beliefs about emotions since an early age and for years—if not decades—of their lives, it is understandable that these beliefs would persist for some time. Further, because thoughts (like emotions) cannot be directly controlled, suggesting to clients that the goal of this ERT is to get rid of these beliefs is likely to paradoxically increase the frequency and severity of these thoughts. Therefore, it is important to make it clear to clients throughout the session that the goal of this treatment is not to eliminate these negative beliefs about emotions but to teach clients more effective ways of responding to them when they arise, so that they don't buy into these beliefs as facts or let them influence their behaviors or how they respond to their emotions. We also recommend that clients be informed explicitly that even if they use the skills they learned during this session to change their relationship to these negative beliefs and respond to them in a more effective way, you would expect these beliefs to persist for some time, as beliefs this ingrained cannot be expected to change overnight.

It is also important to normalize the presence of negative beliefs about emotions throughout the session, making it clear that such beliefs are common and to be expected. Given that the goal of the skills covered in this chapter is to increase emotional acceptance, it is important to present this material to clients in a way that does not increase their self-judgments. As we've discussed previously in this book, it is common for clients who struggle with emotion regulation difficulties to judge themselves for their internal experiences. Thus, to ensure that clients will not judge themselves for their judgments about emotions, it is important to normalize these beliefs and emphasize repeatedly throughout the session that negative beliefs about emotions are understandable and present for a reason.

The final theme to emphasize throughout this session is that the presence of negative beliefs about emotions doesn't have to cause problems in your client's life. Simply having these beliefs doesn't have to influence their behaviors or how they respond to their emotions. Basically, it's not the beliefs themselves but how they respond to these beliefs that matters. It's only when they buy into these beliefs and allow them to influence their behaviors that these beliefs can negatively affect their life. By identifying new ways of responding to these beliefs and taking a step back from them when they arise, these beliefs will have less control over their behaviors and how they respond to their emotions.

Emotional Acceptance: In-Session Exercise 1
Beliefs About Emotions

1. Negative feelings are harmful.

   Alternative approach: _____

   _____

2. Having some emotions is a sign of weakness.

   Alternative approach: _____

   _____

3. Certain emotions should be controlled at all costs.

   Alternative approach: _____

   _____

4. Negative feelings should be avoided.

   Alternative approach: _____

   _____

5. Emotions are not important.

   Alternative approach: _____

   _____

6. If I tried hard enough, I could stop myself from feeling bad.

   Alternative approach: _____

   _____

7. Some emotions should never be felt.

   Alternative approach: _____

   _____

8. Becoming more in touch with my emotions may cause me to lose control of them.

   Alternative approach: _____

   _____

Emotional Acceptance: In-Session Handout 1
Facts About Emotions

Emotions are universal

- Emotions are hardwired
- All humans experience basic emotions, both negative and positive
  - Sadness, anger, fear, joy, surprise, disgust

Emotions are evolutionarily adaptive

- Emotions provide important information about the environment
  - Emotions signal the presence of threat, danger, loss, violation
    - e.g., anger signals that a person's rights have been infringed upon or violated
- Emotions prepare people for action and help organize behavior
  - Emotions give direction
  - Emotions guide actions
  - Emotions help people make choices
- Emotions help people respond quickly
  - When you're in danger, you don't need to think; you can act quickly to save yourself

Emotions serve other important functions

- Emotions communicate to others
  - Scowling sends the message to stay away
  - Smiling sends the message to come closer, engage
- Positive and negative emotions deepen people's experience of life
  - Positive emotions are positive only in comparison to negative emotions

Emotional Acceptance: Outside-of-Session Exercise 1

Exploring Your Negative Beliefs About Emotions

Please list the specific negative beliefs about emotions that are most relevant to you.

_____
_____
_____
_____
_____
_____

When are these beliefs most present? Are there certain times when these beliefs are strongest? Are there certain contexts or situations in which these beliefs are most believable or influential?

_____
_____
_____
_____
_____
_____
_____

When are these beliefs less present? Are there certain times when these beliefs are less strong? Are there certain contexts or situations in which these beliefs seem less believable or influential?

_____
_____
_____
_____
_____
_____
_____

CHAPTER 7

Increasing Emotional Awareness

Emotional awareness is considered another foundational emotion regulation skill within this ERT. Specifically, because emotions provide important information about the environment, it's essential that clients learn to identify their emotions and the information those emotions are providing them. This is what helps clients respond most effectively to their environment. In addition, the ability to label emotions can make them feel less overwhelming and unpredictable, lessening clients' emotional suffering (Lane & Smith, 2021). Finally, identifying and labeling emotions can be regulating in their own right, as it provides the opportunity for clients to respond to, modulate, and learn from those emotions in the moment—when they are clearer.

There are three steps for increasing emotional awareness within this ERT. First, clients are provided with psychoeducation on the different components of emotional responses, as well as the different levels of emotional awareness. Second, clients are assisted in identifying the different components of specific emotional responses for them, including the types of situations or cues that tend to evoke different emotions, as well as the thoughts, physical sensations, action tendencies, and actual actions associated with a variety of emotions. Finally, clients are assisted in identifying effective ways of responding to, acting on, and/or expressing various emotions, depending on the situation and the information provided by that emotion.

As we discussed in chapter 1, the original group therapy version of this ERT dedicates two sessions to increasing emotional awareness. Many clients who struggle with emotion regulation difficulties know very little about emotions or how they experience their emotions. Thus, two sessions is often necessary for clients to both learn about a variety of different emotions and have sufficient time outside of session to practice identifying and labeling their emotions, as well as identifying the information provided by these emotions in their daily lives.

Psychoeducation on Emotions and Levels of Emotional Awareness

The first step in increasing clients' emotional awareness within this ERT is to provide them with psychoeducation on the different components of an emotional response and levels of emotional awareness. Emotional Awareness: In-Session Handout 1 (Emotional Awareness I) can be used to guide this discussion. This handout can be found at the end of this chapter and is available for download at http://www.newharbinger.com/53622. There are several key points to emphasize when you're reviewing this handout with your client. These are summarized below.

Components of Emotions

All emotions consist of three components: physical/bodily (the way your client's body responds when they experience an emotion), cognitive (the thoughts that go along with the emotion), and behavioral (the things your client does or has urges to do when they experience an emotion). Increasing their awareness of the different components of their emotions will make it easier for your client to recognize and label their emotions. Common components of several different emotions, along with example prompting events for these emotions, are described in table 7.1., and can be used to guide this discussion.

Levels of Emotional Awareness

Emotional awareness exists on a continuum, ranging from lower to higher levels of awareness, and is not static (Lane & Smith, 2021). Thus, your client's level of emotional awareness can vary depending on a number of different factors, including the emotion(s) they're experiencing and their intensity, how many distinct emotions they're experiencing, the situation that prompted the emotion(s), and other contextual factors. Clients often find that they have a higher level of awareness for some emotions (e.g., anger) than others (e.g., sadness), or that repeated attempts to avoid or suppress certain emotions have led to lower levels of awareness for those emotions. The key is to help clients connect with the fact that emotional awareness exists on a continuum that varies over time. Framing emotional awareness in this way can help offset the shame some clients experience when they connect with their difficulties identifying emotions and increase their recognition of the emotional awareness they already have. Indeed, even if your client isn't able to label their emotion or identify all of its components, the ability to identify even one or two components of an emotion can be helpful in determining what emotion is present.

FIRST LEVEL OF EMOTIONAL AWARENESS

The first level of emotional awareness corresponds to a complete lack of emotional awareness. This is the level of awareness someone experiences when they are not in touch with any component of an emotional response and are not aware that an emotion is even present.

SECOND LEVEL OF EMOTIONAL AWARENESS

The second level of emotional awareness is awareness of an emotion's action urges, or urges to respond or behave in a certain way. For example, clients may report feeling like they want to punch a wall (an action urge associated with anger) or hide (an action urge associated with fear). Because particular emotions tend to be associated with specific action urges, being aware of their action urges can help clients begin to narrow down what emotion may be present.

TABLE 7.1. Common Prompting Events and Components of Different Emotions

	Fear	Sadness	Anger	Joy	Guilt
Prompt	Encountering a reminder of a past traumatic event Receiving an email from your teacher or supervisor asking for a meeting Walking outside alone late at night Getting lost	Death of a loved one Being rejected by someone Being turned down for a promotion Losing a friend or intimate partner Having a child move away from home	Being stood up by a friend Having something stolen Having your rights violated Having your boundaries crossed	Receiving an unexpected gift Becoming immersed in a valued hobby Getting a visit or card from a loved one Engaging in a valued or pleasurable activity	Doing something that hurt someone else Lying to a loved one or close friend Breaking a law or violating social mores
Physical Sensations	increased heart rate, tunnel vision, muscle tension, sweating, shortness of breath, dry mouth	fatigue, loss of appetite, sluggishness, pit in the stomach	increased heart rate, muscle tension, shortness of breath, flushing, headache	increased heart rate, increased attention and focus, increased energy	pit in the stomach, tension, flushing of the face, wanting to crawl out of one's skin
Thoughts	"I am in danger." "This is unsafe." "I will be harmed." "I can't escape." "What if something bad happens?"	"I am alone." "I miss them." "I have no one." "No one loves me." "I can't win."	"I hate them." "I don't deserve this." "This is unfair." "This shouldn't be happening to me."	"I am lucky." "I am fortunate." "I am having fun." "I don't want this to end."	"I hurt someone." "I regret what I did." "I made a mistake." "I screwed up." "I wish I could take that back."
Action Urges	avoid, escape, freeze	cry, isolate, seek out support	lash out, fight, yell	approach, engage	make amends, hide, rectify, apologize, look away, collapse into oneself, make oneself smaller
Actions	run away, leave the situation, flee, freeze	cry, isolate, hide, curl up in a ball, seek out support	yell, throw something, scream, hit something, cry, clench one's fists	smile, dance, laugh, reach out to a friend, talk to others	look away, look down, lower one's head, cry, apologize, freeze, hide

THIRD LEVEL OF EMOTIONAL AWARENESS

The third level of emotional awareness is awareness of the physical sensations associated with an emotion, such as a racing heart, muscle tension, or pit in the stomach. Awareness of these physical sensations can also help clients begin to identify possible emotions that may be present.

FOURTH LEVEL OF EMOTIONAL AWARENESS

At the fourth level of emotional awareness, clients are aware that they are experiencing an emotion but are not able to identify the specific emotion that is present. At this level, clients are experiencing undifferentiated emotions. Although they are aware of the presence of an emotion and attempting to label that experience, the label is likely to be broad ("bad," "good," "upset," "distressed," or "overwhelmed") and focused more on the valence (positive or negative) of the emotion versus a specific emotional state.

Based on our experience, this is the level of emotional awareness that clients experience the most when they begin this ERT. Clients who struggle with emotion regulation difficulties are often very aware that they are feeling terrible and struggling with painful emotions; they just can't quite identify the precise emotion they are experiencing. This is likely due to their high level of emotional avoidance. When a client repeatedly attempts to avoid their emotions, those emotions tend to build up and form an undifferentiated and unpleasant mass that is difficult to unravel.

FIFTH LEVEL OF EMOTIONAL AWARENESS

The next level of emotional awareness involves the experience of differentiated emotions. At this level, clients can place a more specific label on their emotions and delineate between different emotional states, such as sadness, shame, guilt, anger, fear, or happiness, and so on. They are connecting with all components of their emotional response and using this information, as well as contextual information, to determine the specific emotion they are experiencing.

SIXTH LEVEL OF EMOTIONAL AWARENESS

The last level of emotional awareness is awareness of blended emotions, as people often experience more than one emotion at a time. An example that can be helpful in illustrating this concept to clients is having them imagine what it would feel like to send a child to college. Although this event could bring up feelings of happiness, pride, and excitement related to such an important milestone, it could also bring up feelings of sadness and loneliness as the child moves out of the home and enters a new stage of their life. At this level of emotional awareness, clients can connect with all of the mixed emotions that may occur in response to different situations (positive and negative, weak or strong) and put a label on each. During this part of the discussion, it can be helpful to highlight how often both positive and negative emotions can co-occur and how rare it is for people to experience only one emotion at a time.

When discussing the levels of emotional awareness with your client, assist them in identifying the levels of emotional awareness that are most common for them. Are there specific emotions that tend to be associated with lower or higher levels of emotional awareness? What kinds of situations, emotions, or other experiences influence their level of emotional awareness? Helping your client connect with the varying levels of emotional awareness they experience can help offset the tendency to approach emotional awareness as all or nothing and/or judge themselves for struggling to label their emotions.

Increasing Awareness of the Components of Emotions

The next step in increasing your client's emotional awareness is to assist them in identifying the specific prompting events, physical sensations, thoughts, action urges, and actions associated with a variety of emotional states for them. Emotional Awareness: In-Session Handout 2 (Emotional Awareness II) and Emotional Awareness: In-Session Exercise 1 (Increasing Emotional Awareness) can assist with this; both of these documents can be found at the end of this chapter and are available for download at http://www.newharbinger.com/53622. The in-session exercise gives clients the opportunity to reflect on how they experience specific emotions and the particular internal experiences (i.e., thoughts, sensations, urges) that may serve as signs that the emotion in question is present. The more components of an emotion your client can identify, the better able they will be to recognize and label that emotion when it arises.

We recommend having clients begin this exercise by focusing on some of the basic emotions that are often relevant to clients receiving this ERT, such as fear or anxiety, sadness, and anger. Even if your client isn't always able to identify these emotions when they arise, they probably have some basic knowledge of these emotions and their components that can be a starting point for this exercise. We also find it helpful to have clients identify the different components of one or two positive emotions, such as joy or excitement. We recommend saving more complex emotions, such as guilt or shame, for the second session on emotional awareness, after clients have experience using these skills with more basic emotions.

Specific questions you can use to assist your client in completing this exercise and identifying the various components of each of the emotions they select are provided in table 7.2. You can use these questions to help guide this in-session exercise.

We recommend taking your time with this exercise and using it as an opportunity to assist clients in cultivating a stance of curiosity and openness toward their emotions. This exercise is intended to assist clients in discovering more about how they experience their emotions, with the goal of providing clients with a road map for identifying and understanding different emotional experiences.

TABLE 7.2. Questions for Guiding the In-Session Exercise on Increasing Awareness of the Different Components of Emotional Responses

What prompts this emotion?	• What types of situations tend to bring up this emotion? • What kinds of interactions with others tend to bring up this emotion? • Are there specific internal experiences (e.g., thoughts) that tend to bring up this emotion for you?
What thoughts are associated with this emotion?	• What thoughts come up when you have this emotion? • Do you think about the past or the future? What do those thoughts look like? • Do your thoughts slow down or speed up? • Do you tend to have pleasant or unpleasant thoughts?
What physical sensations are associated with this emotion?	• How does this emotion feel in your body? • Where do you feel this emotion? • Do you feel more or less activated when this emotion occurs? • How does your breathing, heart rate, and/or muscle tension change when this emotion occurs?
What action urges are associated with this emotion?	• What do you feel like doing when this emotion occurs? • Do you find yourself having urges to act in a certain way (for example, avoid, cry, lash out) when experiencing this emotion?
How do you tend to act in response to this emotion?	• What do you typically do when you are experiencing this emotion? • Do you act that way regardless of the situation you are in at the time? Or, do you act in different ways depending on the situation? • Do you tend to act in ways that are consistent with the action urges associated with that emotion? Or do you act counter to those action urges?

The completed worksheets can also be used to guide your client through the process of increasing their level of emotional awareness in the moment. For example, if your client is able to connect with the action urges or physical sensations associated with an emotion but has difficulty identifying the specific emotion they are experiencing, they can use their worksheets to identify the specific emotions that may be associated with those action urges or physical sensations. Then, once they've identified the emotion (or emotions) that correspond to those components, they can use the additional information on the worksheets to assist them in connecting with the other components of the emotion they are experiencing and identifying the specific emotion present in the moment.

Distinguishing Between Fear and Anxiety

When you're assisting clients with this exercise, we have found that it is helpful to distinguish between fear and anxiety. Although these emotions can seem similar, they can be distinguished by the situations that prompt them, as well as their associated thoughts. Specifically, whereas fear tends to be prompted by the presence of actual danger or threat, anxiety tends to occur in response to situations involving the potential for or expectations of danger or harm. As a result, thoughts associated with fear tend to be present-focused (e.g., *I am in danger*), whereas thoughts associated with anxiety tend to be future-focused (e.g., *I will get hurt*).

Distinguishing Between Guilt and Shame

It can also be helpful during this exercise to assist your client in distinguishing between guilt and shame. Specifically, because guilt and shame are both unpleasant self-conscious emotions that arise when people negatively evaluate some aspect of themselves or their behavior (Tangney & Tracy, 2012), the experience of these emotions can be similar, and many clients don't know the differences between these emotions and, thus, use these terms interchangeably. However, there are important differences between guilt and shame that make distinguishing between them important. Specifically, whereas guilt stems from negative evaluations of certain things your client did or said and can be helpful in motivating them to make amends for the behavior or avoid it in the future, shame tends to stem from negative evaluations of themselves as a whole and can actually interfere with behavior change. For this reason, although guilt can be a helpful emotion that can guide effective behavior, shame is generally not helpful and tends to prompt ineffective behaviors (e.g., isolation, avoidance, self-punishment, or self-judgment). As we mentioned previously, due to the complexity of these emotions, we strongly recommend waiting until the second session on emotional awareness to assist clients in identifying the different components of guilt and shame (and distinguishing between them).

Identifying Effective Ways of Responding to Emotions

The final step in increasing clients' emotional awareness is to assist them in identifying both the information provided by their emotions and effective ways of acting on this information and expressing their emotions. Table 7.3 provides example language for describing this final step in improving emotional awareness to your clients.

TABLE 7.3. Example Therapist Language: Identifying the Information Provided by Emotions
Emotions don't randomly occur. They are always tied to some kind of event or cue inside or outside your body, and they are there to provide you with important information about yourself and your environment. Remember, emotions are your body's way of communicating with you. Therefore, if you know what you are feeling, you can start to learn from your emotions. The information provided by your emotions can help you determine how to respond most effectively to the situation. Your emotions can serve as a guide for effective behavior.

Specifically, once you've assisted your client in completing the in-session exercise for several emotions, return to Emotional Awareness: In-Session Handout 2 to review the second half of this handout. When reviewing this part of the handout with your client, there are several key points that are important to emphasize. These are summarized below.

Identifying the Information Provided by Emotions

When assisting clients in identifying the information provided by their emotions, it can be helpful to revisit the psychoeducation on the function of emotions from the session on emotional acceptance (reviewed in chapter 6), particularly the information in table 6.2. During this discussion, it can be helpful to highlight for clients that the information provided by their emotions can vary depending on the situation and context at hand. Specifically, although an understanding of the evolutionary basis of emotions and the basic information provided by emotions can help clients identify general themes of the information provided by specific emotions, it is only by considering the particular situation that cued the emotion and the context in which the emotion is occurring that clients can identify the precise information being provided by their emotion in the moment.

For example, although a client's anxiety in response to learning that their company expects to have layoffs in the near future may provide information of an upcoming or expected threat, anxiety in response to receiving a desired job interview may provide more nuanced information. Although the presence of anxiety in the latter situation may speak to the potential threat of not getting the job or being evaluated negatively, it is also providing information that the person is doing something that is important to them.

Acting on This Information in an Effective Way

Once clients have identified the information provided by their emotions, the next step is to assist them in identifying how to act on this information in an effective way. The key point to emphasize during this part of the discussion is that identifying effective ways of acting on the information provided by emotions requires clients to consider both their overarching goals and the nuances of the current context and situation at hand. In particular, although all emotions are comprised of specific action urges, acting on those urges is not always effective.

For example, if your client received news during a meeting that there could be layoffs at their workplace, this would likely elicit anxiety due to the anticipated threat. However, acting on one of the primary action urges associated with anxiety (i.e., to avoid) by leaving the room would most likely not be effective. Instead, one effective way of acting on the information provided by the anxiety would be to ask questions or seek out more information (e.g., asking about the likelihood of the layoffs, who is going to be laid off, support available should a layoff occur, etc.). On the other hand, if your client was out for a run one day and saw a suspicious figure lurking in an alleyway, acting on the action urge associated with that anxiety by avoiding the alleyway would likely be effective.

Likewise, although anger may provide information that your client's rights have been violated or infringed upon in some way, standing up for themselves (a behavior that could be very effective in some situations) may not always be effective. Instead, in some contexts, it may be more effective to use the information provided by their anger to limit their contact with this person or build a life without this person in it.

Indeed, it is important during this discussion to highlight for clients that acting on the information provided by their emotions cannot (and should not) always be immediate. Instead, sometimes the most effective way of acting on the information provided by emotions is to use this information to develop a longer-term plan for making changes in their life. For example, if your client was experiencing chronic frustration at work, that emotion may be signaling to them that the position or workplace is not a good fit for them or is interfering with other goals. Although one way of acting on this information could be to leave this position, doing so impulsively would likely not be effective. Instead, more effective ways of acting on this information could involve exploring ways of making the position a better fit, exploring ways of changing their position or taking another position, or seeking out a new position that may be a better fit.

Identifying Healthy Ways of Expressing Emotions

As we noted above, although clients' emotions provide important information about their environment, it will not always be effective or possible for them to act on that information immediately. It may take days, weeks, or even months before an effective course of action can be taken in response to the information provided by an emotion. In these cases, it is important to help clients identify adaptive ways to express their emotions in the moment. Because emotions are comprised of specific action urges, expressing emotions can reduce their intensity and help them pass. Although there are times when expressing an emotion is the same as acting on the information provided by that emotion (such as when your client apologizes to a friend for an insensitive remark), there are many times when acting on the information provided by the emotion may take longer. In those cases, expressing the emotion is something that can be done in the moment to help your client take the edge off their emotion.

During this discussion, it is important to remain mindful of any ineffective ways of expressing emotions clients identify (e.g., lashing out at someone, self-injury, negative self-talk) and assist your client in identifying healthier ways of expressing these emotions. It can be helpful to remind clients to focus on both the long-term and short-term consequences of various ways of expressing emotions when identifying the most effective strategies, as some strategies may work in the short term but have paradoxical consequences in the long term. The key is to identify strategies that will take the edge off of their emotions without the long-term negative consequences associated with more harmful or unhealthy strategies.

The Unique Example of Shame

Although identifying both the information provided by their emotions and effective ways of acting on that information are key skills for effectively regulating most of the emotions your clients experience, they are not effective strategies for responding to shame. As we mentioned previously, unlike other emotions, shame does not provide useful information to your client about their environment. Instead, because shame tends to stem from negative evaluations of themselves as a whole, the information that shame provides clients is that they are flawed, faulty, or otherwise not acceptable as they are— information that is never helpful.

For this reason, the most effective way of responding to shame is to *not* act on the information being provided by the emotion, and, instead, to act opposite to this information and the action urges that accompany shame. Specifically, because shame provides clients with the information that they are unacceptable or faulty and tends to be associated with the action urges of hiding/avoiding, self-punishing, self-judgment, and self-criticism, the most effective way for clients to respond to shame is to act opposite to these urges and information. Strategies for responding effectively to shame include the following:

- Being kind to themselves

- Engaging in self-soothing or self-care activities

- Practicing self-compassion

- Focusing on or reminding themselves of their strengths and positive qualities

- Sharing their emotions, experiences, and/or aspects of their identity with trusted others

- Making eye contact when interacting with others

- Standing or walking with an upright posture and head held high

- Reaching out to or spending time with others

It can also be helpful to pair these strategies with the skills for taking a step back from judgments that clients learned in the session on emotional acceptance, including check the facts, mindfulness, and cognitive defusion (reviewed in chapter 6).

Skill Consolidation and Generalization

By the end of the first session on emotional awareness, your clients will have a better understanding of the components of several basic emotions, how to use that information to increase their emotional awareness in the moment, how to identify the information provided by their emotions, and how to use that information to guide effective behavior. The second session reinforces and expands upon the skills they learned in the first session, helping them identify the components of additional and more complex emotions (like guilt and shame), teaching them effective (and unique) strategies for responding to the emotion of shame in particular, and reviewing their experiences identifying both their emotions and the information provided by those emotions as part of the primary outside-of-session exercise for these sessions.

Specifically, in addition to continuing to complete the same version of the self-destructive behaviors monitoring form they've been completing since the session on emotional acceptance (Emotional Awareness: Outside-of-Session Monitoring Form 2, available for download at http://www.newharbinger.com/53622), the primary outside-of-session exercise for both of the emotional awareness sessions is Emotional Awareness: Outside-of-Session Monitoring Form 1 (Emotional Awareness Monitoring Form). This form can be found at the end of this chapter and is available for download at http://www.newharbinger.com/53622. This form assists clients in applying the skills they learned during the session to the emotions they experience on a daily basis, guiding them to identify their emotions and the information provided by these emotions, as well as effective ways of both acting on this information and expressing these emotions. Clients are instructed to complete this monitoring form at least once per day.

We have found that many clients struggle with this exercise, especially during the week after the first session on increasing emotional awareness. If your client reports that they had difficulties identifying their emotions or the information provided by these emotions, validate and normalize this experience. Clients are not expected to be experts at identifying and understanding their emotions overnight. Increasing emotional awareness is a process that takes time. In fact, we recommend emphasizing the value of process versus outcome when it comes to practicing the skills they learned in these sessions. The goal is for them to commit to the process of increasing their emotional awareness and practicing a new way of responding to their emotions. It can also be helpful to remind clients that long-standing patterns of responding to their emotions are not expected to change overnight, and the simple act of focusing their attention on their emotions and trying to identify the information those emotions are providing will increase their emotional awareness over time.

Finally, an additional resource that may be helpful to give to your client at the end of the emotional awareness sessions is Emotional Awareness: Supplemental Handout 1 (Emotion Words). This handout provides a comprehensive list of emotion words that can be helpful in providing clients with a language for describing their emotions, and is available for download at http://www.newharbinger.com/53622.

Emotional Awareness: In-Session Handout 1
Emotional Awareness I

Emotional responses are made up of three different components

- Physical/bodily
- Cognitive
- Behavioral
  - Expressive
  - Action tendencies

Emotional awareness can take place on several different levels

- No awareness/cognitive thought
  - e.g., "I feel like a loser."
- Action urges
  - e.g., "I feel like punching a wall."
- Physical sensations
  - e.g., stomach hurts, heart races
- Undifferentiated emotional responses
  - e.g., "I feel upset."
- Differentiated emotional responses
  - e.g., "I feel sad."
- Blended emotional responses
  - e.g., "I feel hurt, angry, and somewhat ashamed."

Emotional Awareness: In-Session Handout 2
Emotional Awareness II

The more components of an emotional response you can identify, the more information you will have about your emotional experience and the better able you'll be to identify and label your emotions. By knowing exactly what you're feeling, you will be in a much better position to respond to your emotions in an effective and adaptive way.

To increase awareness of an emotional response, ask yourself the following:

➢ What thoughts are associated with this emotion?

➢ What physical sensations are associated with this emotion?

➢ What action urges are associated with this emotion?

➢ How do I tend to act in response to this emotion?

Once you have identified what you are feeling, ask yourself the following:

➢ What information is this emotion providing me (e.g., information about my environment, about myself, etc.)?

➢ How can I act on this information in a way that is effective?

➢ What are healthy ways of expressing this emotion?

Emotional Awareness: In-Session Exercise 1

Increasing Emotional Awareness

Emotion: _____

What tends to prompt or elicit this emotion? What types of situations or interactions elicit this emotion?	What thoughts or appraisals are associated with this emotion?	What physical sensations are associated with this emotion? How does this emotion feel in my body?	What are the action urges associated with this emotion? What does this emotion make me want to do or say?	What do I tend to do in response to this emotion? How do I tend to act when I feel this way?

Emotional Awareness: Outside-of-Session Monitoring Form 1

Emotional Awareness Monitoring Form *(Please complete at least once per day)*

Situation	Emotion	What information is this emotion providing me about my environment?	How can I act on this information in a way that is healthy and adaptive?	What are healthy ways of expressing this emotion?

CHAPTER 8

Increasing Emotional Clarity and Understanding

One of the foundational emotion regulation skills targeted in this ERT is emotional clarity. As we've discussed in previous chapters, this ERT is grounded in the conceptualization of emotions as functional and adaptive. Within this framework, emotions are considered to provide important information about the environment that can be used to guide a client's behaviors. For this reason, it is imperative that clients understand the complexity of their emotional experiences and are able to distinguish between different emotional states and types of emotions. It is only with emotional clarity that clients can benefit from the information provided by their emotions.

There are two specific strategies for improving emotional clarity within this ERT. The first focuses on helping clients distinguish between primary emotions (i.e., their initial emotional responses to a situation) and secondary emotions (i.e., their emotional reactions to these primary emotional responses). The second helps clients learn to distinguish between clear emotions (i.e., emotions that are proportionate and directly tied to the immediate stimulus/situation) and cloudy emotions (i.e., emotions that are not a direct response to the immediate stimulus/situation, but rather influenced by other factors). As we discussed in chapter 1, the original group therapy version of this ERT dedicates two sessions to covering the skills reviewed in this chapter, with the differences between primary and secondary emotions covered in the first session and the distinctions between clear and cloudy emotions covered in the second session. Therefore, we recommend breaking up the skills reviewed in this chapter across at least two sessions so that clients have sufficient time to learn and practice these skills. We will discuss each of the strategies for improving emotional clarity in turn below.

Distinguishing Between Primary and Secondary Emotions

Distinguishing between primary and secondary emotions can be a challenging skill for many clients. The shift from a primary emotion to a secondary emotion can be so fast and automatic that it can be difficult for clients to recognize their initial emotional response. As challenging as it can be to implement this skill, however, this is also a skill that tends to resonate with clients in a more immediate way than the emotional acceptance and awareness skills do. Specifically, it is during this session that clients first see their personal experience of emotions as overwhelming and enduring being highlighted—an experience that can be validating for clients who struggle with their emotions.

Indeed, it's common for clients to express some skepticism in response to the psychoeducation provided in the sessions aimed at increasing emotional awareness, particularly the idea that emotions tend to pass relatively quickly (provided that they are acknowledged and allowed to run their course). This idea tends to conflict with clients' lived experience of painful emotions as sticking around for an extended period of time. What they learn during this session, however, is that the reason for the discrepancy between their experience and what they learned about emotions in the previous sessions is that the previous sessions were focused on primary emotions whereas the emotions they tend to experience and struggle with are secondary emotions. Thus, although distinguishing between primary and secondary emotions can be difficult for clients, this strategy often resonates with them and validates their experience of long-lasting emotional suffering.

Psychoeducation on Primary vs. Secondary Emotions

The first step in teaching clients how to distinguish between primary and secondary emotions is to orient clients to these concepts and provide psychoeducation on the differences between these types of emotional experiences. This information is summarized in a handout that can be given to your client during the session, Emotional Clarity: In-Session Handout 1 (Primary vs. Secondary Emotional Responses). This handout can be found at the end of this chapter and is available for download at http://www.newharbinger.com/53622.

When you're reviewing this handout with your clients, it can be helpful to explicitly acknowledge that the emotions they've learned about so far in this treatment are primary emotions. Although you haven't labeled them as such up to this point, these were the emotions you were talking about in the sessions focused on emotional acceptance and emotional awareness. Specifically, primary emotions are those that occur directly in response to a situation or event and that provide clients with important information about their environments and themselves. As such, these are the emotions that are functional, adaptive, and can be used to guide their behaviors. These are also the emotions that tend to pass relatively quickly—they arise in response to a particular situation, provide information about that situation and potential effective ways of responding, and then pass.

Once you've oriented your client to the concept of primary emotions and the fact that these have been the main focus of this ERT so far, the next step is to introduce your client to the concept of secondary emotions and acknowledge how pervasive these emotions tend to be. It can be incredibly validating for clients to learn that the emotions they tend to experience are common enough to have a name and are different from the emotions they've learned about so far in this treatment. When introducing your client to the concept of secondary emotions, it is important to emphasize the following points:

SECONDARY EMOTIONS ARE EMOTIONAL RESPONSES TO PRIMARY EMOTIONS

Unlike primary emotions, secondary emotions do not arise in response to some situation or event, and, as such, do not provide clients with important information about their environment. Instead, secondary emotions are emotional responses to clients' primary emotions that are driven by clients' negative beliefs about their primary emotions. Therefore, the only information these emotions provide is that clients are judging their primary emotions.

SECONDARY EMOTIONS ARE NOT FUNCTIONAL

For this reason, and unlike primary emotions, secondary emotions are not adaptive, as they do not provide clients with information about anything other than their negative beliefs about emotions. Further, secondary emotions often occur so quickly following a primary emotional response that they can interfere with clients connecting with and learning from their primary emotions. Specifically, secondary emotions can mask a client's primary emotions, making it difficult to identify the information provided by those emotions and interfering with effective responses.

SECONDARY EMOTIONS INCREASE EMOTIONAL SUFFERING

Because secondary emotions are driven by negative beliefs about primary emotions, they generally do not pass quickly. Instead, secondary emotions tend to stick around and increase a client's emotional suffering. In fact, this is why so many clients experience their emotions as distressing and overwhelming—when clients struggle with emotional acceptance and hold long-standing and pervasive negative beliefs about emotions, they tend to experience secondary emotions much more frequently and for longer durations than their primary emotions. And, because these emotions tend to be far more persistent than primary emotions, clients can experience this emotional suffering much of the time.

SECONDARY EMOTIONS CAN BECOME AN ESCALATING CYCLE

Another downside of secondary emotions is that they can become cyclical, with judgments about primary emotions leading to secondary emotions and then judgments about these secondary emotions leading to additional secondary emotions (or tertiary emotions), and so on. As this process unfolds, clients will experience an increasingly complex and painful array of emotions that are very intense, challenging to decipher, and hard to manage. In addition, the more secondary emotional responses your client experiences, the more they will lose touch with their primary emotional response, making it even more difficult to identify this primary emotion and the information it was providing. See figure 8.1 for a visual representation of this escalating cycle of secondary emotional responses.

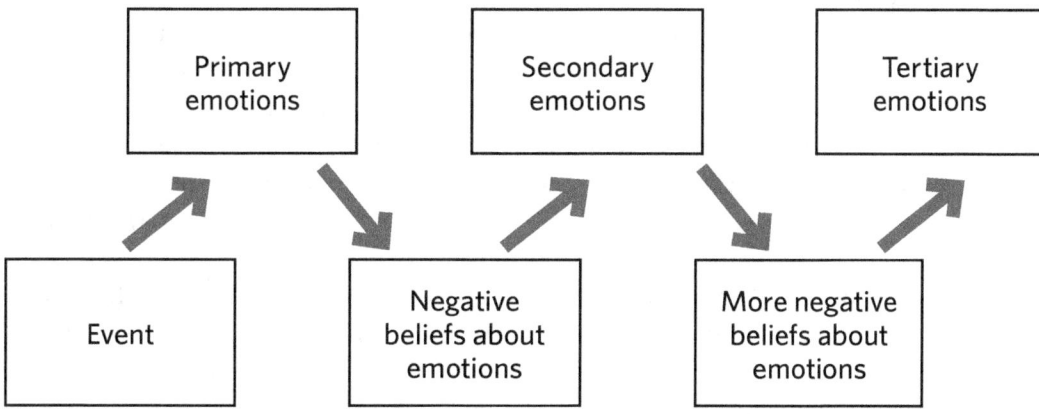

Figure 8.1. Cycle of escalating secondary emotions

Increasing Emotional Clarity and Understanding

Distinguishing Emotional Pain from Emotional Suffering

It can be incredibly helpful at this point in the session to draw a distinction between emotional pain and emotional suffering, to illustrate to clients the downsides of secondary emotional responses. Specifically, whereas emotional pain is an unavoidable part of being human and living one's life, emotional suffering stems from maladaptive responses to emotional pain that only serve to paradoxically intensify and worsen this pain. These maladaptive responses to emotional pain include negative beliefs about emotions and attempts to avoid primary emotions. For this reason, emotional suffering is much more intense and long-lasting than emotional pain and doesn't have the same benefits as the primary emotions that clients experience (emotions that, despite being painful, serve important functions and can help guide their behaviors).

Given how common secondary emotions are for clients who struggle with emotion regulation difficulties, it is highly likely that most of the clients you believe could benefit from this treatment will experience the intense emotional suffering associated with secondary emotions far more often than the emotional pain of primary emotions. The upside of this, though, is that teaching them skills for decreasing their secondary emotions and getting more in touch with their primary emotions will be a powerful tool for alleviating their emotional suffering and decreasing their distress. Although clients will continue to experience emotional pain, their level of emotional suffering will be greatly reduced.

Identifying Secondary Emotions

Once your client has learned about the differences between primary and secondary emotions, the next step is to teach them strategies for distinguishing between the two and identifying secondary emotions when they arise. As we mentioned previously, identifying secondary emotions can be challenging, as they tend to arise so quickly in response to primary emotions that clients may not even be aware of their initial emotional response or the negative beliefs about their emotions that prompted the secondary emotion.

Further complicating efforts to identify secondary emotions is the fact that all emotions can be primary or secondary emotions. If certain emotions were primary emotions and others were secondary emotions, it would likely be far easier for clients to distinguish between the two—they would just need to identify what emotion was present by using the skills they learned in the sessions on emotional awareness (reviewed in chapter 7). This is not the case, however. Instead, any emotion can be a primary or secondary emotion; what distinguishes one from the other is when the emotion occurs in the sequence of unfolding emotions and thoughts and what is driving it. Therefore, as you work with your client to increase their understanding of secondary emotions and distinguish these from a new primary emotion that may occur after the initial primary emotion, the key is to have them focus their attention on what is driving the emotion. If the emotion is in response to a negative belief or judgment about the primary emotion, it is a secondary emotion. If the emotion arises in response to another type of thought that isn't a judgment about a primary emotion, then it is most likely simply a new primary emotion driven by an internal stimulus.

The examples in table 8.1 illustrate these differences and can be used to guide this discussion with your client and ensure that they understand the difference between a secondary emotion and a new primary emotion. We recommend leading your client through several of these examples to illustrate how the second emotion in a sequence of emotions and thoughts could be either a secondary emotion or a new primary emotion, depending on the context.

Effective Ways of Responding to Primary and Secondary Emotions

Once you've taught your client the differences between primary and secondary emotions and how to distinguish between the two, the next step is to teach them strategies for responding adaptively to each type of emotion. Specifically, because primary and secondary emotions differ from one another in such important ways, the most adaptive ways of responding to these emotions differ as well.

When teaching your client how to respond adaptively to these different types of emotions, it is important to highlight that the skills they learned in the sessions on emotional awareness are really only applicable to their primary emotions. Specifically, because primary emotions are the emotions that are functional and adaptive, the most effective way for clients to respond to these emotions is to bring their attention to the emotion, label the emotion, identify the information the emotion is providing, and identify effective ways of acting on and expressing the emotion.

Conversely, the most adaptive way for clients to respond to secondary emotions is to use the skills they learned in the session on emotional acceptance (reviewed in chapter 6) to change how they relate and respond to their negative beliefs about their primary emotions (e.g., by approaching these beliefs as simply objects in their mind versus an indication of truth). It can be helpful to revisit the in-session exercise on beliefs about emotions that clients completed during the emotional acceptance session, Emotional Acceptance: In-Session Exercise 1, to assist them in identifying more adaptive ways of responding to their negative beliefs about emotions. We also recommend reviewing the skills for taking a step back from negative beliefs about emotions that clients learned during that session, including check the facts, mindfulness, and cognitive defusion.

The different approaches for responding effectively to primary versus secondary emotions are reviewed in table 8.2, and summarized in Emotional Clarity: In-Session Handout 1. You can use these materials to guide your discussion of these skills with your client.

TABLE 8.1. Identifying Secondary Emotions: Distinguishing a Secondary Emotion from a New Primary Emotion

Example #	1	2	3	4	5	6	7
Primary emotion	Sadness	Anxiety/Fear	Anger	Anger	Sadness	Happiness	Guilt
Thoughts	This sadness is only going to get worse. I am going to fall into a depression.	I am weak for feeling this way. Only losers feel anxious.	The world isn't fair, so why bother? Everyone will leave me eventually.	I hate feeling this way. I can't control this feeling.	My life will never get better. I don't have any kind of future.	I wonder when this feeling will end. It just means I have farther to fall.	I really messed up. I'm going to get into trouble.
Next emotion	Fear	Shame	Sadness	Anger	Sadness	Fear	Fear
Is this a primary or secondary emotion?	Secondary	Secondary	Primary	Secondary	Primary	Secondary	Primary
Explanation	In this case, the thoughts reflect judgments of the primary emotion of sadness: i.e., that sadness is not able to be regulated and will always escalate into depression.	In this case, the thoughts reflect judgments of the primary emotion of anxiety as unacceptable and a sign of weakness.	In this case, the thoughts are not judgments of the primary emotion of anger. They are thoughts that occurred after the anger and cued a new primary emotion of sadness.	In this case, the thoughts reflect judgments of anger as unacceptable and out of control—judgments that then drive a secondary emotion of anger.	In this case, the thoughts reflect sadness-related thoughts that cue further sadness. These thoughts are not judgments about the primary emotion of sadness.	In this case, the thoughts reflect judgments about the primary emotion of happiness as dangerous and threatening.	In this case, the primary emotion of guilt leads to thoughts that cue a new primary emotion of fear. These thoughts do not reflect judgments of the emotion of guilt itself.

TABLE 8.2. Adaptive Ways of Responding to Primary and Secondary Emotions

Primary Emotions

- Focus on the emotion
- Notice and observe the emotion and its action tendencies
- Identify the information the emotion is providing
- Identify effective ways to act on and express the emotion

Secondary Emotions

- Focus on the thought—do not act on the emotion!
- Identify the thought that led to the emotion
- Change one's relationship to the thought (e.g., mindfulness, cognitive defusion, check the facts)

Identifying Typical Secondary Emotions to Primary Emotions

Because secondary emotions can occur so quickly in response to primary emotions, one helpful strategy for increasing clients' awareness of secondary emotions in the moment is to have them identify in advance the typical secondary emotions they have in response to a variety of common primary emotions. Within this ERT, this is done in the context of an in-session exercise, Emotional Clarity: In-Session Exercise 1 (Identifying and Challenging Secondary Emotional Responses). This exercise can be found at the end of this chapter, and is available for download at http://www.newharbinger.com/53622. The goal of this exercise is to help clients identify the judgments that typically arise in response to specific primary emotions, as well as the secondary emotions that stem from these judgments. This helps clients increase their awareness of the secondary emotions that tend to follow different primary emotions, as well as the specific negative beliefs about emotions that may be driving these secondary emotions. Increased awareness of these patterns will make it easier for them to identify these beliefs in the moment so that they can use the skills they learned in this session to take a step back from these beliefs and return their attention to the primary emotion.

During this exercise, assist your client in identifying the specific judgments that accompany different primary emotions and then connecting each of these to a specific secondary emotion. For example, if your client judges a primary emotion as bad or unacceptable, they are likely to experience a secondary emotion of shame. Conversely, judgments of an emotion as dangerous or threatening are likely to lead to a secondary emotion of fear. Help your client determine the specific secondary emotion linked to each of their judgments about their primary emotions. Finally, assist your client in identifying more adaptive ways of responding to the negative beliefs about emotions they identified, including using the skills they learned during the session on emotional acceptance to help them check the facts about their negative beliefs or take a step back from these beliefs by practicing mindfulness or cognitive defusion.

To ensure that clients leave the session with a guide to the secondary emotions likely to arise in response to specific primary emotions, it is most helpful to have clients complete a separate worksheet for each of the primary emotions they tend to judge. Thus, we recommend making several copies of this worksheet to give to your client in session.

Skill Consolidation and Generalization

Given how difficult it can be for clients to identify their secondary emotions (particularly in the moment), the outside-of-session exercises for this set of skills are particularly important for helping clients increase their awareness of their secondary emotions and apply the skills they learned for responding adaptively to primary and secondary emotions in their daily lives. The more that clients practice these skills and increase their awareness of the ways in which their judgments about emotions lead to secondary emotional responses, the better able they will be to notice these judgments in the moment and take a step back from them before secondary emotions arise.

The primary outside-of-session exercise for this set of skills is a monitoring form that asks clients to track their primary emotions, judgments about these emotions, resultant secondary emotions, and distress on a daily basis, Emotional Clarity: Outside-of-Session Monitoring Form 1 (Primary and Secondary Emotional Response Monitoring Form). This monitoring form can be found at the end of this chapter, and is available for download at http://www.newharbinger.com/53622. The goal of this form is to help clients identify the secondary emotions stemming from their negative beliefs about their primary emotions, as well as the emotional consequences of buying into these negative beliefs and experiencing secondary emotions. The expectation is that monitoring the distress associated with their primary and secondary emotions will further reinforce the link between secondary emotions and emotional suffering, thereby motivating clients to use the skills they learned in this session to respond more adaptively to their judgments about emotions.

We also recommend encouraging your client to revisit the worksheets from the in-session exercise (Emotional Clarity: In-Session Exercise 1) over the course of the next week to continue to identify the specific judgments and related secondary emotions they experience in response to different primary emotions. The more detailed these worksheets are, the more useful they will be for increasing clients' awareness of secondary emotions in the moment (before they respond). Finally, clients should continue to use the outside-of-session self-destructive behaviors monitoring form first introduced in chapter 6 to continue to increase their awareness of the role of negative beliefs about emotions in self-destructive behaviors, Emotional Clarity: Outside-of-Session Monitoring Form 3, available for download at http://www.newharbinger.com/53622.

Tips for Teaching This Skill

As we discussed in chapter 6, when you're teaching clients skills for managing negative beliefs about emotions, it is important not to suggest that the presence of these beliefs is necessarily problematic or that the goal of treatment is to get rid of these beliefs entirely. It's also important to let clients know that they will likely continue to experience secondary emotions for some time, even if they use the skills they learned in this session regularly. Beliefs as ingrained as clients' negative beliefs about emotions cannot be expected to change overnight. Therefore, we find it very helpful to emphasize throughout the session that the goal of these skills is not to eliminate secondary emotions entirely (as that is not possible) but to help clients find ways of connecting with and acting on their primary emotions and reducing the extent to which they buy into the negative beliefs about emotions that can prompt secondary emotions.

Distinguishing Between Clear and Cloudy Emotions

The second strategy for improving emotional clarity within this ERT focuses on helping clients distinguish between clear and cloudy emotions. This set of skills is a lot more straightforward than the skills focused on distinguishing between primary and secondary emotions, and tends to be easier for clients to learn and apply. Therefore, if you choose to break up the material in this chapter across at least two separate sessions (as we recommend), you will often have time in the session focused on clear and cloudy emotions to revisit the material on primary and secondary emotions and continue to have your client practice monitoring these emotions outside of session.

The goal of this set of skills is to continue to increase clients' awareness of the complexity of emotional responses and the particular types of emotions that are most helpful in guiding behavior. These skills build on the idea introduced in the prior session that certain types of emotions are more useful in informing responses and guiding behavior than others. Specifically, in the same way that primary emotions are more adaptive than secondary emotions (and provide more useful information about the environment), clear emotions are more helpful than cloudy emotions. Thus, it is important that clients know how to distinguish between the two, as well as the best strategies for managing and responding to each. An overview of these skills is provided in a handout that can be given to clients during the session and used to guide this discussion, Emotional Clarity: In-Session Handout 2 (Clear vs. Cloudy Emotional Responses). This handout can be found at the end of this chapter, and is available for download at http://www.newharbinger.com/53622.

Psychoeducation on Clear vs. Cloudy Emotions

The first step in teaching clients how to distinguish between clear and cloudy emotions is to introduce clients to these concepts and provide psychoeducation on the differences between these types of emotions. Specifically, clear emotions are emotions that arise directly in response to a particular stimulus or situation (i.e., they are proportionate and tied directly to the immediate situation/stimulus). As such, clear emotions are the emotions that provide the most useful information about your client's environment and can be most helpful in guiding their behavior.

When discussing clear emotions with your client, it is important to emphasize that clear emotions can vary in intensity, depending on the situation at hand. Simply because an emotion is very intense does not mean that it is not a clear emotion; what matters is whether the emotion is proportionate to the situation or stimulus. Therefore, whereas having an intense emotional reaction to a mild stressor may be indicative of a cloudy emotional response, experiencing intense emotions in response to other stimuli may be a proportionate response (e.g., feeling profoundly sad when a friend moves away or feeling very anxious when giving an important presentation at work).

It can be helpful when orienting clients to the concept of clear emotions to tie these emotions back to the types of emotions they learned about in earlier sessions of this treatment. You can let your client know that even though you didn't label them as such, it was clear emotions that were the focus of the sessions on emotional acceptance and awareness: these are the emotions that are the most functional, adaptive, and helpful in guiding their behavior.

Once your client has a solid understanding of clear emotions, the next step is to introduce the concept of cloudy emotions and how they differ from clear emotions. Specifically, unlike clear emotions, cloudy emotions are not tied directly to the situation or stimulus at hand; that is, they are not a direct response to the immediate stimulus. Instead, cloudy emotions are emotions that are influenced by, or "clouded by," other factors, including physiological vulnerabilities or other emotions or aspects of an emotional response. We'll describe these factors and the particular ways in which they can influence or cloud a client's emotional responses in more detail below. At this point in the session, however, the key elements for you to emphasize are that (1) cloudy emotions are influenced by factors not directly related to the situation at hand, and, (2) as a result, cloudy emotions are often (although not always) more intense than the corresponding clear emotion would have been. For example, your client may be more reactive to a disagreement with a coworker if they had an argument with their romantic partner earlier in the day and hadn't yet had the opportunity to process their emotions related to that argument. To ensure that clients have a basic understanding of the concept of cloudy emotions, it can be helpful to walk them through several examples of cloudy emotions and the corresponding clear emotion in that scenario. Table 8.3 provides several examples of cloudy emotions that can assist you in this discussion.

When having this discussion with your client, it's important to emphasize that cloudy emotions are normal, natural, and to be expected. Not only do all human beings experience cloudy emotions, they are actually more common than clear emotions (as most of the emotions that people experience are clouded to some extent by other factors). Thus, the goal is not for your client to stop having cloudy emotions. Rather, the goal is for them to become more aware of their cloudy emotions and the factors contributing to these, as well as to connect with their clear emotion before responding.

TABLE 8.3. Examples of Cloudy Emotions and Their Corresponding Clear Emotions

Situation	Cloudy emotional response (including intensity)	Clear emotional response (including intensity)
While heading to work in the morning, you spill your coffee.	You burst into tears and begin to sob uncontrollably.	Mild frustration, irritation, or sadness
While driving home from work, someone cuts you off on the highway.	You experience intense rage and begin to scream, swear, and shake.	Mild frustration, anger, or fear
You are watching a movie where a boy's pet runs away.	You experience intense and overwhelming sadness and begin to cry uncontrollably.	Mild to moderate sadness
Your supervisor at work gives you constructive feedback.	You experience intense dread and gloom, along with overwhelming feelings of shame and anger.	Mild to moderate concern, disappointment, guilt, or gratitude

Psychoeducation on Factors That May Cloud Emotions

Once your client understands the differences between clear and cloudy emotions, the next step is to provide them with psychoeducation on the various factors that may cloud their emotional responses on a daily basis. These factors fall into four main categories. Each of these categories is reviewed below, along with some key points to emphasize during your discussion of these factors with your client. They are also summarized on the Emotional Clarity: In-Session Handout 2.

- *Failures in self-care.* One of the main factors that can cloud a client's emotions is not attending to or caring for their physical health. Because emotions have a physical/bodily component, whether and to what extent clients take care of themselves physically can have a major impact on their emotional responses, with failures to care for their health and their body increasing a client's vulnerability for more intense and reactive emotions. Common examples of failures in self-care that can cloud emotions include not sleeping well or not sleeping enough, not eating well (including not eating enough or eating too much), being sick or hungover, not taking medications as prescribed, and using alcohol or drugs.

- *Emotions connected to future, imagined events.* Another factor that can intensify a client's emotional responses in the moment is a focus on the future versus the present. When clients focus on what the current situation could mean for the future (versus what is happening in the present moment), their emotional responses in the moment can be influenced by their worries of what may occur. This tends to intensify a client's emotional response, as it is clouded by worries and fears about the future.

- *Unprocessed or unacknowledged emotional responses to past events.* This set of factors is similar to the concept of emotional baggage. When clients have unprocessed or unacknowledged emotions about a past event, these can influence their reactions to a similar event in the moment, often intensifying their emotions in response to the current situation. For example, if your client has a history of chronic invalidation by their parents, they may be more sensitive or reactive to experiences of invalidation by people in their life currently. Their unprocessed emotions about past invalidation may intensify their emotional reactions to even mild instances of invalidation in the present, as their response is not just about the immediate experience but all of the similar experiences they've had in the past.

- *Secondary emotional reactions.* As we discussed in the previous section on primary and secondary emotional responses, one downside of secondary emotions is that they can obscure a client's primary emotions, making it more difficult to identify the information provided by those emotions. In this way, secondary emotions can also be thought of as something that can cloud a client's emotional response to a situation. Highlighting this for clients can help them integrate the two sets of skills covered in this chapter and further reinforce the importance of working to decrease secondary emotions by responding to judgments about emotions in more adaptive ways.

Once you've discussed each of these sets of factors with your client, the next step is to assist your client in identifying the factors that are most likely to lead to cloudy emotions for them. It can be helpful to ask them to reflect on past experiences of cloudy emotions and then assist them in identifying the factors that may have clouded their emotions in those moments. Pay attention to any themes that arise during this discussion (e.g., a lack of sleep increasing emotional intensity and reactivity across the examples they give) and then highlight these for your client. The goal of this discussion is to increase your client's awareness of the key factors that most commonly cloud their emotions so that they can take steps to reduce those.

Effective Responses to Clear and Cloudy Emotions

Once your client has a better understanding of the differences between clear and cloudy emotions and the factors that may cloud their emotions, the final step is to teach your client the most effective ways of responding to each type of emotion. Similar to the discussion you had with your client when teaching them how to respond effectively to primary versus secondary emotions, the key point to emphasize during this discussion is that it is their clear emotions that provide important information about their environment and can be used to guide their behavior. Therefore, effective ways of responding to their clear emotions include the skills they learned in the sessions on emotional awareness and are similar to effective ways of responding to primary emotions: identify the clear emotion and its action tendencies, identify the information the emotion is providing, and then identify effective ways to act on and express the emotion.

Conversely, the most effective way to respond to cloudy emotions is to not act on the emotion. Instead, the goal is for clients to increase their awareness of cloudy emotions and separate the clear emotion from the cloudy emotion before they act. Specifically, as clients become more aware of their cloudy emotions, the goal is for them to use the presence of these emotions as a cue to take a step back from their emotions, identify the factors clouding their emotional response, and then identify the clear emotion prior to responding.

Additionally, once clients have identified the factors that are most likely to lead to cloudy emotions for them, the goal is for clients to take steps to minimize these factors or limit their exposure to them. Although not all of these factors are entirely avoidable, there are numerous skills clients can use to minimize the impact of these factors on their emotional responses, such as the PLEASE skills of DBT (Linehan, 1993b; 2015) and the skills they learned in previous sessions of this ERT for decreasing secondary emotions and increasing emotional acceptance and awareness.

The different approaches for responding effectively to clear versus cloudy emotions are reviewed in table 8.4, and can be used to guide your discussion of these skills with your client.

TABLE 8.4. Adaptive Ways of Responding to Clear and Cloudy Emotions

Clear Emotions

- Identify the clear emotion.
- Notice and observe the emotion and its action tendencies.
- Identify the information the emotion is providing.
- Identify effective ways to act on and express the emotion.

Cloudy Emotions

- Increase awareness of cloudy emotions before responding.
- Separate the cloudy emotion from the clear emotion before acting—do not act on the cloudy emotion!
- Increase awareness of the factors that contribute to cloudy emotions and take steps to minimize these.

Skill Consolidation and Generalization

Similar to the outside-of-session exercises focused on primary and secondary emotions, the primary outside-of-session exercise for this particular set of skills is a monitoring form that asks clients to track their clear and cloudy emotions on a daily basis throughout the week, as well as to identify adaptive ways of acting on the information provided by their clear emotions, Emotional Clarity: Outside-of-Session Monitoring Form 2 (Clear and Cloudy Emotional Response Monitoring Form). This form can be found at the end of this chapter, and is available for download at http://www.newharbinger.com/53622. The goal of this form is to help clients increase their awareness of their cloudy emotions and the factors contributing to these, as well as to learn to identify the clear emotional response prior to acting on or expressing their emotions. Clients are also asked to continue completing the same version of the self-destructive behaviors monitoring form they've been completing on a daily basis since the session focused on increasing emotional acceptance, Emotional Clarity: Outside-of-Session Monitoring Form 3.

Tips for Teaching This Skill

When you're teaching clients this set of skills, it is important not to imply that the goal of these skills is to eliminate cloudy emotions entirely. As we mentioned previously, cloudy emotions are a natural part of the human experience and far more common than clear emotions. Therefore, it's important that clients do not leave the session thinking that they can or should eliminate their cloudy emotions. Instead, the goals of these skills are to (1) reduce vulnerability to cloudy emotions and (2) increase awareness of cloudy emotions so that clients are able to take a step back from these emotions and connect with the clear emotion before responding. Emphasizing throughout your discussion of these skills how human and natural cloudy emotions are can help offset any expectations clients may have about the need to get rid of these emotions entirely, decreasing the potential for shame or self-judgments when clients experience cloudy emotions in the future.

Consistent with this, we highly recommend that you use examples from your own life to illustrate the concept of cloudy emotions with clients. Doing so normalizes the experience of cloudy emotions and reinforces the message that clients do not need to get rid of this type of emotion. It can also be a helpful strategy for minimizing the shame some clients experience for having cloudy emotions. We suggest identifying relevant examples of cloudy emotions ahead of time, so that you are prepared to incorporate them into the session as needed. Particularly helpful examples are those that demonstrate the ubiquity of cloudy emotions and illustrate the various factors that can contribute to cloudy emotions.

Emotional Clarity: In-Session Handout 1
Primary vs. Secondary Emotional Responses

Primary emotional responses are initial emotional responses to a situation

- Functional
- Adaptive
- Motivate behavior (through associated action tendencies)
- Pass rather quickly—come and go

Secondary emotional responses are emotional reactions to primary emotions

- Driven by negative beliefs and judgments about primary emotions
- Mask primary emotions and make one's overall emotional experience less clear
- Interfere with functionality of primary emotions
- Increase distress and emotional suffering
- Don't pass quickly—tend to stick around

These different emotional responses are best responded to in different ways:

- Primary emotional responses
  - Notice, observe, and identify the emotion
  - Observe the action tendencies associated with the emotion
  - Identify effective ways to act on and express the emotion
- Secondary emotional responses
  - Identify negative beliefs about emotions that precede this emotional response
  - Identify more adaptive ways of responding to these negative beliefs about primary emotions

Emotional Clarity: In-Session Handout 2
Clear vs. Cloudy Emotional Responses

Clear emotional responses are directly related to, and in response to, a stimulus

- ➢ Proportionate
- ➢ Tied directly to the immediate stimulus/situation
- ➢ Adaptive
    - ➢ Provide important information about the situation/stimulus/environment
    - ➢ May be useful in informing behavior
- ➢ May be intense/strong reactions

Emotional responses are often clouded by other factors

- ➢ May be influenced by, or colored by, other factors
- ➢ Are not directly in response to the immediate environment

Cloudy emotional responses may result from:

- ➢ Failures in self-care
    - ➢ For example, not eating, not sleeping, too much caffeine, drugs, etc.
    - ➢ Can increase reactivity: emotions may be more intense than usual and thus prompt more of an extreme response than is effective
- ➢ Focusing on the future versus the present moment
    - ➢ Emotions connected to future imagined events can intensify emotions in response to what is happening in the moment (as you are not responding to the present situation but to your fears of what it could mean for the future)
- ➢ Unprocessed or unacknowledged emotional responses to past events
    - ➢ For example, an earlier fight with your partner may influence responses to a current interaction with your boss
- ➢ Secondary emotional responses

You can know how to respond to a situation by identifying the clear emotion

Emotional Clarity: In-Session Exercise 1

Identifying and Challenging Secondary Emotional Responses

Primary emotion	What do you usually say to yourself after you have this emotion? What beliefs do you have about yourself for having had this emotion? What thoughts run through your head about having had this emotion?	When you say these things to yourself, do you start to feel a certain way? Do you have another emotional reaction in response to the initial one (e.g., do you feel angry, ashamed, scared)?
	What are alternative perspectives to these negative beliefs? How might you respond differently to these negative beliefs?	

Increasing Emotional Clarity and Understanding

Emotional Clarity: Outside-of-Session Monitoring Form 1

Primary and Secondary Emotional Response Monitoring Form (*Please complete at least once per day*)

Situation	Primary emotional response: What was your immediate emotional response to the situation? What feelings did you initially experience in response to the situation?	Distress level: Rate your distress (0-100)	Reactions to your emotions: What did you say to yourself about your initial emotional response? Did you criticize yourself for feeling that way? Did you judge the primary emotional response?	Secondary emotional response: Did you experience another emotional reaction in response to the initial one? (e.g., did you start to feel bad about yourself for having the primary emotion, or angry, scared, or ashamed?)	Distress level: Rate your distress (0-100)

Emotional Clarity: Outside-of-Session Monitoring Form 2

Clear and Cloudy Emotional Response Monitoring Form (*Please complete at least once per day*)

Situation	Emotion	Is there anything that may be clouding this emotional response? If so, what?	What is the clear emotional response? (Identify the emotion and level of intensity)	What information is the **clear emotion** providing me about my environment?	How can I act on this information in a way that is adaptive?	What are healthy ways of expressing the **clear emotion**?

Increasing Emotional Clarity and Understanding

CHAPTER 9

Increasing Emotional Willingness

Although this is the first session in this ERT explicitly focused on increasing emotional willingness and decreasing emotional unwillingness, clients have been exposed to these concepts throughout this treatment (for example, when learning about the paradoxical consequences of emotionally-avoidant behaviors or the benefits of approaching, labeling, and listening to their emotions) and, thus, should be familiar with them to some extent. In fact, as we discussed in chapter 4, the downsides of emotional unwillingness and benefits of emotional willingness are two central themes of this ERT that we recommend highlighting across all sessions of this treatment.

Nonetheless, despite the informal focus on these concepts throughout the treatment, it is important at this stage of the treatment to target emotional willingness directly by actively teaching clients skills for approaching their emotions with an open and willing stance and decreasing efforts to escape or avoid emotions. Indeed, the skills clients have learned up to this point in this ERT are only useful to the extent that clients are willing to experience their emotions. And, as much as clients have learned about the benefits of emotional acceptance and the functions of emotions by this point in the treatment, most still struggle with emotional unwillingness.

Given that emotional willingness is considered such an important and foundational emotion regulation skill within ERT, the original group therapy version of this ERT dedicates two sessions to covering the skills reviewed in this chapter, with the first session focused on the downsides of emotional unwillingness and the second session focused on emotional willingness as the more adaptive alternative to emotional unwillingness. Therefore, we recommend breaking up the skills reviewed in this chapter across at least two sessions so that clients have sufficient time to learn and practice these skills. We also want to highlight that these two sessions are different than the previous ERT sessions, as they are designed to be less didactic and more experiential. Although clients have previously learned about the downsides of emotional avoidance and control, this information can be further reinforced and cemented by having clients connect experientially with the negative consequences of emotional unwillingness and the benefits of emotional willingness. Thus, both of the sessions reviewed in this chapter rely heavily on experiential exercises, metaphors, and client self-reflection and self-monitoring to teach these concepts to clients.

Decreasing Emotional Unwillingness

The focus of the first of these two sessions is exclusively on emotional unwillingness. The goal of this session is to help clients connect experientially with the futility of trying to avoid or control their emotions in the long term, with an emphasis on their paradoxical consequences. If you are familiar with ACT, then you will probably recognize the focus of this session on instilling creative hopelessness, or assisting clients in connecting with the hopelessness of adhering to an emotional control agenda. By the end of this session, the hope is that clients will begin to connect with the idea that their emotional control agenda is not sustainable or effective.

Identifying the Consequences of Emotional Avoidance/Control

To this end, this session begins with an in-session exercise, Emotional Willingness: In-Session Exercise 1 (Emotional Unwillingness: Think of a time you were unwilling to have your feelings), focused on helping clients reflect on their past experiences trying to directly control or avoid their emotions. This exercise can be found at the end of this chapter and is available for download at http://www.newharbinger.com/53622. The goal of this exercise is to assist clients in connecting with the consequences of efforts to control or avoid their emotions, with a particular emphasis on the paradoxical emotional consequences of these efforts. First, ask your client to think of a time when they tried to avoid or control their emotions. Once they have an instance or two in mind, use the questions in table 9.1 to assist them in reflecting on their experiences and identifying the ways in which these efforts to control or avoid their emotions did and did not work. Then, have them write down their responses in the appropriate column on the worksheet.

TABLE 9.1. Questions to Guide Emotional Willingness: In-Session Exercise 1
What did you do to control or avoid your feelings? This can take the form of more subtle avoidance strategies like "checking out" or automatically suppressing emotions, or more overt unhealthy or self-destructive behaviors like binge-eating or self-injury.
Did that strategy really work? Were you successful in controlling or avoiding your feelings in the short term? In the long term? Did your feelings go away and stay away, or did they return?
What were the consequences of attempting to control or avoid your feelings? What thoughts did you have as a result? Did you beat yourself up or judge yourself for engaging in these behaviors? Did you experience any other feelings as a result of your attempts to control or avoid your feelings? For example, feelings of shame or guilt?
Did you feel more or less prepared to manage these feelings in the future?
Thinking about all of the times you've tried to avoid or control your emotions in the past, when are these efforts more or less effective? Do they tend to work when your emotions are very intense? How about when you really want them to work, or really don't want to feel whatever it is you're feeling?

Once your client has completed the worksheet, assist them in reflecting on what they learned from the exercise and any patterns they noticed. We recommend incorporating the following points into this discussion.

HIGHLIGHT BOTH SUBTLE AND OVERT AVOIDANCE AND CONTROL BEHAVIORS

First, it can be very helpful to highlight all of the ways in which clients may attempt to avoid or control their emotions, focusing on both overt self-destructive behaviors and more subtle behaviors like pushing away their emotions or shutting down. By this point, most clients are easily able to identify the more overt behaviors they engage in to avoid their emotions. However, it can be much more challenging for them to identify more subtle avoidance or control behaviors. An important point to emphasize during this discussion is that the more people try to avoid their emotions, the more skilled they can become at doing so and the more automatic this process can become (until they don't even realize they are doing this).

REINFORCE MATERIAL FROM PREVIOUS SESSIONS

Second, when you're reviewing the consequences of your client's efforts to control or avoid their emotions, use this as an opportunity to review and reinforce the skills they've already learned in this treatment (e.g., by highlighting how emotional avoidance can reduce emotional awareness or cloud emotional responses, thereby interfering with their ability to access and use the information provided by their emotions). It can also be helpful to tie this exercise back to the exercise they completed in the first session on the functions of self-destructive behaviors (chapter 5), which highlighted how efforts to avoid emotions tend to have paradoxical emotional consequences. Finally, it can be helpful to remind your client that attempts to avoid primary emotions can intensify and worsen emotional pain, leading to emotional suffering (covered in chapter 8).

HIGHLIGHT ADDITIONAL DOWNSIDES OF EMOTIONAL CONTROL/AVOIDANCE

Third, there are two additional downsides of efforts to control or avoid emotions that haven't been addressed directly in this ERT so far and, thus, should be emphasized here. The first of these focuses on the ways in which efforts to avoid emotions can result in secondary emotional responses and self-judgments—both of which only increase your client's suffering. Specifically, when clients' efforts to avoid their primary emotions don't work, they can experience even more emotional distress due to judgments about their primary emotions or judgments about themselves for being unable to avoid their emotions. The second is that efforts to control or avoid emotions—especially if these efforts aren't effective—can reduce a client's emotional self-efficacy (i.e., their perception of their ability to effectively manage their emotions in the future). The basic idea is that the more clients try to avoid their emotions, the more they teach themselves that emotions are threatening and need to be avoided and the less likely they are to learn that they are capable of managing and tolerating their emotions.

ACKNOWLEDGE THE PROS AND CONS OF EMOTIONAL CONTROL/AVOIDANCE

Finally, when you're reviewing the short- and long-term consequences of attempts to avoid or control emotions, make sure to give your client the space to identify both positive and negative consequences. Similar to the in-session exercise in the first session of this ERT (reviewed in chapter 5), clients may be able to identify some positive consequences of emotional avoidance, as well as times when emotional control or avoidance worked for them. If they do, it's important to validate those experiences and acknowledge the ways in which they reinforce further avoidance. Then, assist your client in reflecting on the negative consequences of emotional avoidance and times when their efforts to avoid their emotions didn't work. Usually, clients will notice that efforts to avoid their emotions are more likely to be successful at times when their emotions aren't too intense or when the situation isn't that important or relevant to their life. Conversely, efforts to avoid their emotions tend to be less successful at times when their emotions are very intense or stem from a situation that is far more personally relevant or meaningful to them. Basically, emotional avoidance is most likely to fail in the very contexts and situations that clients most want it to work.

Psychoeducation on Why People Try to Avoid Emotions

Once you've finished discussing this exercise with your client, pose this question to them: "If you know that your attempts to control or avoid your emotions often don't work and tend to ultimately backfire, why do you think you still continue to do this?" Then, provide your client with Emotional Willingness: In-Session Handout 1 (Emotional Unwillingness). This handout can be found at the end of this chapter and is available for download at http://www.newharbinger.com/53622. The first section of this handout provides psychoeducation on the reasons why people try to avoid or control their emotions and can be helpful in both validating your client's experience and reducing any shame they may feel when connecting with the downsides of emotional avoidance. Similar to our discussion of judgments about emotions in chapter 6, it is important to normalize clients' efforts to avoid emotions and emphasize how human it is to want to avoid pain. The key points to focus on during this part of the session are summarized below.

EMOTIONAL CONTROL SEEMS LIKE A REASONABLE GOAL

Being in control of one's emotions is commonly framed as a key goal of mental health. People are often taught that not only is being in control of their emotions possible, it is the ideal state. In addition, being in control of one's emotions is equated with positive qualities (for example, strength, confidence, competence) in society. As a result, it is common for people to receive the message that they must learn to control, push aside, or not express their emotions in order to be positively regarded.

SOMETIMES PEOPLE CAN CONTROL THEIR EMOTIONS

As we discussed in chapter 5, human beings tend to be motivated and influenced by the short-term versus long-term consequences of behaviors. Thus, because efforts to control or avoid emotions often work in the short term (providing temporary relief from emotional distress), they tend to be reinforced. Indeed, it is precisely because efforts to control emotions sometimes work that it can be so hard for clients to stop these behaviors. Moreover, because these efforts do sometimes work, the natural inclination when they aren't working is for clients to try harder or enact even greater control efforts. Basically, once clients learn that efforts to avoid or control emotions can provide temporary emotional relief, it is incredibly challenging to connect with the longer-term negative consequences of these efforts or the times when these efforts do not work.

OTHER PEOPLE APPEAR TO CONTROL THEIR EMOTIONS

One reason why it can seem like emotional control is possible is that other people can appear to be successfully controlling their emotions. Often, clients will fall into a trap of comparing how they feel on the inside to how others look on the outside. And, because people can control the expression of their emotions (even if they can't control whether they have an emotion), it can appear as if the world is full of people who can control their emotions.

Another reason why it can seem like other people can control their emotions is that many people are taught at an early age that they need to control the experience or expression of their emotions. Messages like this are common in society and can be both explicit, such as when children are instructed to stop crying in a public place or told that they will be punished if they express certain emotions, and more indirect, such as when clients repeatedly hear phrases like, "Just relax," "Don't worry," "Put on a happy face," or "Get over it." These messages become part of a client's learning history and can influence their behavior, cementing the idea that it is possible (and preferable) to control their emotions.

CONTROL WORKS IN OTHER AREAS OF LIFE

When it comes to the external world and accomplishing goals in life, control can work very well. Goals are often achieved through diligent discipline, attention, and perseverance—all of which require some level of control. Thus, enacting control has likely paid off for your clients in many areas of their lives (e.g., when pursuing an education or trying to advance in their career). When clients have experiences such as this, it makes sense that they would try to enact this same level of control over their internal experiences. The problem, though, is that trying to control internal experiences doesn't work in the same way (or as well) as exerting control over external experiences.

Connecting with the Paradoxical Consequences of Emotional Control

One effective strategy for teaching clients that internal experiences cannot be controlled in the same way as external experiences is to lead them through the experiential exercise in table 9.2 (based on a study by Wegner, Schneider, Carter, & White, 1987).

TABLE 9.2. In-Session Exercise: The White Bear
There have been a number of studies looking at whether people can control their thoughts and what the consequences are of trying to do so. Rather than telling you what those studies have found, I think it will be more helpful (and interesting) to lead you through an exercise used in many of these studies. Let's try that now. First, start by closing your eyes. Now, bring your attention to your thoughts. Just notice any thoughts that are in your mind right now. [Pause for thirty seconds.] You can have any thought that enters your mind. [Pause for thirty seconds.] Now, beginning in this moment, I want you to NOT think of a white bear. Whatever you do, do NOT think of a white bear. You can think of anything except a white bear. [Wait one minute.] Allow any thoughts to be present in your mind except for a white bear. Do not allow yourself to think of cute polar bears frolicking in the snow or the white bear that was associated with Coca-Cola commercials. Just don't think of any white bears. [Pause for one minute.] Okay, you can open your eyes now. Did that work? Were you able to not think of a white bear? Or, was that almost all you could think about when I instructed you not to do so? [Collect feedback from your client.] Of course you had thoughts of white bears. In fact, I'm guessing that before I told you not to think about white bears, you weren't thinking about them at all, and yet as soon as I told you not to think about them, it was probably difficult to think about anything else. This exercise provides an excellent demonstration of how trying to control our internal experience doesn't work so well. The problem with trying to control your thoughts—or really any internal experience—is that this necessitates that you constantly monitor your internal environment to see if whatever thought or emotion you don't want to have or are trying to control is occurring. However, as you experienced here, by monitoring yourself for thoughts of white bears, you inadvertently thought a lot more about white bears than you probably ever have. By setting the rule that you can't think of something, you pretty much guarantee that you will think of that thing.

An additional experiential exercise that you can use with your client to help them connect experientially with the difficulties of trying to control internal experiences involves asking them to close their eyes and think of some kind of food (e.g., warm jelly donuts) or beverage (e.g., a cold glass of milk) (Hayes et al., 1999). For example, if you choose to focus the exercise on a cold glass of milk, ask your client to close their eyes and then try not to think about a cold glass of milk. Instruct them not to think about how a cold glass of milk would feel in their hands, what the milk would feel like in their mouth, what it would taste like, or how refreshing it would be after eating a warm chocolate chip cookie. After you lead your client through this exercise, ask them to reflect again on how trying to not think about the cold milk actually made them think about it more and put them more in touch with the experience of drinking the milk and the imagery and thoughts associated with cold milk.

Once clients have connected with the paradoxical consequences of trying to control these aspects of their internal experience, the next step is to help them connect with the paradox of trying to control their emotional experiences. Metaphors are a particularly powerful tool in this regard. Thus, this ERT incorporates two metaphors adapted from ACT (Hayes et al., 1999) to help clients connect with the futility of trying to control their emotional experiences. These are described in table 9.3.

TABLE 9.3. Metaphors for Conveying the Paradoxical Consequences of Emotional Control

Metaphor	Script
Million Dollars to Fall in Love (Hayes et al., 1999)	To illustrate this concept a bit more, I want you to consider this scenario. Let's say that I just so happen to have a lot of extra money lying around and I am willing to give it to you if you will fall in love with the next stranger you meet. In fact, I'll give you a million dollars, and all you need to do is fall in love with this person. That's it. Just fall in love with them. Could you do it? Even with that much incentive to control your emotions and feel a certain way, it really wouldn't be possible. I'm sure you could act as if you were in love, or do things to make it look like you were in love. However, could you really force yourself to feel that way? Even with all that incentive? I doubt it. Emotions just can't be controlled like that, even if we really want to control them.
Polygraph Test (Hayes et al., 1999)	Now let me give you another example in which you would have the ultimate motivation to control a negative emotion, in this case anxiety. Imagine that I had you hooked up to the best polygraph machine that was ever built. This is a perfect machine, the most sensitive ever made. It never fails. When you are connected to it, there is no way that you can be the slightest bit anxious without the machine knowing. The only thing you have to do in this scenario is to stay relaxed and not feel anxious. If you get the least bit anxious, the machine will detect it, and I will know. Now, because I know you want to succeed at this task and I am all about supporting you in these efforts, I want to make sure that your motivation for passing this polygraph is as high as it can be. I just want to make sure you have as much incentive as possible to not feel anxious. Therefore, to really motivate you, I have brought with me—right outside this room—the thing that you fear the most in the world (for example, a snake, rat, spider, etc.), and, if you show even the slightest twinge of anxiety, I'm going to bring it in here and make you confront it. What would happen? How would you feel? Of course you would feel anxious in this example. Despite your strong motivation to control your anxiety, it would be almost impossible not to feel that way under these circumstances.

The first metaphor illustrates that even when there is a strong desire and motivation to experience a pleasant emotion, it is just not possible to simply conjure up that emotion. The second metaphor illustrates how difficult it can be to prevent the experience of an emotion even when there is strong motivation to do so. In fact, trying to prevent an emotion can actually increase the likelihood that the emotion is experienced. Specifically, the same process that caused your client to think of white bears or a glass of milk in the previous exercises operates when they try to control their emotions. If they set a rule that a certain thought or emotion is not acceptable, their mind begins a process of scanning their internal environment to see if that rule is being broken. In so doing, this process inadvertently brings up and increases awareness of the very experiences they are trying to avoid. After sharing these metaphors with your client, it can be helpful to spend some time getting their feedback about the metaphors and how they apply to their experiences.

Psychoeducation on the Paradoxical Consequences of Emotional Control

The next step is to provide your client with psychoeducation on the paradoxical consequences of emotional control. The remaining sections of Emotional Willingness: In-Session Handout 1 can aid you in this discussion. As you review this handout, it can be helpful to highlight how your client's experiences completing the exercises in this session are consistent with the research on the paradoxical consequences of emotional control, and introduce the possibility that perhaps the problem isn't that your client hasn't tried hard enough or found the right strategy to control their emotions. Instead, perhaps emotional control just isn't an effective strategy in the long term.

During your discussion of this handout with your client, it can be helpful to emphasize the following key points. First, studies have shown that attempts to control internal experiences like thoughts and emotions generally only work in the short term and tend to backfire in the long term. For example, in the classic white bear study that formed the basis of the exercise you led your client through earlier in the session, the researchers found that even people who were able to suppress thoughts of a white bear initially later experienced a surge of thoughts about white bears. The same thing happens with emotions. When people try not to feel something, that same emotion tends to come back more frequently and with greater intensity.

Second, studies have found that attempts to avoid or control emotions can actually make people feel worse in the long term. Because emotions are a biological process, it takes a lot of effort to suppress them or try to push them away. Therefore, trying to avoid emotions can actually increase physiological arousal (Gross & Levenson, 1997). In addition, repeated attempts to control emotions can actually reduce your client's tolerance for those emotions. As we discussed in chapter 5, by not allowing themselves to experience emotions on a regular basis, and by shutting down their emotions whenever they reach a certain intolerable level, clients can gradually lose their tolerance for those emotions until even low levels of those emotions feel incredibly overwhelming. Third, when someone's goal is to control their emotions, even the slightest hint of that emotion can feel threatening and contribute to feelings of failure, inadequacy, or low self-efficacy. Basically, if clients have the rule that they cannot experience some emotion, then experiencing any level of that emotion, even if it's weak in intensity and barely present, can make them feel as if they failed in their attempts to control their emotions and further increase their distress.

Once you've reviewed the remainder of this handout with your client, give them some time to reflect on what they've learned and how this information maps onto their experiences of their emotions. Then, end the session with the following for your client to contemplate over the course of the next week: "So, what does it mean that you have put so much energy and time into trying to control something that can't really be controlled? Does this mean that you must give up or resign yourself to a lifetime of emotional suffering and not doing the things in life that you want to do? Fortunately, the answer is no. You don't need to control your feelings to live a life that is meaningful. Emotions don't have to be obstacles to living the life you want to live. In the next session, we will discuss what you can do instead."

Ending the session in this way, without providing clients with the alternative to emotional unwillingness, was done purposefully, in order to give clients the week between these two sessions to connect with the ways in which emotional unwillingness may not be working for them in their lives. Doing so will make them more open to considering emotional willingness as an alternative in the next session.

Learning Consolidation

The primary outside-of-session exercise for this session, Emotional Willingness: Outside-of-Session Monitoring Form 1 (Emotional Willingness and Unwillingness Monitoring Form), focuses on helping clients connect with the experiential consequences of efforts to avoid their emotions in their daily lives. This monitoring form can be found at the end of this chapter and is available for download at http://www.newharbinger.com/53622. We recommend that you instruct your client that they do not need to change how they respond to their emotions in any way throughout the week. Instead, the goal is for them to monitor the consequences of their typical responses to their emotions, whether they choose to avoid their emotions or allow themselves to experience their emotions. We frame this exercise to clients as an information-gathering exercise.

Clients are also asked to complete a modified version of the outside-of-session self-destructive behaviors monitoring form that they've been completing on a daily basis since the first session. Specifically, this version of the form, Emotional Willingness: Outside-of-Session Monitoring Form 2, incorporates two new columns assessing if clients were willing to experience their emotions and if they tried to avoid their emotions. The goal of this version of the form is to increase clients' awareness of the ways in which efforts to avoid emotions may prompt engagement in self-destructive behaviors. This monitoring form is available for download at http://www.newharbinger.com/53622.

Increasing Emotional Willingness

The session on increasing emotional willingness begins with a review of clients' experiences monitoring the consequences of emotional unwillingness (versus willingness) in their daily lives using Emotional Willingness: Outside-of-Session Monitoring Form 1. Ask your client to share their experiences and observations of the consequences of emotional unwillingness and avoidance, as well as any differences in the consequences of choosing emotional unwillingness versus willingness (if in fact they did at times choose emotional willingness during the past week). During this discussion, highlight for clients all of the negative consequences of choosing unwillingness, particularly any increases in emotional distress and suffering they experienced. In addition, if your client did choose emotional willingness during the week, assist them in reflecting on what that experience was like and the longer-term emotional consequences of that choice (relative to emotional unwillingness).

After reviewing your client's outside-of-session exercises, the next step is to introduce clients to the alternative to emotional control and avoidance: emotional willingness. We recommend highlighting for clients that if emotional control was possible, it would have worked by now. Then suggest that perhaps the fact that it hasn't worked means that it won't and that your client needs to find an alternative that will work better. Sample language for discussing this with your client is provided in table 9.4.

TABLE 9.4. Example Therapist Language: Introducing Emotional Willingness

I wonder if trying to manage your emotions by making them go away or avoiding them entirely is the best idea. From what we've discussed and you've observed in your own life, this just doesn't seem to work. And, my guess is that if avoiding or controlling emotions was going to work for someone, then it would have worked for you. You have put a lot of time and effort into trying to do this; therefore, if it was simply a matter of effort, or trying hard enough, I have no doubt that it would have worked for you. The fact that it hasn't makes me wonder if perhaps this will never work. Perhaps what seems to be the solution to emotional distress is actually the problem, and is making you feel even worse. Perhaps it would be helpful to find another way of responding to your emotions.

Introducing Clients to the Concept of Emotional Willingness

This is the point in the session where you can formally introduce your client to the alternative to emotional unwillingness: emotional willingness. Given that the prospect of approaching emotions with willingness can be a scary and challenging concept for clients who have a long history of struggling with their emotions, we recommend using a metaphor to introduce clients to this concept. The metaphor used in this ERT to introduce the concept of emotional willingness is the "Tug-of-War with a Monster" metaphor from ACT (Hayes et al., 1999), described in table 9.5.

TABLE 9.5. Tug-of-War with a Monster Metaphor

It's like you've been in this massive tug-of-war with a monster. This monster is all of the painful emotions you've been wanting to avoid: your anxiety, fear, sadness, anger, shame, and despair. It personifies all of the emotions you've been trying to get away from. Now, consider that in between you and this monster is a bottomless pit. If you lose this tug-of-war and fall into this pit, you will be destroyed. However, if you could just figure out a way to win this tug-of-war and pull the monster into the pit, you could live your life free from pain. So, you put all of your time and energy into winning this tug-of-war. You pull and pull on the rope, harder and harder. However, the harder you pull, the harder the monster pulls. And so you pull back even harder. And because the stakes are so high, your entire life becomes about winning this battle. As you focus all of your attention on how to pull the monster into the pit, your life is going on around you and yet you can't participate in it. All of your time and energy is being spent trying to win this tug-of-war. However, even when you try changing your grip or your footing or drawing upon some deep reserves of energy to pull as hard as you can, nothing seems to work. All of your energy is going into a fight that is impossible to win. The hardest thing to see is that your job here is not to win the tug-of-war—your job is simply to drop the rope.

After you share this metaphor, we recommend giving your client the space to process what it would mean to drop the rope by remaining silent until they speak. When they do speak, the next step is to elicit their reactions to the metaphor. What do they think about this solution? What would it mean to drop the rope? During this discussion, it can be helpful to emphasize the following key points: Dropping the rope is the opposite of resignation. Although clients sometimes share that dropping the rope seems like giving up, it is actually the opposite of that: it is making an active choice to do something more effective. In the end, this is not a battle that can be won. Therefore, an active choice can be made to not engage in this battle. Although the monster will still be there, by choosing not to pick up the rope, your client can't fall into the pit. The only times they inch closer to the pit are when they pick up the rope and give the monster the opportunity to pull them closer to the pit. In addition, by not picking up the rope, direct contact with the monster is reduced and all of the energy they've spent trying to win this unwinnable battle can now be focused elsewhere, such as on building a meaningful life. Although the monster may still taunt or yell at your client, this can only negatively affect them if they decide to engage in the battle.

Once your client has processed their reactions to the metaphor, let them know that the alternative to emotional control and avoidance—the equivalent of dropping the rope—is emotional willingness. Then, elicit their initial reactions to this concept and what they think it may mean.

Psychoeducation on Emotional Willingness

After your client has shared their initial reactions to the concept of emotional willingness, the next step is to provide your client with psychoeducation on emotional willingness and debunk any misconceptions they have about this concept. Emotional Willingness: In-Session

Handout 2 (Emotional Willingness) summarizes this information and can be used to guide this discussion with your client. This handout can be found at the end of this chapter and is available for download at http://www.newharbinger.com/53622. Key points to emphasize when reviewing this handout with your client are summarized below.

DEFINITION OF EMOTIONAL WILLINGNESS

Willingness refers to being open to internal experiences (e.g., emotions, thoughts) as they arise, whenever they arise, without trying to avoid, escape, control, change, or manipulate them in any way.

WILLINGNESS IS NOT ABOUT RESIGNATION OR GIVING UP

Whereas resignation is passive and future-focused, willingness is active and present-moment focused. In fact, willingness can be thought of as the opposite of giving up (Orsillo & Roemer, 2016). It takes a lot more courage and strength for clients to allow themselves to experience whatever emotions are present in the moment than to try to get rid of their emotions. If willingness was an easy choice, clients would have been doing it already.

WILLINGNESS CAN BE CHOSEN IN ANY MOMENT

Every time your client experiences an emotion, they can choose to be willing or unwilling. It is a moment-to-moment choice. Thus, even if there are times when your client chooses unwillingness, that doesn't preclude them from choosing willingness in the very next moment. What's more, because willingness is an active choice rather than a feeling, clients can make the choice to be willing even if they don't *feel* willing or don't want to be willing (Orsillo & Roemer, 2011).

WILLINGNESS IS NOT ABOUT LIKING OR PURSUING EMOTIONAL PAIN

The goal of willingness is not for your client to seek out or relish emotional pain. There is nothing noble about experiencing pain for pain's sake (Orsillo & Roemer, 2011). If there was a way for your client to live a meaningful life without experiencing painful emotions, then willingness wouldn't be necessary. The problem is that this is not possible. Emotional pain is a part of life and cannot be avoided. Thus, your client doesn't have to want, enjoy, or attempt to generate uncomfortable emotions. Their "job" is just to be open to their emotions as they live their lives. The Annoying Joe metaphor (adapted from an ACT metaphor; Hayes et al., 1999) in table 9.6 can be useful in conveying the distinction between willingness and wanting.

TABLE 9.6. Annoying Joe Metaphor
Imagine that you just moved into a new house and invited all of your neighbors to a housewarming party. On the day of the party, people begin showing up and things are going really well. However, partway through the party you realize that Joe, your annoying neighbor, has also shown up. Joe is one person in the neighborhood whom you don't really like. He complains a lot, makes insensitive remarks, and often starts arguments. Others seem to find him difficult to interact with as well. So when you see him at your party, you think, "Oh no! Why did he show up?" Because you did say everyone in the neighborhood was invited, though, what options do you have? You could decide that even though you said everyone was welcome, he really is not welcome. However, that would mean that you would have to spend all of your time guarding the door to the house to make sure he doesn't come back. Or, you could decide that it is best to monitor him and try to contain him while he is at the party. Maybe you could restrict him to one area of the house or make sure he only talks to certain people. The problem is that this choice means that all of your attention will have to be focused on trying to control Joe. In fact, both of these options are going to put you into even greater contact with Joe and take your attention away from your party. Or, maybe you could just let Joe attend the party like everyone else and focus on enjoying the party yourself. Can you see how it is possible to allow him to be at the party even though you don't care for him? You don't have to like him. You don't have to seek him out. Joe can be at your party *and* you can enjoy your party. There may be moments when you bump into Joe or overhear him; and in these moments you may experience some distress or frustration. However, you can notice that and bring your attention back to enjoying your party. Your opinion or evaluation of Joe is distinct from your willingness to have him as a guest in your home.

WILLINGNESS CAN DECREASE EMOTIONAL SUFFERING

Clients in ERT often express concerns that choosing willingness means that they will be constantly overwhelmed by their emotions. On the contrary, willingness helps decrease emotional suffering and can help clients feel far less overwhelmed than they did previously. It can be helpful when discussing this point to remind your client of the paradoxical emotional consequences of efforts to control or avoid their emotions. You may want to refer back to the outside-of-session exercise you reviewed at the start of this session or the in-session handout from the previous session (Emotional Willingness: In-Session Handout 1).

The key points to emphasize are the following: Although emotional pain is a part of life and cannot be avoided, it does not have to turn into emotional suffering. Emotional suffering occurs when clients are unwilling to experience emotional pain and attempt to control, avoid, or escape it. It is this fight with their emotions that increases distress. The key to combatting emotional suffering, on the other hand, is emotional willingness. By practicing willingness, clients will experience far less distress than they did previously. There are two metaphors used in this ERT to convey the benefits of emotional willingness. One of these is described in table 9.7 and the other (the "Two Scales" metaphor from ACT; Hayes et al., 1999) is available for download at http://www.newharbinger.com/53622 in the addendum to table 9.7 (Additional Metaphor for Conveying the Benefits of Emotional Willingness).

TABLE 9.7. Metaphor for Conveying the Benefits of Emotional Willingness	
Metaphor	Script
Swimming in a Riptide	One of the original clients who received this treatment came up with a really helpful metaphor for capturing the experience of emotional willingness. She was a lifeguard and so this metaphor resonated with her. Are you a swimmer? Do you know what to do when you are caught in a riptide? Well, when you are caught in a riptide, the way to save yourself is to swim parallel to the shore. People drown because they get caught in the riptide and the thing that seems to make the most sense— the thing that seems like the best option—is to swim toward the shore in order to get safely back to dry land as soon as possible. And, on the surface, that makes a lot of sense. Of course, trying to get to shore as quickly as possible seems like the best option when you are getting tired and feel like you may drown. However, despite how logical it may seem, that is actually not the way to survive. Instead, the way to survive a riptide and save your life is to go against all of your natural urges and instincts and swim away from the shore so that you can get around the riptide. Doing this thing that feels like it is so wrong and cannot possibly help—going against your urges and what your mind is telling you will work—is the only way to save your life. And that is what willingness is.

This metaphor was shared by a client in the original trial of ERGT who viewed emotional willingness as both incredibly challenging and life-saving. As a lifeguard, she compared choosing emotional willingness to the choice swimmers have to make when they are swimming in the ocean and get caught in a riptide.

Skill Generalization and Consolidation

The primary outside-of-session exercise for this session is the same exercise clients completed following the previous session on emotional unwillingness, although with a twist. Specifically, although clients are once again asked to complete Emotional Willingness: Outside-of-Session Monitoring Form 1 on a daily basis, the goal for this week is to practice choosing emotional willingness more often than they have in the past. When discussing this exercise with your client, remind them that the goal is not to choose willingness 100 percent of the time. The goal of this exercise is simply for clients to recognize that emotional willingness is a choice they can make, choose this more often than they have in the past, and observe what happens as a result.

If your client expresses hesitancy to choose willingness, validate how scary it can be to approach emotions in a new way and then gently ask them to reflect on how well unwillingness has been working for them. You do not need to try to convince your client that willingness is the answer. In fact, that can be counterproductive. The goal is simply to have your client leave the session with a commitment to try out willingness some of the time this week. Finally, clients are also asked to continue completing the same self-destructive behaviors monitoring form they completed following the last session to increase their awareness of the impact of emotional unwillingness versus willingness on engagement in self-destructive behaviors.

Emotional Willingness: In-Session Handout 1
Emotional Unwillingness

Human beings often attempt to control emotions

- Seems like a reasonable goal
- Being "in control of emotions" is equated with positive qualities such as competence, balance, achievement, etc.
- Sometimes emotional control seems to work
  - Avoiding or distracting from emotions can provide temporary relief from emotional distress in the short term
  - Because control seems to work, the natural response when it isn't working is to try harder and engage in even more control strategies
- It seems like other people can control their feelings
  - Children are given the message to control their emotions ("Don't be sad" or "There's nothing to be afraid of")
  - Many adults limit the outward expression of their emotions
- Control works well in other aspects of life
  - Other accomplishments (educational, career, physical) are often achieved through diligent discipline, training, and control

Research suggests it is not possible to gain complete control over feelings

- Attempts to control/avoid feelings are not effective in the long term
- Attempts to control/avoid feelings don't work when you really need them to
- Attempts to control/avoid feelings often backfire
  - Increase the likelihood of those feelings
  - Increase the intensity of those feelings

Attempts to avoid or control emotions may actually make you feel worse

- Increase physiological arousal
- Interfere with distress tolerance
- Failures at control/avoidance (which are inevitable) increase distress

Emotional Willingness: In-Session Handout 2
Emotional Willingness

If emotional control doesn't work, what can you do?

- ➤ You don't need to control your feelings in order to do the things in life you want to do

- ➤ You just need to change your focus

Answer: Willingness

- ➤ Willingness refers to how open you are to experiencing your own internal experience as it happens—without trying to manipulate it, avoid it, escape it, or change it

- ➤ Willingness is not about giving up

- ➤ Willingness is not about resigning yourself to living with unbearable emotional pain

- ➤ Willingness does not mean you will feel constantly overwhelmed
    - ➤ Willingness will ultimately help you feel less overwhelmed
    - ➤ Willingness can prevent emotional pain from turning into emotional suffering
    - ➤ **Remember:** Being unwilling to have your feelings—attempting to control them—increases distress and emotional suffering

Emotional Willingness: In-Session Exercise 1

Emotional Unwillingness: Think of a time you were unwilling to have your feelings

What did you do to try to avoid your feelings? What behavior(s) did you engage in?	Were these attempts to avoid your emotions successful?	What thoughts did you experience as a result of trying to avoid your emotions?	Did any other feelings (i.e., secondary emotions, cloudy emotions) arise as a result of trying to avoid your emotions? (e.g., fear, shame, etc.)	Other (longer-term) consequences of attempts to avoid emotions? (e.g., are you more or less prepared to manage these feelings in the future?)	When is emotional avoidance least effective? (i.e., what factors make it less likely to work?)
	In the short term?				
	In the long term?				

Emotional Willingness: Outside-of-Session Monitoring Form 1

Emotional Willingness and Unwillingness Monitoring Form (*Please complete at least once per day*)

Situation	Emotion	Initial distress level (0-100)	Willingness: Were you willing to have your emotions?	As a result of this choice, did you engage in any unhealthy behaviors? If yes, what did you do?	As a result of this choice, did you experience any other feelings (i.e., cloudy emotions, secondary emotions)?	As a result of this choice, did you experience any thoughts?	Subsequent distress level (0-100)
			NO, Unwilling: Attempted to avoid and get rid of feelings				
			YES, Willing: Allowed myself to experience feeling				

Increasing Emotional Willingness

CHAPTER 10

Increasing Emotion Modulation Effectiveness and Flexibility

Up until this point in the treatment, the focus of this ERT has been on the functionality of emotions and the importance of being able to access and experience the full range of human emotions. In fact, all of the skills taught to clients so far in this treatment have focused on accepting, experiencing, labeling, and learning from one's emotions as they arise.

As we mentioned in chapter 1, we made a conscious decision to wait to teach clients specific skills for modulating emotional arousal until later in the treatment, to ensure that they would have a strong foundation in emotional acceptance and willingness prior to discussing distraction skills that can be used to take the edge off of emotions. We've found that when clients are taught distraction skills too early in treatment—before they have a solid foundation in emotional acceptance and willingness—they can misinterpret distraction as a form of avoidance, leading to the use of distraction skills to avoid their emotions and therefore interfering with the effectiveness and adaptiveness of these skills. Instead, it is much more helpful to emphasize the benefits of approaching, experiencing, and learning from emotions early on in treatment, and to only move to a discussion of the potential utility of distraction skills once clients have become more willing to experience their emotions. That's why this is the first chapter to focus on specific skills clients can use to modulate emotional arousal, or take the edge off of their emotions.

When orienting your client to the emotion modulation skills of ERT, it can be helpful to frame these in the context of the skills they've learned so far, noting that even though accepting, experiencing, and labeling emotions are some of the most helpful strategies for regulating emotions, that doesn't mean that it isn't also important for people to know that there are things they can do to modulate their emotions, or lessen the intensity of these emotions so that they are less overwhelming. This is another place where the use of the word *and* is so important within ERT. We can acknowledge the utility of emotions and the importance of experiencing them *and* still understand the benefits of strategies for taking the edge off of emotions and reducing their intensity. Knowing that there are things they can do to help their emotions pass can go a long way toward improving a client's emotion regulation self-efficacy, or their belief in their ability to regulate their emotions effectively. The key is for clients to use these strategies to modulate their emotional arousal so that they are better able to control their behaviors when experiencing these emotions, rather than to try to avoid these emotions entirely. This is what distinguishes adaptive emotion modulation from nonadaptive or ineffective emotion modulation efforts.

There are several steps for teaching clients effective emotion modulation skills within this ERT. Each of these will be reviewed in turn here.

Review the Modulation Strategies Clients Have Used in the Past

The first step is to help clients identify how they've tried to modulate their emotions in the past, with an emphasis on efforts to avoid emotions. The goal is to assist clients in connecting with their reliance on avoidance strategies in the past, and to reinforce previous discussions you've had with them about the paradoxical, negative consequences of emotional avoidance. This discussion can provide a helpful starting point for introducing your client to the need for more adaptive emotion modulation strategies like the ones you'll be teaching them in this session. We recommend highlighting the following three points in this discussion:

- People often try to modulate their emotions by avoiding their emotions.

- Although this may seem to work in the short term, it is not ultimately effective, because it actually increases the intensity and duration of these emotions.

- Attempts to avoid emotions can take the form of unhealthy and self-destructive behaviors, like self-injury, alcohol or drug use, bingeing or purging behaviors, risky sexual behaviors, or gambling, among others.

Framework for Conceptualizing Different Types of Modulation Strategies

After this brief review of the downsides of avoidance strategies, the next step is to provide clients with a framework for conceptualizing the different types of emotion modulation strategies and how they differ from one another. This overview of emotion modulation strategies is summarized on a handout that can be given to your client during the session, Emotion Modulation: In-Session Handout 1 (Emotion Modulation Strategies: Effective Ways to Modulate Emotions). This handout can be found at the end of this chapter and is available for download at http://www.newharbinger.com/53622.

Within this ERT, emotion modulation strategies are conceptualized as falling into one of three broad categories that exist on a continuum: avoidance, distraction, and approach strategies (see figure 10.1 for a visual representation).

Figure 10.1. Continuum of strategies for modulating emotions

On one end of the continuum are avoidance strategies—strategies that are meant to cut off all contact with emotions and shut them down completely. By this point in the treatment, you can expect your client to be very familiar with the concept of avoidance strategies. The downsides of these strategies are discussed in earlier sessions of this treatment (including the prior sessions on emotional willingness and unwillingness), and reviewed at the start of this session. Therefore, when introducing this category of emotion modulation strategies to your client, all you need to do is remind them that although these are the strategies that a lot of people turn to when they're experiencing unwanted emotions, they don't tend to work very well in the long term and have a lot of downsides. And, that's why you are going to focus on teaching them more adaptive emotion modulation strategies during this session.

We find it helpful to move to the other end of the continuum next, focusing on approach strategies and how these can be thought of as the opposite of avoidance strategies. Let your client know that much of the treatment so far has focused on helping them learn approach strategies, as getting in touch with their emotions, understanding their emotions, paying attention to the information provided by their emotions, and allowing themselves to experience their emotions are all approach strategies that will allow emotions to pass. Indeed, one of the most helpful points to emphasize when discussing approach strategies with your client is that these are some of the most helpful strategies for modulating emotions and allowing them to pass.

Once you've reviewed the strategies on each end of the continuum and reminded your client about the information they've already learned about these strategies, you can move on to introducing your client to distraction strategies. We placed distraction strategies in the middle of the continuum because they fall between approach and avoidance strategies conceptually. Specifically, distraction involves putting aside the emotion for a while by redirecting attention toward something else, and yet necessitates a willingness to return to the emotion and experience it in the future.

When you're teaching your client about distraction strategies, it is important to distinguish distraction from avoidance. As we mentioned previously, it can be easy for clients to mistake avoidance for distraction, or to think they are engaging in distraction strategies when they are really engaging in avoidance strategies. For this reason, discussing distraction within this ERT requires explicitly distinguishing distraction from avoidance, and teaching clients the important differences between these strategies. There are three key differences between distraction and avoidance that are emphasized within this ERT.

The first focuses on the length of time their attention is being redirected toward something other than the emotion. Specifically, unlike avoidance, where the goal is to get away from an emotion permanently, the goal of distraction is to redirect attention toward something else for a short period of time with the plan to return one's attention to the emotion in the near future. For this reason, distraction implies a willingness to experience the emotion in the future. This is an important distinction to emphasize when discussing distraction with your clients. We had quite a few clients in the ERGT clinical trials who believed they were using distraction strategies and then discovered that they were using these strategies as avoidance. For example, one client in an early ERGT trial reported playing video games to distract herself from distressing emotions—something that could very well be a helpful distraction strategy in some contexts. Upon discussing this with her further, however, we discovered that she was using this strategy every single time she experienced emotional distress, and that the purpose of this strategy was to avoid her emotions. She never had any intention of returning her attention to the emotion and would use this strategy for extended periods of time (sometimes upwards of ten hours) in an effort to escape her emotions entirely. If you're finding it challenging to determine whether a client is engaging in distraction or avoidance, it can be helpful to ask them the function of the strategy and what their goal is in using the strategy. Is it to take a break from their emotion so that they are better equipped to process it later on, or is it to escape or avoid the emotion entirely? If your client says that they hope the emotion will go away, this is a good sign that they may be using the strategy as avoidance and not distraction.

The second difference between distraction and avoidance emphasized within this ERT involves the focus of a client's attention and whether they are distracting *away from* the emotion (in an effort to escape or avoid that emotion) or distracting *toward* something else (e.g., a desired activity). These are expected to have different consequences, with the former resembling avoidance and the latter likely being more effective. The key point here is that focusing on shifting their attention *away from* the emotion functions as avoidance because the goal in that moment is to not be in touch with the emotion. As such, distracting attention away from the emotion is expected to have the same paradoxical consequences of avoidance that you discussed with your client previously. Conversely, focusing attention toward something else may provide enough of a healthy distraction to allow the emotion to lessen in intensity without the downsides that accompany active attempts to avoid emotions.

The final difference focuses on the behaviors used to distract attention toward something other than the emotion. Specifically, whereas avoidance strategies often take the form of unhealthy or harmful behaviors, distraction strategies involve healthy behaviors, such as reading, going for a walk, seeing a movie, or talking to a friend about something unrelated to the emotion. An important point to emphasize with your client is that any behavior that is unhealthy or harmful to them cannot, by definition, be a distraction strategy.

Key differences between distraction and avoidance strategies are summarized in table 10.1, and can be used to help guide your discussion of the ways in which these strategies differ.

TABLE 10.1. Key Differences Between Avoidance and Distraction Strategies

Avoidance	Distraction
• You are trying to permanently get away from or stop an emotion. • You are unwilling to experience the emotion. • Often takes the form of unhealthy behaviors (drinking, drug use, harming yourself)	• You are redirecting your attention toward something else for a short period of time. • You are willing to approach and experience the emotion later on. • Takes the form of behaviors that aren't unhealthy or harmful (exercise, watching a movie, playing a game on your phone)

Psychoeducation on the Role of Context in Effective Emotion Modulation

Once your client has an understanding of the differences between approach, distraction, and avoidance strategies, the next step is to provide them with psychoeducation on the contextually-dependent nature of adaptive emotion regulation and the importance of considering the context when determining what strategy to use and whether it is likely to be effective. Thinking about the specific context in which they'll be using the strategy can help your client decide whether to use a distraction or approach strategy in general, as well as whether there are particular distraction or approach strategies that would be most effective in that context.

When discussing the importance of context for selecting an emotion modulation strategy, it is important to highlight for clients that context can refer to both external factors (like the time of day, location or setting, or presence versus absence of other people) and internal factors (like the specific emotion they're experiencing at the time). The goal is for them to consider both the situation they are in and what they are trying to accomplish. This will help them determine what strategies are most likely to be helpful in the moment. A key point to emphasize in this discussion is that no distraction or approach strategies are inherently better or worse than others. All of these strategies have the potential to be helpful; what determines their helpfulness in the moment is the context your client is in and what they are trying to accomplish in that moment.

It can also be helpful to highlight for clients times when distraction strategies may be preferable to approach strategies in the moment; in particular, when approach strategies aren't possible or won't work as well. For example, if your client received some unpleasant news right before a big meeting at work and experienced anxiety in response, they may not have the time or ability to process their emotions in the moment and, thus, may need to wait until later to do so. Therefore, they may need to do something else in the moment to modulate their emotions so that they can perform well in the meeting. Distraction strategies would be a helpful option in this situation. Table 10.2 outlines times when distraction strategies may be particularly helpful or preferred over an approach strategy, and can be used to guide this discussion.

TABLE 10.2. Times When Distraction May Be Preferred Over Approach Strategies
Distraction strategies can be particularly helpful at the following times: • When it isn't safe to experience an emotion in that moment • When the situation your client is in is not supportive of an approach strategy • As a first-line strategy for taking the edge off of an intense emotion so that your client can think more clearly and connect with the information that the emotion is providing

Finally, when discussing effective emotion modulation in the context of this ERT, there are two other points that are important to highlight for clients. The first is the benefit of using distraction and approach strategies together, in sequence, to modulate emotions. The goal of this discussion is to introduce even more flexibility in emotion modulation strategy use by describing to clients how different strategies can be used in sequence to more effectively modulate emotions. The second point that's important to emphasize in this ERT is the importance of emotion modulation flexibility for adaptive emotion regulation. Specifically, it is helpful to teach clients that the more strategies they have access to, the more flexibility they will have in choosing strategies that are the best fit for any given context—which, in turn, will likely increase the effectiveness of their emotion modulation efforts. Clients often aren't aware of just how helpful it is to have a wide range of emotion modulation strategies to choose from, in order to be able to effectively modulate their emotions across a number of different situations and contexts. Therefore, emphasizing this point explicitly is considered very helpful in this ERT.

Identifying Effective Emotion Modulation Strategies

Once you've provided this psychoeducation to your client and fully reviewed the in-session handout with them (Emotion Modulation: In-Session Handout 1), the next step is to assist your client in identifying a number of healthy approach and distraction strategies they can use to modulate their emotions in different contexts. The worksheet for this in-session exercise, Emotion Modulation: In-Session Exercise 1 (Healthy Ways to Modulate Emotions), will assist with this. This exercise can be found at the end of this chapter and is available for download at http://www.newharbinger.com/53622. Using this worksheet, assist your client in identifying a variety of strategies they can use to modulate their emotions at different times of the day, in different settings, when experiencing different emotions, and when alone or with others. Throughout this discussion, keep in mind the importance of emotion modulation flexibility and ensuring that your client is identifying a variety of emotion modulation strategies, both approach and distraction. Examples of different approach and distraction strategies are provided in table 10.3. You can use this table to help guide this exercise with your client.

TABLE 10.3. Examples of Approach and Distraction Modulation Strategies

Approach	Distraction
• Identify and label the emotion you are experiencing. Connect with the different parts of an emotion (for example, thoughts, physical sensations, etc.). • Identify the information the emotion is providing you. • Express your emotion: talk to a trusted friend or loved one about how you feel; write about how you feel; express how you feel through music or artwork. • Connect with your emotion by listening to a song that brings up that emotion. • Sit with your emotion and be willing to experience it. Ride out the emotion like a wave.	• Do something active or something that captures your attention (for example, do housework, watch a movie, or go for a long walk outside on a nice day). • Keep your mind busy, such as with a puzzle, game, or work. • Do something that activates one of your five senses, such as eating spicy food, petting your cat, taking a cold shower, listening to loud music, or smelling a strongly scented candle. • Visualize being in your favorite location. • Talk to a friend about something other than your emotions (sports, current events, your friend's life).

Replacing Unhealthy Strategies with Adaptive Strategies

The final step in improving emotion modulation effectiveness within this ERT is assisting clients in replacing avoidance strategies with the new (more adaptive) emotion modulation strategies they identified in the previous exercise. The worksheet for this exercise, Emotion Modulation: In-Session Exercise 2 (Replacing Unhealthy Modulation Strategies with Adaptive Strategies), can be found at the end of this chapter and is available for download at http://www.newharbinger.com/53622. Completing this exercise with your client in session ensures that they leave the session with a written plan for replacing avoidance strategies with approach and distraction strategies.

The goal of this exercise is to help clients identify specific approach and distraction strategies that serve the same function as the avoidance strategies they used previously and, thus, could be helpful substitutes for these strategies. To begin this exercise, work with your client to identify the avoidance strategies they use most often, with an emphasis on strategies that are harmful or have other negative consequences. Have them write these down in the first column. Next, assist your client in identifying the contexts in which they are most likely to use each of these avoidance strategies, focusing on factors such as the time, place, situation, and their emotional state. They can write down this information in the middle column.

Finally, using the worksheet for the previous in-session exercise (Emotion Modulation: In-Session Exercise 1) as a guide, help your client identify more adaptive approach and distraction strategies they could use instead of the avoidance strategies they identified. During this discussion, assist your client in identifying the function of their avoidance strategies and selecting relevant approach or distraction strategies that serve a similar function. For example, if your client reports using self-injury to obtain relief from feelings of anger, the best substitute strategies would be those that are effective at modulating anger, such as vigorous exercise or throwing ice at an outside wall. Conversely, if your client engages in binge-eating to avoid feelings of sadness, you'd want to assist them in identifying approach or distraction strategies that can help them modulate feelings of sadness in particular, such as talking to a close friend, spending time with a loved one, or watching a funny movie or TV show.

It is also important during this exercise to focus on identifying substitute strategies that will be effective in the specific contexts your client identified for each of the avoidance strategies. For example, if your client reported using certain avoidance strategies only when they are at work, make sure to assist them in identifying alternative strategies that they can also use at work. If the substitute strategy is not helpful in the same context as the original avoidance strategy, then it will not be an effective substitute. Work with your clients to identify several different approach and distraction strategies they could use instead of each of the avoidance strategies.

Skill Consolidation and Generalization

The outside-of-session exercises for this session focus on helping clients practice the new approach and distraction strategies they identified in the session, monitor the consequences of these strategies, and increase their emotion modulation flexibility. The goals of these exercises are for your client to increase their use of adaptive emotion modulation strategies, replace avoidance strategies with approach or distraction strategies, and increase their emotion modulation flexibility by using a variety of approach and distraction strategies.

These outside-of-session exercises include a form your client can use to monitor their use of different emotion modulation strategies on a daily basis, Emotion Modulation: Outside-of-Session Monitoring Form 1 (Emotion Modulation Strategy Practice: Monitoring Form), as well as a worksheet they can complete at the end of the week that prompts them to identify the strategies that were most effective for them throughout the week and ways to increase their emotion modulation flexibility, Emotion Modulation: Outside-of-Session Exercise 1 (Emotion Modulation Strategy Practice Review). Both of these can be found at the end of this chapter and are available for download at http://www.newharbinger.com/53622.

Finally, to continue to facilitate skills integration across ERT sessions, clients are also asked to complete an updated version of the outside-of-session self-destructive behaviors monitoring form that incorporates a column on the emotion modulation strategies your client used during the week to help prevent engagement in self-destructive behaviors. This form, Emotion Modulation: Outside-of-Session Monitoring Form 2, is available for download at http://www.newharbinger.com/53622.

Emotion Modulation: In-Session Handout 1

Emotion Modulation Strategies: Effective Ways to Modulate Emotions

Being able to modulate emotional arousal is an important skill

- It is useful to know that there are things you can do to take the edge off your emotions
- It is useful to know that there are things you can do so that you are not flooded by intense emotions for a very long time

Strategies for modulating emotions (i.e., lowering emotional arousal) can be seen as falling into one of three categories on a continuum

- Avoidance
    - People often try to modulate emotions by actively avoiding them
    - Although this may work in the short term, it is not effective in the long term (increases the intensity and duration of these emotions)
    - Attempts to avoid emotions may take the form of unhealthy/impulsive behaviors (e.g., alcohol, drugs, binge-eating, self-injury)
- Distraction
    - Put the emotion aside for *a while* (not forever), and come back to it
    - Distract until the intensity of the emotion lessens somewhat
    - Distract until it is safe to experience the emotion
    - Distract until you have the resources to manage the emotion
    - Distract until the situation is more supportive of approach strategies
- Approach
    - Label the emotion
    - Experience the emotion so that it runs its course and lessens in intensity
    - Identify the information it is providing
    - Process the emotion

One important dimension of emotion regulation is the flexible use of situationally appropriate, nonavoidant emotion regulation strategies

- The more strategies you have available, the more flexibility you have
- The effectiveness of any emotion regulation strategy is context dependent
- Distraction and approach strategies can be used together to modulate emotional arousal across a wide range of contexts

Emotion Modulation: In-Session Exercise 1

Healthy Ways to Modulate Emotions

Approach	Context (i.e., times, situations, emotions) when this works best
1.	1.
2.	2.
3.	3.
4.	4.
5.	5.
6.	6.
7.	7.
8.	8.
Distract	Context (i.e., times, situations, emotions) when this works best
1.	1.
2.	2.
3.	3.
4.	4.
5.	5.
6.	6.
7.	7.
8.	8.

Increasing Emotion Modulation Effectiveness and Flexibility

Emotion Modulation: In-Session Exercise 2

Replacing Unhealthy Modulation Strategies with Adaptive Strategies

What have you done in the past to try to avoid feeling a certain way (i.e., how have you tried to avoid your emotions in the past)?	Is there a particular context (e.g., a certain type of situation or time of day) in which you are more likely to use these strategies?	What healthy emotion modulation strategies could you substitute in the future that would serve a similar function?
1.	1. 2. 3.	1. 2. 3.
2.	1. 2. 3.	1. 2. 3.
3.	1. 2. 3.	1. 2. 3.
4.	1. 2 3.	1. 2. 3.
5.	1. 2. 3.	1. 2. 3.

Emotion Modulation: Outside-of-Session Monitoring Form 1

Emotion Modulation Strategy Practice: Monitoring Form *(Please complete at least once per day)*

Situation: Include a description of contextual factors (time, situation, etc.)	Emotional response: What emotions did you experience in response to the situation?	Emotional intensity: Intensity of the emotion (0–100)	Emotion modulation strategy: What emotion modulation strategy did you use?	Effectiveness of strategy: Was this strategy effective in modulating your emotion? Why or why not?	Emotional intensity: Intensity of the emotion (0–100)

Increasing Emotion Modulation Effectiveness and Flexibility

Emotion Modulation: Outside-of-Session Exercise 1

Emotion Modulation Strategy Practice Review

Which emotion modulation strategies did you practice this week?

_____
_____
_____
_____

In what contexts do distraction strategies tend to be the most effective? Which distraction strategies seem to work the best for you?

_____
_____
_____
_____
_____
_____

In what contexts do approach strategies tend to be the most effective? Which approach strategies seem to work the best for you?

_____
_____
_____
_____
_____
_____

Do you have a tendency to rely on distraction or approach strategies, to the exclusion of the other? If you repeatedly use one type as opposed to the other, how might you increase your access to the other type of strategy? What might you do to increase your flexibility with regard to the use of emotion modulation strategies?

_____
_____
_____
_____
_____
_____

CHAPTER 11

Increasing Impulse Control

One of the key dimensions of emotion regulation targeted in this ERT is the ability to control impulsive behaviors when distressed. Difficulties in this domain have particular clinical significance, as this is one of the dimensions of emotion dysregulation most strongly related to engagement in a variety of self-destructive and health-compromising behaviors. For this reason, it's imperative that clients who struggle with emotion regulation learn skills for controlling impulsive behaviors specifically.

Importantly, some of the skills described in previous chapters in this book are relevant to this domain of emotion dysregulation as well, and may be helpful in minimizing the risk for impulsive behaviors among your clients. For example, if your client engages in impulsive binge-eating or substance use to avoid unwanted emotions, then assisting them in increasing their willingness to experience painful emotions through the skills reviewed in chapter 9 should help reduce their reliance on these behaviors. Likewise, if your client impulsively self-injures to punish themselves for experiencing emotions they judge to be unacceptable or bad, then improving their emotional acceptance should minimize their desire for self-injury.

Nonetheless, as much as many of the emotion regulation skills we've reviewed thus far can be helpful for reducing self-destructive and impulsive behaviors among clients, additional skills aimed at improving impulse control may also be needed. Specifically, even if many impulsive behaviors are driven by emotional nonacceptance and unwillingness, these behaviors can, over time, become overlearned and habitual, occurring with limited awareness or planning. It is at that point that impulse control strategies can be a key intervention for reducing these behaviors, as these strategies focus specifically on increasing clients' awareness of the negative consequences of these behaviors, as well as the moment between the impulse and the behavior when clients have an opportunity to resist their impulses and engage in more adaptive behaviors.

Within this ERT, impulsive behaviors are targeted directly via four basic impulse control strategies: distraction/delay, behavioral substitution (i.e., replacing the impulsive behavior with a more effective and less harmful behavior that serves the same function as the impulsive behavior), increasing awareness of the negative consequences of impulsive behaviors, and consequence modification (i.e., changing the consequences of impulsive behaviors by having clients reward themselves for resisting urges to engage in these behaviors and remove the positive consequences typically associated with these behaviors). These strategies are discussed in greater detail later in this chapter, and are summarized in a handout that can be given to clients during the session, Impulse Control: In-Session Handout 2 (Impulse Control Strategies: Techniques for Resisting Impulses). This handout can be found at the end of this chapter and is available for download at http://www.newharbinger.com/53622.

Introducing the Concept of Impulsive Behaviors

The first step in teaching clients impulse control strategies in this ERT is to orient them to the concept of impulsive behaviors. Although previous sessions in this therapy helped clients identify both their self-destructive behaviors and the functions of these behaviors, the emphasis was on the emotion-regulating function of these behaviors and how they are used to help clients avoid emotions. This is the first session to specifically introduce the concept of impulsive behaviors to clients and provide them with a behavioral approach to understanding and resisting impulses. Thus, the start of this session focuses on defining impulsive behaviors and orienting clients to the concept of impulses. Impulse Control: In-Session Handout 1 (Impulsive Behaviors) summarizes this information for clients and can be used to help guide this discussion. This handout can be found at the end of this chapter and is available for download at http://www.newharbinger.com/53622. Key points to emphasize during this discussion can be found in table 11.1.

TABLE 11.1. Key Points to Emphasize when Discussing Impulsive Behaviors

- Impulsive behaviors tend to occur so quickly and with such immediacy that clients may not be able to notice the moment between the impulse and the behavior.
- It can feel to clients as if the impulse and the behavior are the same and occur at the same time, with no possible way of inhibiting or stopping the behavior because it happens too quickly.
- Impulsive behaviors are typically accompanied by a sense of immediacy—a compelling urge to do something in the moment. This sense of immediacy can make it even harder not to act on an impulse and is one of the things that can make resisting impulses so uncomfortable.
- Impulsive behaviors tend to have both substantial positive consequences in the short term and significant downsides in the long term.
- Impulses are, by definition, very short-lived. Although they tend to be very strong, they pass relatively quickly. Therefore, if clients can resist the impulse long enough—often for a relatively brief period of time—it will lessen in intensity and become easier to resist.

Distraction and Delay Strategies

The first set of impulse control strategies covered in this session includes distraction and delay strategies. These strategies stem from the fact that impulses are, by nature, fairly short-lived and will thus pass relatively quickly if a client can resist the urge to act on them in the moment. Therefore, the goal of these strategies is simply to create some space between the impulse and the behavior in order to give the impulse time to dissipate. This set of strategies can take two different but related forms: distraction and delay.

With regard to distraction, the goal is for your client to distract from their impulses by engaging in any healthy or adaptive activity that captures their attention. When discussing this strategy with your client, it can be helpful to refer back to the in-session exercise on emotion modulation strategies they completed in the previous session, Emotion Modulation: In-Session Exercise 1 (Healthy Ways to Modulate Emotions), as many of the distraction strategies they identified during that exercise will be relevant here as well. The goal is to assist your client in identifying a number of different activities they can use to distract themselves from their impulses so that they have time to pass. In the context of this discussion, it's most helpful to focus on distraction techniques that are compelling enough to capture your client's attention.

The alternative to distraction is delay, which involves delaying responding for long enough to allow your client's impulses to lessen or dissipate. The idea behind this strategy is that because impulses pass relatively quickly, one way to avoid acting on these is to build in a delay between the impulse and the behavior in order to give the impulse the opportunity to pass. This particular strategy can be done in two ways. The first is to simply have your client commit to delaying action for a set period of time, such as five, fifteen, or thirty minutes. Work with your client to choose an amount of time that feels tolerable to them and to which they can commit. The goal is for them to commit to delaying action for just a small period of time to give the impulses time to lessen. At the end of that period, the impulses may have passed, or your client could use the skill again to delay for a second period of time. The key is just to delay acting long enough for the impulse to pass.

The second way to use this strategy is to work with your client to build in a delay between the impulse and the behavior ahead of time, so that they must wait to act on the behavior when the impulse arises. For example, for behaviors that require an implement of some kind (e.g., a razor blade for self-injury), preventing immediate access to this implement may introduce enough of a delay between the onset of the impulse and the client's ability to engage in the behavior (i.e., access the implement) for the impulse to lessen. Table 11.2 provides examples of different delay techniques that may be helpful and can be used to help guide the discussion of this strategy with your client.

TABLE 11.2. Examples of Delay Techniques

- Have your client commit to not acting on their impulses for fifteen minutes; have them set a timer for this period of time.
- If your client struggles with binge-eating or overeating, ask them to commit to waiting thirty minutes before acting on urges to binge or overeat.
- Have your client freeze self-injury implements in a block of ice so that they will need to wait for the ice to melt before they can access the implement (building in a delay ahead of time).
- If your client struggles with impulsive spending, have them freeze their credit cards in a block of ice.
- Have your client get someone to hide their credit cards (for those who struggle with impulsive spending) or cigarettes (for those who struggle with smoking) in their house so that there is a built-in delay as they have to search for them.
- If your client struggles with binge-eating, ask them to avoid keeping their preferred food for bingeing in the house so that there is a built-in delay as they try to obtain the food.

Behavioral Substitution

The next strategy that can be very helpful for controlling impulsive behaviors is behavioral substitution, or replacing the impulsive behavior with a more adaptive behavior that serves the same function as the impulsive behavior. If this strategy sounds familiar to you, that's because we reviewed a very similar skill in chapter 10 when discussing how to assist clients in replacing avoidance strategies with more adaptive emotion modulation strategies. The same principles we discussed in that chapter apply here as well: the best substitute behaviors for impulsive behaviors are those that serve a similar function to the impulsive behavior. The needs clients are trying to meet with impulsive behaviors tend to be important and valid needs: feeling better, obtaining relief from emotional pain, obtaining comfort, obtaining social connection, making their pain more manageable, and establishing a sense of control, among others. Therefore, it's important to provide them with some other way of getting those needs met, rather than just asking them to stop the behavior and tolerate the unmet needs. Helping clients identify more adaptive behaviors that serve the same function as their impulsive behaviors will provide them with a more adequate and tolerable substitute, increasing the likelihood that this substitution will be effective.

Increasing Awareness of the Negative Consequences of Impulsive Behaviors

The next strategy for controlling impulsive behaviors within this ERT is increasing a client's awareness of the negative consequences of these behaviors. This strategy is based on the fact that human beings tend to be motivated and influenced by the short-term consequences of behaviors, rather than their long-term consequences. Consequences that occur closer in time to a behavior, particularly those that follow the behavior immediately, become more closely linked to that behavior and, as such, are more likely to shape future behaviors. This means that it tends to be the short-term consequences of behaviors—those that are most closely linked to the behaviors in time—that shape behaviors and influence their future likelihood.

The reason that this makes it more difficult to control impulsive behaviors is that impulsive behaviors tend to have positive short-term consequences and negative long-term consequences. Thus, the consequences that become most strongly associated with these behaviors for clients are the positive consequences, reinforcing these behaviors and making them more likely to persist in the future. The long-term consequences of these behaviors, even when they are extremely harmful, do not become as closely associated with the behaviors because they are too far removed from the behaviors in time. It's easier to discount these consequences than those that follow a behavior immediately.

One way to counteract this (and, thus, the basis of this strategy) is to increase a client's awareness of the negative consequences of their impulsive behaviors, bringing their attention to these consequences and thereby strengthening the association between the behavior and its negative consequences. There are a number of ways that this can be done. The key is simply to increase your client's connection to the negative consequences of their impulsive behaviors whenever they experience an urge to engage in these behaviors. Table 11.3 provides several specific strategies for increasing clients' awareness of the negative consequences of their impulsive behaviors. As you can see, most of these involve having clients identify all of the negative consequences of their impulsive behaviors ahead of time (when they are not experiencing impulses to engage in these behaviors) and then take steps to increase their awareness of and connection to these consequences when they're experiencing urges. That's why so many of these strategies start out with instructions to have your client list all of the negative consequences of their impulsive behavior. To facilitate this discussion, it can be helpful to assist your client in completing Impulse Control: In-Session Exercise 1 (Consequences of Impulsive Behavior) so that they leave the session with a solid understanding of many of the negative consequences of their impulsive behaviors. This exercise can be found at the end of this chapter and is available for download at http://www.newharbinger.com/53622.

TABLE 11.3. Strategies for Increasing Awareness of the Negative Consequences of Impulsive Behaviors

- Have your client list every possible negative consequence of their impulsive behavior they can think of, and then post copies of this list everywhere they tend to engage in this behavior. For example, if your client overeats, have them post this list in their kitchen or anywhere else they tend to eat.

- Have your client create a list of all of the negative consequences of their impulsive behavior on their phone and read the list whenever they have urges to engage in the behavior.

- If your client engages in self-injury, have them place a list of all of the negative consequences of this behavior right next to the implements they use to engage in this behavior.

- We've had multiple clients who impulsively contact someone in their life in a way that is ineffective, e.g., by repeatedly calling or contacting someone who is not healthy for them, who has asked the client not to contact them, or who has expressed concerns about the frequency of the contact. In all of these situations, the behavior has been both impulsive and ineffective, and has had serious negative consequences for the client. In cases like this, one strategy that has been helpful is to have the client program that person's name in their phone with the negative consequences of contacting them. For example, they could rename the person in their contact list as one of the negative consequences of contacting them, or simply as a reference to the fact that they will regret doing so (e.g., changing their ex-partner's name to "you will regret calling" or "calling me is an unwise idea").

Consequence Modification

The final strategy for controlling impulsive behaviors within this ERT is consequence modification. This strategy is based on the fact that impulsive behaviors are maintained by their positive short-term consequences. As we discussed above, it is the powerful positive consequences that immediately follow impulsive behaviors that reinforce these behaviors. When a client experiences rewarding consequences following a behavior, that behavior will be reinforced and more likely to occur again in the future.

On the contrary, when a client tries to resist an impulse and refrain from engaging in an impulsive behavior, this is generally not reinforcing in the moment. Instead, resisting an impulse is often incredibly uncomfortable and painful. This is why it can be so challenging for clients to control impulsive behaviors even when they are able to connect with the ways in which these behaviors are harming them in the long term: in the moment, engaging in the behaviors is reinforcing whereas resisting impulses is not reinforcing (and is actually punishing).

That's where this particular impulse control strategy comes in. The idea behind this strategy is to invert the consequences of engaging in versus resisting impulsive behaviors in the moment so that engaging in these behaviors is not rewarding and resisting them is rewarding. This will make it easier for your client to resist these behaviors in the future.

The first step of this two-step strategy is for your client to reward themselves every time they resist an impulse. Although this may sound simple, it can actually be quite difficult to do, as this reward needs to occur immediately after your client resists the impulse. This means that the reward must be relatively small and inexpensive, as well as something that can be done in the moment (whenever your client resists an urge to engage in their impulsive behavior).

One of our favorite examples of this type of reward came from one of the first clients to receive this ERT. This client was artistic and found great pleasure in creating artwork. After we reviewed this strategy in session, this client visited an art store and bought a number of small art supplies (e.g., colored pencils, different colored paints, brushes, etc.). She then kept these in a box in her closet. Then, every time she resisted an urge to harm herself, she went into the closet and rewarded herself with one art supply from this box. It was a highly personalized and effective reward, and the use of this strategy resulted in an immediate reduction in her self-injurious behaviors. Other rewards that clients have identified in the past are described in table 11.4, and can be used to guide your discussion of this strategy with your clients.

TABLE 11.4. Small and Immediate Rewards for Resisting Impulsive Behaviors

When your client resists an urge to engage in an impulsive behavior, the following are things they can do to reward themselves in the moment:

- Give themselves a ten-minute break to listen to their favorite music or look at self-soothing pictures on their phone or computer.
- Treat themselves to their favorite snack or beverage.
- Go for a walk outside to connect to nature.
- Buy fresh flowers for their home.
- Give themselves a sticker (and collect these in one place so that they can connect to the growing number of times they've been able to resist their impulses).
- Watch their favorite TV show.
- Take a few minutes to snuggle with a pet or loved one.

The second step of this strategy is for your client to remove the rewards that typically follow engagement in their impulsive behavior. The idea behind this step is that if you can help your client strip their impulsive behavior of its positive short-term consequences, this behavior will be far less rewarding and, thus, far less likely to continue to occur.

Even more than the previous step, however, this step of the consequence modification strategy requires a nuanced approach. The key is for your client to remove the positive consequences of the behavior without punishing themselves for engaging in the behavior or making themselves feel worse than they did before they engaged in the behavior. We let clients know that the goal is for them to get back to the state they were in right before they engaged in the behavior—not to make themselves feel worse than they did initially or to do something else to punish themselves. If they can get back to the state they were in right before they engaged in the behavior, they have an opportunity for a redo—a chance to use the skills they've learned in this treatment to more effectively regulate their emotions. Indeed, this latter point is key to the effective application of this strategy: once clients take away the positive consequences associated with the impulsive behavior and get back to the state they were in immediately before engaging in the behavior, they have the opportunity to get their needs met in another, more adaptive, way. The goal isn't for them to remain miserable or resign themselves to having unmet needs; instead, the goal is for them to use an adaptive emotion modulation strategy or healthy behavior that serves the same function as their impulsive behavior to get their needs met in a more effective way.

One thing to keep in mind as you're teaching your client this strategy is that it is easy for clients to shift into a self-punishment focus, even if you've explained to them that this is not the goal of this step of the strategy. Thus, it is important that you remain mindful of any references your client makes to self-punishment, or any ideas they generate for removing the rewards associated with their impulsive behavior that function as self-punishment or are intended to make themselves feel worse than they did before. When you notice these, point them out to your client and assist them in identifying ways to remove the positive consequences of the behavior only. To assist you with this discussion, we have included examples of how this step of the strategy can be applied ineffectively (in a self-punishing way) versus effectively for several different impulsive behaviors in table 11.5 below. These examples will provide a framework for discussing this strategy with your client and assisting them in applying this step of the strategy as intended.

TABLE 11.5. Example Impulsive Behaviors and Ineffective vs. Effective Strategies for Removing the Positive Consequences of These Behaviors

Impulsive Behavior	Positive Consequence	Ineffective/Self-Punishing Applications of This Strategy	Adaptive/Effective Applications of This Strategy
Alcohol abuse	Avoid hangover and withdrawal symptoms	Bang their head on the wall (to cause a headache) Force themselves to vomit (to reduce the physiological effects of the alcohol and increase the likelihood of withdrawal symptoms)	Exercise (to bring on physiological arousal and sweating) Listen to loud music (may result in a minor headache, irritation, concentration problems, and/or physiological arousal)
Self-injury	Avoid shame	Ruminate about their most shameful and intolerable experiences or characteristics (to induce intense distress and shame) Ask someone else to berate them (to bring up feelings of worthlessness and shame)	Imaginal exposure (imagine the situation that led to their feelings of shame) Conduct a chain analysis (i.e., work back from the self-injury to come into contact with the thoughts and feelings that prompted the self-injury)
Risky sex	Avoid feelings of loneliness	End a meaningful relationship or cut themselves off permanently from people they care about	Spend some time alone Listen to songs or watch movies that involve loneliness or isolation
Overspending	Get a high and feel less empty	Give away their possessions and meaningful belongings (to induce intense distress and punish themselves)	Return the purchased items

Now that you've reviewed the examples in table 11.5, we hope that the distinction between a client removing the positive consequences associated with an impulsive behavior and punishing themselves for engaging in an impulsive behavior is clear. Because this can be a challenging distinction for clients to grasp, we recommend emphasizing repeatedly throughout your discussion of this strategy that the goal is not for your client to make themselves feel worse than they did before engaging in the impulsive behavior, but to return to the emotional state that was present immediately prior to the impulsive behavior—no worse or better. Tips for teaching this strategy effectively are provided in table 11.6.

TABLE 11.6. Tips for Effectively Teaching Your Client Consequence Modification

- Make sure to emphasize the distinction between removing the positive consequences of an impulsive behavior and punishing oneself for having engaged in that behavior.
- Remind your client repeatedly that the goal of this strategy is to remove the positive consequences of an impulsive behavior immediately after they engage in that behavior in order to return to the state they were in right before they engaged in that behavior (i.e., their baseline state)—not to make themselves feel worse than they did before. Once clients have returned to their baseline state, they can use any of the skills they've learned in this therapy so far to regulate their emotions or get another need met in a more effective way.
- Stay alert and mindful to any references clients make to wanting to punish themselves for engaging in the impulsive behavior.
- Remind clients that this strategy is most effective when the modified consequences of resisting impulses and engaging in impulsive behaviors are implemented immediately. The goal is to ensure that these modified consequences follow the behavior immediately.
- Ensure that the rewards clients identify for resisting impulses are personally meaningful and reinforcing for them.

Skills Consolidation and Generalization

There are two outside-of-session exercises for this session. The first, Impulse Control: Outside-of-Session Exercise 1 (Consequence Modification), focuses on helping clients personalize and apply the consequence modification strategy. Specifically, this exercise assists clients in identifying particular techniques for both rewarding themselves when they resist an impulsive behavior and removing the positive consequences of impulsive behaviors. The goal is for your client to complete this exercise early in the week so that they have time to practice this strategy before the next session. This exercise can be found at the end of this chapter and is available for download at http://www.newharbinger.com/53622.

The second (and primary) outside-of-session exercise assists clients in practicing the impulse control strategies they learned during the session and monitoring their consequences using an updated version of the outside-of-session self-destructive behaviors monitoring form, Impulse Control: Outside-of-Session Monitoring Form 1. Specifically, the updated version of this form includes two additional columns that prompt clients to practice the impulse control strategies they learned. This form is available for download at http://www.newharbinger.com/53622.

Impulse Control: In-Session Handout 1
Impulsive Behaviors

Impulsive behaviors are behaviors that occur:

- Without control, inhibition, restraint
- Without thinking, reflection, or consideration
- Without foresight, adequate planning, or regard for the consequences
- With a sense of immediacy and spontaneity

Impulsive behaviors tend to be associated with:

- Positive short-term consequences
- Negative long-term consequences

Although they may be strong, impulses are (by their very nature) short-lived

Strategies for managing impulsive behaviors and resisting impulses include:

- Distraction/delay
- Behavioral substitution
- Increasing awareness of the negative consequences of impulsive behaviors
- Consequence modification

(see Impulse Control: In-Session Handout 2 for complete descriptions of each strategy)

Impulse Control: In-Session Handout 2

Impulse Control Strategies: Techniques for Resisting Impulses

Distraction/Delay

- Distracting from an impulse or delaying a response may help you "ride out" the impulse until it lessens in intensity
- **Interventions:** Engage in any healthy activity that distracts you from the impulse (Distraction) or delay responding for a set period of time or by building in delays in advance (Delay)

Behavioral substitution

- Impulsive behaviors serve important functions and meet important needs
- Finding alternative ways to get these needs met may decrease the need for the impulsive behavior
- **Intervention:** Identify alternative (more adaptive) behaviors that serve the same function as the impulsive behavior and engage in these instead

Increasing awareness of the behavior's negative long-term consequences

- Short-term consequences exert more influence over behaviors than long-term consequences because they are more closely linked to the behaviors
- Increasing awareness of the long-term negative consequences of impulsive behaviors can help you resist your impulses
- **Intervention:** Identify the short- and long-term, positive and negative consequences of impulsive behaviors and then focus on the negative consequences

Consequence modification

- Impulsive behaviors are maintained by their positive short-term consequences (e.g., the relief they provide)
- One way to reduce impulsive behaviors is to change their consequences
- **Intervention:** Reward yourself for resisting urges to engage in the impulsive behavior and remove the positive consequences typically associated with the impulsive behavior

Impulse Control: In-Session Exercise 1

Consequences of Impulsive Behavior

	Positive	Negative
Short-term consequences		
Long-term consequences		

Impulse Control: Outside-of-Session Exercise 1

Consequence Modification

When you do not act impulsively: How can you reward yourself when you resist the urge to engage in an impulsive behavior?

_____
_____
_____
_____
_____
_____
_____
_____
_____
_____

When you do act impulsively: How can you remove some of the positive consequences you gain from engaging in the impulsive behavior?

_____
_____
_____
_____
_____
_____
_____
_____
_____
_____

CHAPTER 12

Clarifying Valued Directions in Life

By this point in the treatment, clients have learned numerous emotion regulation skills and likely noticed improvements in the behaviors and symptoms that brought them to treatment. Even though these treatment gains are expected to increase clients' quality of life, however, we have found that many clients who receive this ERT continue to be unsure at this point in the treatment of who they are and the type of life they want to live. Many of them had put so much effort into trying to escape their emotional pain that they didn't have the resources to devote to building a meaningful life. Others report having actively avoided meaningful activities due to their potential to bring about emotional pain, and still others describe repeated experiences where their desires and choices were diminished, punished, or invalidated, leading them to live a life that did not feel like their own.

Given this, we decided to focus the final sessions of this ERT on valued directions (referred to as "values" from this point forward) from ACT (Hayes et al., 1999). Values refer to the things in life that are meaningful and important to a client and can be used to guide their actions and the choices they make. Specifically, as clients start to identify and clarify their values, they can begin to make choices focused on building a more fulfilling and meaningful life as opposed to temporarily escaping unpleasant internal experiences. Moreover, by connecting day-to-day actions to values, those actions take on new meaning and can become far more reinforcing (Hayes et al., 1999; Twohig, Levin, & Ong, 2021). For example, many clients report urges to skip therapy sessions or drop out of treatment due to the association of therapy with the potential for emotional pain. However, the meaning of the action of attending therapy can be changed if clients recognize that attending therapy is consistent with a value of self-care. Even though therapy may still result in distress, connecting this action to a value changes its meaning and makes it more reinforcing.

We view values as integral to this ERT, as doing this work gives clients the opportunity to put the skills they've learned in this treatment into action to build the life they want to live. In fact, it is often during these final sessions on values when the skills clients have been working so hard to incorporate into their lives seem to "click" and clients display notable shifts in their overall functioning and emotional well-being. Thus, given the importance of values to this treatment, the original group therapy version of this ERT dedicates four sessions to clarifying valued directions and increasing valued actions. The first of the sessions devoted to values (reviewed in this chapter) focuses exclusively on introducing the concept of values and assisting clients in the process of clarifying their values. The next three sessions focus on helping clients identify doable actions in line with their values and increase engagement in valued actions (reviewed in chapter 13).

Introducing the Concept of Values

At the start of the first session focused on values, clients are informed that the focus of this ERT is shifting from the previous sessions, moving from learning skills for responding more effectively to their emotions to building the life they want to live.

Identifying the Downsides of Goals

When posed with the question "What do you want to move toward in your life?," it is common for clients to immediately begin thinking about goals they can set for themselves. This is the approach most people learn for building the life they want to live. Yet, as much as goals can be helpful, they are associated with some downsides. Therefore, it is important to spend some time at the start of this session distinguishing values from goals. We recommend beginning this process by asking clients to share what comes to mind when they hear the word "goals." Often clients will respond to this question with words such as "achievement," "aspiration," "progress," and "growth." However, most clients will also bring up painful or unpleasant associations with the concept of goals, such as "failure," "trapped," "overwhelming," and "disappointment." If your client doesn't initially bring up any of the negative associations with the word "goals," it can be helpful to ask them if they can identify any downsides to goals, or if they have had experiences where setting goals made them feel overwhelmed, trapped, or like a failure.

Once your client has shared their associations with the concept of goals, the next step is to provide psychoeducation on some of the downsides of goals. There are two primary downsides of goals emphasized within this ERT. (1) Goals are, by their nature, future focused. One consequence of this is that setting a goal implies that where clients are in the moment is not good enough (as they are striving to be different in some way) (Orsillo & Roemer, 2016). In addition, this focus on the future can be overwhelming and make it challenging for clients to determine the steps they need to take to reach their goal. In this way, goals can increase anxiety, helplessness, hopelessness, and feelings of low self-efficacy. The future-focused nature of goals also means that they may lose their meaning and importance to clients in the midst of pursuing them. Specifically, when goals are set far in the future, clients' interest and investment in these goals can change, and yet it can be difficult for clients to change course or move on from these goals after they've invested so much time and energy into trying to achieve them. Thus, clients often find that they continue to pursue these goals even after they lose their meaning. (2) Goals are rigid and all or nothing. Once a goal is set, that goal will either be reached or not reached. For this reason, success is determined by reaching a particular outcome in the future as opposed to the moment-by-moment journey of pursuing the goal (Orsillo & Roemer, 2016).

Values Are an Alternative to Goals

The next step is to introduce your client to the concept of valued directions as an alternative to goals. Valued Directions: In-Session Handout 1 (Valued Directions) can be used to guide this discussion. This handout can be found at the end of this chapter and is available for download at http://www.newharbinger.com/53622.

It can be helpful to frame this discussion as providing clients with an alternative to goals that doesn't have the same downsides you just discussed. Prior to giving them the handout on valued directions, it can be helpful to ask your client what comes to mind when they hear the word "values." This will give you the opportunity to learn about your client's current associations with this concept. Not surprisingly, most clients think of values differently than how the term is used within this ERT. Clients typically mention family values, morals, ethics, or religion when they hear the word "values." Once they share what comes up for them, it can be helpful to clarify that values mean something different in the context of this ERT. Specifically, the term *valued directions* (or *values*, for short) refers to the things in life that matter to your client and are meaningful to them.

This is the point at which it can be helpful to give your client the in-session handout on valued directions and use this to guide your discussion of the definition and meaning of values within this ERT. The key points to emphasize when describing values to clients are summarized below, along with different metaphors you can use to capture these concepts.

VALUES ARE A MOMENT-TO-MOMENT PROCESS

Contrary to goals, values are focused on the present moment (versus the future) and process (versus outcome). As such, values can be thought of as an ongoing and enduring guide for your client's life. Because values reflect a moment-to-moment process, they are often described in an active way, such as "being compassionate" or "helping others." These values do not have an end point. They cannot be achieved or crossed off a list. Instead, clients can engage in actions consistent with these values in perpetuity, with each action they take moving them in the direction of this value.

In addition, because values are a process rather than an outcome, "success" is defined as taking any actions consistent with these values (rather than by achieving a specific outcome, as in the case of goals). This means that any actions your client takes consistent with their values are meaningful and important, and move them forward in their life—no matter how big or small those actions are. This also means that your client can make meaningful changes in their life right now, in every moment. As a result, focusing on values versus goals can increase a client's sense of agency, self-efficacy, and control over their life.

The "Skiing" metaphor from ACT (Hayes et al., 1999), described in table 12.1, can be a useful technique for conveying the benefits of focusing on the process versus outcome and the differences between values and goals in this regard.

TABLE 12.1. Skiing Metaphor (Hayes et al., 1999)
Let's say that you absolutely love snow skiing and go to your favorite slope one day. You take the lift all the way to the top of the slope and just as you are about to make your way down the mountain, you hear someone calling out for you. You look over your shoulder and see a man standing next to a helicopter. He asks you where you are going, and when you tell him you are going down the mountain, he responds, "Great! That's where I'm going. Jump on in and I'll take you down there." You think to yourself, "Well, riding in the helicopter would be efficient. I do want to get to the bottom of the mountain." So, after some deliberation, you decide to get into the helicopter and ride to the bottom of the mountain. After you get to the bottom, you ride the lift to the top of the slope again. Once again, though, just as you are about to head down the mountain, you see the man in the helicopter. He tells you that he is taking another ride to the bottom of the mountain and invites you to get in. So, once again you jump into the helicopter and ride to your destination at the bottom of the mountain. The rest of the day proceeds in the same way: you take the lift up to the top of the mountain and the helicopter then brings you down to the bottom of the mountain. At the end of the day, how would you rate your day of skiing? Would you find the experience meaningful or enjoyable? Ultimately, you reached your goal every time; however, is that what you were looking forward to at the start of the day? Of course not. What's meaningful and rewarding about skiing is not the outcome of reaching the bottom of the mountain but the journey you take to get there: navigating obstacles, connecting with the scenery or the feeling of the wind against your face, feeling yourself glide through the snow. That's skiing. And that's what really matters—the process.

Another benefit of focusing on the process versus a specific end point is that this means that progress does not have to be linear. When your client sets goals for themselves, they can evaluate their progress toward those goals by comparing where they want to be to where they are now and where they started. This leaves two options—either your client is consistently making progress toward their goal or they are not. There is no space in this scenario for making process in a nonlinear way or for veering off the direct path from where they started to their end point. The downside of approaching progress in this way is that it sets up clients for negative evaluations of themselves and their progress any time they encounter a roadblock or fail to make linear progress (which is often inevitable). When this occurs, clients often report judgments such as "I am not making any progress" or "I'll never achieve this" or "I am a failure." The "Path Up the Mountain" metaphor from ACT (Hayes et al., 1999), described in table 12.2, can be used to illustrate to clients how progress is defined in the context of values.

TABLE 12.2. Path Up the Mountain Metaphor

It's a perfect day for hiking, so you decide to head out to your favorite trail. Now, if we think about goals, the goal of hiking is to get to the top of the mountain. If you just focused on that goal, there are a lot of ways that you could get there. You could even take a helicopter to the top of the mountain! I'm guessing, though, that you've already connected to the fact that hiking is about more than just getting to the top of the mountain. It's about the process of making your way up the mountain. So, let's focus on that process for now. If you decide you want to hike to the top of the mountain, how would you measure your progress? One option would be to focus on linear progress toward that end point of reaching the top of the mountain. This would mean that any time you are moving up the mountain, you are making progress, and anytime you are moving down the mountain, you are not making progress. You could even decide that the quickest way to reach the top of the mountain is just to scale the side of the mountain, as that is the most direct path. If you have ever hiked, though, then you probably know that this isn't how it works. There generally isn't a straight path from the bottom of the mountain to the top of the mountain. Instead, you usually end up making your way up the mountain on paths that wind and bend. Sometimes you may be heading up the mountain. Sometimes you may be staying at a constant elevation. And, sometimes you may even notice that you have to head down the mountain a little in order to stay on the windy path or make it around some obstacle. What this means is that, depending on where you are on the path (or in the process of hiking), you may not always be able to see that you are moving forward. If you were to stop at certain points in the trail, such as a point where you are heading down the mountain, it may even seem like you are not making progress at all. However, this wouldn't be accurate. Focusing on that one moment and assuming that progress should be linear doesn't take into account the bigger picture and the fact that sometimes turning down the mountain is a necessary step in making progress toward the top. Even though in a certain moment it may feel as though you are not making progress, you are still moving forward in making your way along the trail. You are doing exactly what you need to do at any given moment to get to where you want to go. And that is consistent with values.

Once you've shared this metaphor with your client, spend some time asking them about their impressions of and reactions to this metaphor. What are some benefits of approaching progress in this way? What comes to mind as they shift their focus from the end point to the process?

Next, clarify for your client how focusing on the process increases behavioral flexibility and the potential to act in ways consistent with values in any moment. Specifically, when clients focus on values, there are numerous choices they can make in the moment that will be consistent with these values. And, as long as the choice they make is consistent with one of their values, they will be moving forward in their lives. Indeed, one of the benefits of values is that they open up clients to a range of potentially rewarding possibilities. For example, if your client had a goal of being in a committed relationship, there are all kinds of things they would need to do before they could achieve that goal (e.g., finding someone to be in a relationship with, going on dates, establishing a connection with that person, maintaining that connection, etc.), and many of these would not be in their control. However, by connecting to the value that may underlie that goal (for example, caring for others), there are multiple actions they can take in the moment that are in service of that value: listening to another person, validating another's emotions, reaching out to someone to provide them with support, making eye contact with someone else, and even caring for themselves. And, engaging in these actions would allow your client to build the life they want and be the person they want to be *right now*, in this very moment.

VALUES ARE PERSONAL

Another key feature of values is that they are highly personal and can only be determined by the individual. Clarifying for clients that only they can determine their values can be both freeing and anxiety provoking for them. As we mentioned earlier, many clients who struggle with emotion regulation difficulties report feeling as if they have not been living their own life. Before entering this ERT, they may have felt the need to hide aspects of their identity or make choices to please others or avoid conflict. The consequence of this is that many of the clients who receive this ERT are not living the life *they* want to live. Therefore, informing clients that they alone get to determine their values can help foster a sense of agency and control.

That said, it is also common for clients to experience anxiety about identifying their values, especially if they haven't really explored what matters to them before or have experienced repeated invalidation of their internal experiences or identity. If your client reports anxiety about the process of identifying values, we recommend leaning into the dialectical stance underlying this ERT by simultaneously validating how difficult and anxiety-provoking it can be to begin to build a meaningful life and acknowledging the benefits and importance of doing so. Remind clients that it is perfectly natural for them to experience doubts or fear as they move through this uncharted territory *and* (as they learned in earlier sessions of this treatment) it is also possible to experience these feelings and thoughts and move forward with them.

VALUES ARE CONSTANT

At this point in the treatment, clients are generally able to recognize that many of the choices they've made in their lives were driven by efforts to achieve or avoid particular internal states. Although basing choices on the presence or absence of particular internal states can sometime work, however, internal experiences are not always the most useful or stable guides for behavior. Specifically, because thoughts and emotions are transitory and can change with each moment, basing choices solely on these internal experiences can lead to inconsistent and even erratic choices as your client's thoughts and emotions change. Your client may feel as if they are a pinball bouncing around through life without any stability, predictability, or direction. This is particularly the case when choices are driven by efforts to avoid certain internal experiences, as making choices to avoid emotional pain can actively interfere with building a meaningful life.

Likewise, making choices based on reasons stemming from desired thoughts or emotions can also introduce challenges to consistency when these thoughts or emotions change or disappear. Specifically, because it is not possible to control specific thoughts or emotions, making choices based on the expected presence of these can introduce challenges to maintaining valued actions when these internal experiences inevitably change. Values, on the other hand, provide constancy and stability. Unlike reasons for engaging in certain actions that stem from momentary emotions or thoughts (and, thus, are subject to change at any time), values are consistent and never end. Table 12.3 provides example language that can be helpful in explaining to clients the differences between basing choices on values (which are constant) versus reasons stemming from thoughts or feelings (which are momentary).

TABLE 12.3. Example Therapist Language: Values Are Constant
If something is going to guide your choices in life, it makes sense to rely on something that is constant and stable. For example, let's consider the choice of signing up for a challenging class or project at work. What are the reasons someone might give for that choice? Maybe the material is interesting, or taking on that challenge would make you feel good about yourself, or doing so will give you the opportunity to meet new people. Those are all incredibly good reasons. However, what happens to your choice when those reasons aren't present? There could be times when you don't find the work interesting, or you encounter a barrier that makes you doubt yourself, or you experience stress, boredom, frustration, or disappointment. In those moments, when the initial reasons for taking on this challenge aren't present, should you drop the class or stop working on the project? Of course not. There are going to be times when you are not able to connect with all (or even any) of your reasons for doing something and yet the most effective thing to do is to continue to move forward with that class or project. This is because there is something deeper than those reasons you initially identified that is driving your pursuit of this class or project: your values. It may be that the values of learning, challenging yourself, or growing in your position drove your choice to take on this class or project. Unlike reasons, these values aren't going to change. They are always going to be there to guide you and move you forward, especially during those times when your emotions, thoughts, or other internal experiences are telling you otherwise.

It can also be helpful to clarify for clients that using values to guide their choices has advantages over simply weighing the pros and cons of a decision, which clients have likely done in the past. Ask your client if they have ever created a list of pros and cons of a possible decision before and, if so, what the experience was like for them. Clients will sometimes report experiences of generating numerous pros and cons and still ending up feeling stuck. Or, they may identify a number of cons for making a particular choice and yet still decide to move forward with that choice. The key point to emphasize during this part of the discussion is that values are larger than the specific reasons that can be generated for or against a certain choice. Values can provide guidance on the most effective path to take (that is, the path in service of building a meaningful life) even when your client's mind is focusing on all of the reasons not to take that path.

There are two metaphors that can be used in this ERT to illustrate this feature of values to your client. One of these is described in table 12.4 and the other (the "Gardening" metaphor from ACT; Hayes et al., 1999) is available for download at http://www.newharbinger.com/53622 in the addendum to table 12.4 (Additional Metaphor for Conveying the Constancy and Stability of Values).

TABLE 12.4. Metaphor for Conveying the Constancy and Stability of Values

Metaphor	Script
Lighthouse in a Storm	You can think of your values as a lighthouse in a storm. During intense storms, boat captains can lose their bearings. They may not be able to see the coastline and may run the risk of losing their way and running aground or crashing into the rocks at the shore. The intense light from a lighthouse permeates through the storm and provides a guide to the captain. It lets the captain know where the shore is and can provide a guidepost for safe navigation. So, even when the captain can't trust everything going on around them, they know that lighthouse light is going to stay constant and steady, helping them get to where they need to go. Similarly, values can serve as a stable guide in those moments when it is challenging to navigate our lives—when we are struggling with intense emotional pain, when our emotions are cloudy, when we are judging ourselves, or when we aren't sure what the future holds. In those moments, we may not know what decisions to make or what path to take. However, just like the lighthouse, our values can shine through those experiences and guide us in the most helpful direction. You can't go wrong if you use your values as a guide and make choices in line with these values.

VALUES ARE DEFINED BY ACTIONS VS. FEELINGS

A key point to emphasize during your discussion of values with your client is that even though they cannot directly control what they think or feel, they always have control over their behavior. A major benefit of this with regard to values is that clients can choose to act in a way that is consistent with their values regardless of how they feel or what thoughts are present. Specifically, and consistent with the gardening metaphor from ACT (Hayes et al., 1999), values can provide a stable guide for clients' choices even in the presence of worry thoughts, unpleasant emotions, low motivation, desires to avoid, or negative self-focused thoughts. It is possible for your client to experience all of these internal states, as well as doubts about their choices, *and* still engage in valued actions.

That said, it is incredibly important when discussing this particular feature of values with your client not to send the message that emotions shouldn't be listened to or regarded. Not only would this message be inconsistent with the theoretical basis of this ERT, it would interfere with all of the progress clients can make when they use their emotions to inform their behaviors and guide their choices. Thus, we recommend tackling the nuances of this issue head-on by clarifying for clients that this particular feature of values is not meant to contradict everything they've learned about the function of emotions, or to imply that they should not pay attention to the information their emotions provide. Rather, this characteristic of values is consistent with many of the skills they've learned that focus on using the information provided by emotions to guide their behavior in an effective way, given their goals and the situation at hand (rather than acting on emotions without thinking).

If clients have questions about this, it can be helpful to refer them back to the skills they learned for determining how to act on the information provided by their emotions in an effective way in the sessions focused on emotional awareness, clarity, and willingness. Specifically, it can be helpful to remind clients that it isn't always effective to act directly on the action urges associated with their emotions, or to act immediately on the information being provided by their emotions. For example, if your client learned that they had to give a formal presentation at work, they could experience a high level of anxiety and related urges to avoid the presentation. In this case, although experiencing anxiety is valid, avoiding the presentation would not be in your client's best interests, especially if they valued sharing knowledge, teaching others, or challenging themselves. Instead, these values would suggest an action counter to the action urge associated with their anxiety: that is, approaching the feared situation and giving the presentation.

Moreover, connecting with their values could also shed light on the specific information being provided by their emotion. In particular, although anxiety signifies that a potential threat is present, connecting with their values could provide more nuanced information about the nature of this threat for your client; that is, that the threat is present precisely because the presentation matters to your client and is consistent with their values. The goal is to assist clients in utilizing both the information provided by their emotions and their values to guide their behaviors, incorporating all of this information to arrive at the most effective choice consistent with building a meaningful life. Table 12.5 provides sample language for having this discussion with your client.

TABLE 12.5. Example Therapist Language: Using Both the Information Provided by Emotions and Values to Guide Choices

You recently brought up a situation where you were experiencing irritation with your children. Let's use that example as a way to demonstrate how you can listen to the information being provided by your emotions *and* take an effective course of action based on your values. You indicated previously that you value having an honest and caring relationship with your children. In the situation you described, your children were being very disruptive and running around the house yelling. Given that you were trying to get some work done at the time, it makes complete sense that you experienced frustration. This emotion was indicating that you had a goal (work) that was being blocked by your children's behavior. Now, in the past, you may have lost your temper and yelled at your children to go to their rooms. Although that behavior may have provided some immediate relief, it would be counter to the relationship you want to develop with your children. Therefore, given the information being provided by your emotions, as well as your value of wanting an honest and caring relationship with your children, it seems like a more effective choice in that moment could involve using your adaptive emotion regulation skills to modulate your frustration so that you could express it more effectively, having a conversation with your children about their behavior and the behavior you'd prefer to see, or even taking a quick break from your work to play with your children before asking them to play quietly in their rooms. In this situation, you would be recognizing your emotions as valid, connecting with the information they provide, and making a choice to act on that information in a way that is consistent with your values.

As you discuss this characteristic of values with your client, it can be helpful to ask them to think of times when they did something that was in line with their values even though they may have been experiencing thoughts or emotions that were motivating avoidance (e.g., going to the dentist, attending therapy, or resisting self-injury).

VALUES CANNOT INVOLVE CONTROLLING INTERNAL EXPERIENCES

It is also important to clarify for clients that values are not about controlling internal experiences. For example, some clients will initially identify values of being happy or not being anxious. Although the desire to feel better is understandable, it is important to remind clients that internal experiences cannot be directly controlled and that values are not about achieving a particular outcome. Thus, statements focused on controlling internal experiences or achieving desired internal states are not values.

VALUES GIVE LIFE MEANING AND DIRECTION

One of the most important points to emphasize when orienting clients to the concept of values is that values give life meaning and direction. It can be helpful to point out to clients that chronic emotional suffering can be an indication that they are not living their lives in a way that is consistent with their values. Ask your client if they ever feel like they are on automatic pilot or disconnected from their life, or if they have lost interest in their life. These experiences can be a sign that they are not acting consistent with their values. Likewise, some clients will report that they feel stuck, or as if they have little control over the direction their life is going. When clients have a longstanding history of making choices to avoid painful emotions and thoughts, or pursuing goals that are not their own or not associated with an underlying value, their life can begin to lose meaning and they are likely to experience increased emotional suffering.

Values provide a solution to this dilemma. They serve as a compass that can assist clients in continuously moving *toward* something that matters to them. Values can also provide clients with a sense of control, agency, and mastery. Moreover, by connecting their values to concrete actions, those actions begin to stand for something greater: building a life worth living. In this way, acting consistent with values also increases the likelihood that clients will come into contact with positively reinforcing experiences. Finally, just as throwing a small stone into a pond will create expanding ripples across the water, engaging in actions consistent with one's values can also have a ripple effect, opening up more and more opportunities for building a meaningful life.

Assisting clients in distinguishing between values and goals can be challenging. To help you with this, table 12.6 provides a list of answers clients may give when asked about their values, along with information on whether these statements reflect values or goals.

TABLE 12.6. Examples of Values and Goals

Statement	Value or Goal
Being genuine and open in relationships	Value
Being compassionate toward myself and others	Value
Being in a relationship	Goal
Helping others	Value
Maintaining a healthy lifestyle	Value
Being curious in life	Value
Visiting a new country	Goal
Being a nurse	Goal
Teaching and mentoring others	Value
Learning new things and challenging myself	Value
Taking a college-level class	Goal
Not being anxious	Unattainable goal

Clarifying Values

Although much of this session is focused on orienting clients to the concept of values, it is important to save time at the end of the session to begin the process of helping clients identify some initial values. Because identifying and clarifying values is a process in and of itself, we do not expect clients to be able to generate a lengthy list of values by the end of this session. However, it can be useful to check in with clients to see if learning about values sparked any ideas about possible values they may have. Assist your client in clarifying their values by reinforcing an open and curious stance toward the process of discovering their values. It can be helpful to ask your client open-ended questions such as "Tell me more about why that matters to you?" "How does that statement fit with the characteristics of values that we discussed?" or "What thoughts and feelings come to mind when you think of that value?" The goal of this discussion is to assist clients in reaching their own conclusions about their values and identifying the values that are meaningful to them personally, rather than suggesting or recommending certain values to clients.

Table 12.7 contains a list of common values that you can use to facilitate this discussion with your client. However, as much as this list can be a helpful resource, it is important to not lean too heavily on this list when assisting clients in identifying their values, as this discussion is most effective when it is driven by your client. Indeed, some clients may be quick to select particular values because of anxiety related to uncertainty about their values or judgments that certain values *should* be endorsed. Therefore, we recommend only sharing the examples in table 12.7 with your client if they can't identify any values and the open-ended questions recommended above aren't effective. In addition, be mindful of your own anxiety if you are not able to assist a client in immediately identifying a value, or if you are not sure if your client is identifying a value or a goal. It can be incredibly helpful and therapeutic to model to your client that uncertainty with the process of identifying values is both acceptable and to be expected,. Even if they aren't sure of the answers or the specific values that matter most to them, your client can still commit to the process of working to clarify their values.

TABLE 12.7. Examples of Values

Being accepting of myself and/or others	Upholding justice
Being curious and explorative	Being an advocate for others in need
Challenging myself to grow, learn, or discover new experiences	Looking at experiences from multiple perspectives (flexibility)
Being compassionate toward myself and/or others	Being nurturing toward myself and/or others
Being authentic or genuine	Being loving and affectionate
Being attentive toward the needs of others	Being assertive
Being creative	Being self-aware
Encouraging others	Being supportive
Being collaborative	Being loyal
Maintaining my physical health	Being open
Maintaining my mental health	Being responsible
Being flexible	Being patient
Being mindful	Being charitable
Savoring life experiences	Sharing knowledge
Being honest with myself and others	Being humble
Being hardworking	Being grateful
Being independent and self-sufficient	Being kind to yourself and/or others

Skill Consolidation and Generalization

There are three outside-of-session exercises for this session that focus on helping clients continue the process of clarifying their values. Each of these can be found at the end of this chapter and downloaded at http://www.newharbinger.com/53622. In the first exercise, Valued Directions: Outside-of-Session Exercise 1 (Identifying the Importance of Valued Domains), clients are presented with different domains of valued directions (for example, family relations, health/physical well-being, etc.) and asked to rate both the importance of each domain to them and the extent to which they have successfully lived their life in accordance with values within this domain. There are two goals for this exercise. The first is to help clients clarify the specific domains that may be most important and meaningful to them, in order to aid them in identifying values within this domain. The second goal is to help clients identify the areas of their life where they may already be engaging in valued actions, as well as areas that may benefit from additional attention.

The second exercise, Valued Directions: Outside-of-Session Exercise 2 (Identifying What Matters to You), is intended to help clients begin the process of identifying valued directions. This exercise (adapted from Orsillo & Roemer 2011, 2016) is a free-writing exercise that is designed to help clients begin to identify the things in life that matter to them the most. It can be helpful to instruct your client to write freely in response to the prompts on this exercise without any concerns about spelling, punctuation, or grammar.

The third exercise, Valued Directions: Outside-of-Session Exercise 3 (Identifying Valued Directions), asks clients to write down specific values they have within different domains. This exercise was adapted from Orsillo and Roemer (2011, 2016). When you orient your client to this exercise, remind them that this process can be challenging and there are no right or wrong answers. The goal of this exercise is simply to begin the process of identifying some values that may be meaningful to them. Let them know that it's okay if they aren't completely certain about a value or how to phrase it; they can just write down whatever comes to mind. It can also be helpful to introduce clients to the concept of "valuing valuing," or the process of being open to discovering their values by approaching their life with curiosity and seeking to discover what matters to them. The goal of this exercise is to begin the process of discovering their values rather than to achieve the end point of clarifying all of their values. Therefore, if they notice during the week that they are getting caught up in a cycle of perfectionism or anxiety about not being able to identify their values, the most helpful strategy is to redirect their attention back to the present moment and connect with a stance of curiosity, openness, self-compassion, and patience with the process.

Finally, clients are asked to continue to complete the same version of the outside- of-session self-destructive behaviors monitoring form they began completing following the session on impulse control, to facilitate further implementation and practice of the impulse control strategies they learned during that session. This monitoring form, Valued Directions: Outside-of-Session Monitoring Form 1 (Self-Destructive Behaviors Monitoring Form), is available for download at http://www.newharbinger.com/53622.

Common Obstacles Encountered During Values Clarification

As we've discussed throughout this chapter, identifying and clarifying values can be a challenging process for clients. The concept of values is novel to most clients and requires a relatively dramatic shift in how they think about moving forward in their lives. Thus, it is common for clients to struggle with identifying values, particularly early on in this process. Some of the most common obstacles we've encountered when delivering this ERT are described in table 12.8, along with effective strategies for addressing these in session.

TABLE 12.8. Common Obstacles Encountered During Values Clarification and Strategies for Addressing these Obstacles in Session

Obstacle	Strategies for Addressing This Obstacle
Clients identify values focused on obtaining or avoiding a particular emotional state	If your client says that they value "being happy" or "not being anxious," balance validation of the desire behind these statements (i.e., to feel better or avoid emotional pain) with a reminder of what they learned in the sessions on emotional willingness, particularly that it isn't possible to directly control emotions and efforts to do so tend to backfire. Then, redirect your client back to the defining characteristics of values. Ask your client what they would choose to do if they were always happy or never felt anxious. Focus on the choices your client identifies and help them identify values that may be driving those choices. Assist your client in recognizing that those choices can be made regardless of their current emotional state.
Clients identify goals versus values	Clarify the differences between a value and a goal. Assist your client in identifying how the example they gave has a particular outcome or end point that can be reached. To clarify the value underlying the goal, ask your client why that goal matters to them and what motivated them to choose that goal.
Clients struggle to identify any values	Early on in the process of clarifying values, it is common for some clients to struggle to identify any values. If your client is struggling to identify any values, remind them that identifying values is a process and is not expected to occur overnight. The simple act of trying to identify their values (including devoting time and energy to this process and considering what matters to them)—even if they are not able to do so immediately—is meaningful in and of itself. Introduce your client to the concept of "valuing valuing," or the process of being open to discovering their values by approaching their life with curiosity and seeking to discover what matters to them.

Obstacle	Strategies for Addressing This Obstacle
Clients identify values focused on the control of others or having others change their behavior	This is another instance when a dialectical stance can be very helpful. We recommend validating your client's desire to change others' behavior *and* also reminding them that they only have control over their own behavior. In situations like this, irreverence and radical genuineness can be particularly effective (e.g., "I really wish there was a way that I had complete control over everyone's behavior—this treatment would be a lot easier!" Unfortunately, though, and much to my chagrin, I can't control other people. All any of us can do is focus on our own behavior). Assist your client in shifting their focus to how they want to act or behave in this relationship. Remind your client that focusing on their values within this relationship could very well have an impact on the other person and facilitate some of the desired behavior change they were hoping for. In other words, even though they cannot directly control or change the behavior of others, acting consistent with their values within these relationships could strengthen the relationships and elicit desired behaviors from others.
Clients identify competing values	Sometimes clients will identify values that initially seem to be in opposition to one another. For example, clients may indicate that they value self-care and being industrious at work. In situations like this, focusing on one of these values may mean that the other has to take a backseat in that moment. That is okay. As we discussed previously, values are a moment-to-moment process, and clients can act consistent with their values in any given moment. Therefore, it's not a concern if there are some times when one value takes priority over another. The key is to ensure that one value doesn't always take priority over the other and that there are still times when your client acts consistent with both values. Thus, we recommend encouraging your client to remain mindful of both values and work to balance the times when they act consistent with each. It can also be helpful to discuss with your client the importance of staying in the present moment so that they are better able to determine what their needs are from one moment to the next and which of their values to prioritize in any moment. Because acting consistent with values is a moment-to-moment process, there is always an opportunity for clients to shift their focus to and from one value to the next given their current needs, circumstances, or opportunities.

Valued Directions: In-Session Handout 1

Valued Directions

What Are Values?

Values are different from goals

- A goal is an outcome (obtain your degree, start a committed relationship)
  - Although goals are helpful, they keep you focused on the future and suggest that where you are in this moment is not good enough
- A value is a process (learning, being supportive, being compassionate)
  - Values are never ending. You can choose to act in accordance with values all the time and in every moment
  - Values are the glue between goals
  - Progress is not linear

Values are personal

- Only you can determine what kind of life you want to live
- Values are flawless

Values are constant

- Values are not chosen in the moment on the basis of reasons or pros and cons
- Values can remain even if reasons change or disappear entirely in a moment
- Values provide guidance and stability
- Values help you choose among options
  - Every choice you make and action you take leads you in a certain direction

Values are defined by actions, not feelings

- You don't have to feel like you want to do something in order to do it
  - You can feel like you don't want to go to therapy and still go
  - You can feel annoyed with your partner and still act lovingly

Why are values important?

- Values give your life meaning
- Values give life direction and something to move toward (rather than away from)
- Values make your actions stand for something

Clarifying Valued Directions in Life

Valued Directions: Outside-of-Session Exercise 1

Identifying the Importance of Valued Domains

Below are ten areas of life that people may consider important. Please rate each area on the following scales:

> ➢ Rate their importance to you on a scale of 1 to 10, with 1 being high importance and 10 being low importance.

> ➢ Rate them again in terms of how successfully you have lived your values in this area over the last month, with 1 being very successfully and 10 being not at all successfully.

Domain	Importance	Success
Intimate Relationships		
Family Relationships		
Social Relationships		
Employment		
Education/Training		
Spirituality		
Health/Physical Well-being		
Emotional Well-being		
Recreation		
Citizenship		

Valued Directions: Outside-of-Session Exercise 2

Identifying What Matters to You

Please set aside twenty minutes of uninterrupted, private time to complete this writing assignment. The goal of this exercise is to explore your feelings and thoughts about the topics listed below. You can think of this writing as capturing your stream of consciousness about the topics. Thus, write whatever comes to mind without worrying about how it sounds or censoring it in any way.

> - If you could let go of all the obstacles that are in your life right now (e.g., being too busy, being anxious, depressed, or stressed out, feeling unmotivated, etc.), what kinds of things would you want to spend your time doing? For instance, would you work on developing or deepening relationships? Do you have career, educational, or volunteerism goals you want to focus on? Are there some leisure activities that you want to develop? Do you want to pursue some spiritual goals?
>   > - Try to pick one or two things that really matter to you—*not* things that your parents, friends, or therapist might want you to pick.
>
> - Express your thoughts and feelings about why those things are so important to you.
>
> - Write about what you think is getting in the way of you doing the things that are most important to you.
>
> - Write about how it feels to not be working on the things that matter most to you in your life.

Valued Directions: Outside-of-Session Exercise 3

Identifying Valued Directions

This exercise is a first step toward identifying your valued directions in life. Unlike goals, which reflect a specific end point (e.g., I want to get my degree or be married), values (e.g., learning, caring for others) cannot be permanently achieved or checked off a list. Instead, values are an ongoing process and can be used to guide your actions in any moment. You can think of values as a compass for moving forward in your life with meaning and direction.

This exercise contains a list of different areas of life that people may value. If you do not have valued directions in certain areas, feel free to skip those. Not everyone has the same values and you are not expected to identify values in all of these domains. The goal of this exercise is simply to begin the process of identifying the things in life that matter to you and some of the values you may hold. If you find that you have similar values in multiple domains, that's okay. Feel free to write them in any area where they are relevant.

1. *Intimate relationships.* Write down a description of the person you would like to be in an intimate relationship. Write down the type of relationship you would want to have. Try to focus on your role in that relationship.

2. *Family relationships.* In this section, describe the type of sibling/child/parent you want to be. Describe how you would treat your family members if you were the "ideal you" in these various relationships.

3. *Friendships/social relationships.* In this section, write down what it means to you to be a good friend. If you were able to be the best friend possible, how would you behave toward your friends? Try to describe your role in an ideal relationship.

4. *Career/employment.* Describe the type of work you would like to do. This can be specific or general. Remember this is in the context of an ideal world. After writing about the type of work you would like to do, write about why it appeals to you. Next, discuss what kind of worker you would like to be with respect to your boss, coworkers, or supervisees.

5. *Education/personal growth and development.* If you would like to pursue education, formally or informally, or pursue some specialized training, write about that. Reflect on why it matters to you.

6. *Spirituality.* This area is not necessarily about organized religion, although it could be. This is meant to capture whatever spirituality means to you, from communing with nature to participating in an organized religion. If this is an important part of your life, write about how you'd like to be in this area and why it matters to you. Otherwise, feel free to skip this section.

7. *Health/physical well-being.* In this section, include your values related to maintaining your physical health and how you'd like to treat your body, including self-care activities.

8. *Emotional well-being.* In this section, include your values related to maintaining your emotional well-being and mental health, such as therapy and self-care.

9. *Recreation/leisure.* Describe the kind of recreational life you would like to have, including hobbies, sports, leisure activities, and fun.

10. *Citizenship.* For some people, participating in their community and supporting causes that matter to them is an important part of life, such as volunteering, being active in politics, or pursuing activities related to social justice. If these types of activities are important to you, write about the direction you would like to take in this area. Write about what appeals to you in this area.

Domain	Values
Couples/Intimate Relationships	
Family Relationships	
Friendship/Social Relationships	
Career/Employment	
Education/Training	
Spirituality	
Health/Physical Well-being	
Emotional Well-being	
Recreation	
Citizenship	

Clarifying Valued Directions in Life

CHAPTER 13

Increasing Valued Actions

As we mentioned in chapter 12, the final active sessions of this ERT (before the sessions focused on relapse prevention and the maintenance of treatment gains) focus on valued directions, with the original group therapy version of this ERT dedicating four sessions to identifying valued directions and increasing valued actions. Following the session focused on identifying values (reviewed in chapter 12), the remaining sessions discussed in this chapter focus on how to translate identified values into effective action. Specifically, in the second session dedicated to values, clients are assisted in identifying discrete doable actions that they can engage in *right now* that are in line with their identified values. In the third session, clients are assisted in identifying barriers to valued action, as well as strategies for effectively navigating and overcoming those barriers. The final session is focused on the concept of commitment from ACT (Hayes et al., 1999) and how it can facilitate valued action.

Even though there is a shift in the sessions reviewed in this chapter from identifying values to putting those values into action, it is important to remember that identifying values is a process. Clients are not expected to have generated a complete list of their values after just one session. Clarifying values takes some time, especially when the concept is new to a client. Therefore, although the focus of the remaining sessions will be on valued actions, it is important to continue to assist clients in identifying and clarifying their values throughout the remainder of this ERT.

Identifying Valued Actions

At the start of the second session focused on values, it is helpful to spend some time reviewing your client's outside-of-session exercises from the previous session, in order to get a better sense of the things in life that matter to your client and the valued directions they identified. We recommend starting by reviewing your client's free-writing exercise (Valued Directions: Outside-of-Session Exercise 2). Often when completing this exercise, clients identify goals they'd like to accomplish if they were able to remove all the barriers from their life. If this occurs, use it as an opportunity to clarify the distinction between goals and values and assist them in identifying the values that may underlie those goals.

During your discussion of this exercise with your client, keep in mind that as helpful as this exercise can be in assisting clients in clarifying their values, it can also be painful for clients to complete. It is common for clients to report that the exercise elicited distress and made them even more aware of how far they are from living the life they want to live. If your client shares a similar sentiment, validate their experience and acknowledge their willingness to come into contact with and express that emotional pain. Then, remind them that the purpose of this exercise was to help them address that very dilemma by beginning the process of building a more meaningful life.

As you review your client's outside-of-session exercises, assist them in identifying one or two values that stand out as most meaningful to them in the moment. Once they've identified one to two values to focus on, inform your client that the next step in this process is to identify the numerous ways in which they could act consistent with those values. Remind your client that there are innumerable ways to act consistent with their values in any moment throughout the day. With this in mind, assist your client in generating a list of as many small, doable actions as possible consistent with their identified value(s) they could take in the next week.

Tips for Assisting Your Client with This Activity

The following key points are important to keep in mind as you assist your client with this activity. First, the longer the list of doable actions your client identifies for each of their values, the better. Brainstorm with your client and share any ideas you have about possible values-consistent actions they could take. It can also be helpful to assist your client in generating possible actions that could be taken in multiple contexts or situations. This will foster flexibility and increase opportunities for valued action.

In addition, it's important to remain mindful of any comments your client makes aimed at minimizing or discrediting small actions. If your client suggests that small actions aren't sufficient or meaningful, remind them that the point of this exercise is to identify *doable* behaviors. For example, if your client identifies a value of "being connected and present with others," one action consistent with that value could be making eye contact during a conversation. Although clients may judge this action as "too easy" or "too small" or "not important," remind them that valued actions are intended to be actions that can be taken in the moment, at any time, to move the client forward in the direction of their values; the more doable, the better.

Another form that the minimization of small actions can take during this activity is the repeated identification of elaborate or extensive actions, such as "meeting five new people next week." If this occurs, ask your client if they are attaching to judgments about small actions or getting caught up in perfectionistic thoughts. Remind your client that not only do small actions count, they can be even more impactful in building a meaningful life than more elaborate actions that requiring planning or multiple steps. Smaller, more doable actions allow your client to incorporate more valued actions into their daily life on an ongoing basis, putting them in greater contact with their values. It may be helpful to remind your client of the ripple effect metaphor from chapter 12, which captures the ever-expanding number of opportunities for engaging in valued actions and building a meaningful life that can stem from taking just one valued action.

Because clients are identifying discrete actions, it is easy for clients (and even clinicians) to get caught up in a goal-oriented mindset during this exercise. Remind clients that the point of this activity is not to identify multiple goals that must be accomplished in the next week. Instead, the main point of this exercise is to demonstrate to clients that there are numerous ways in which they can act consistent with their values in the moment, at any time, starting right now, thereby fostering flexibility. These actions can be viewed as suggestions or intentions. The goal is simply to increase actions consistent with valued directions by engaging in any valued actions, regardless of what those actions are and whether they were planned ahead of time or not. Finally, highlight for your client the values-consistent actions they've already been taking and encourage them to give themselves credit for these actions and to focus on fully participating in these actions and connecting with their meaning when they engage in them in the future.

In-Session Exercise on Valued Actions

After you've assisted your client in brainstorming multiple actions consistent with their values, give your client the worksheet for the in-session exercise aimed at identifying valued actions for the next week, Valued Actions: In-Session Exercise 1 (Identifying Valued Actions). This exercise can be found at the end of this chapter and is available for download at http://www.newharbinger.com/53622. Assist your client in completing this worksheet by selecting five doable actions from the list of valued actions they generated during the previous discussion. Inform your client that this exercise will aid them in completing the outside-of-session exercise for this session and can serve as a guide for engaging in valued actions over the course of the next week. That said, it is also important to remind them that the valued actions they list on this worksheet are best thought of as options or suggestions rather than rigid goals.

Skill Consolidation and Generalization

The primary outside-of-session exercise for this session, Valued Actions: Outside-of-Session Monitoring Form 1 (Monitoring Valued Actions I), assists clients in monitoring their efforts to engage in valued actions on a daily basis throughout the week. This exercise can be found at the end of this chapter and is available for download at http://www.newharbinger.com/53622. If your client plans to focus on more than one value during the week, it can be helpful to provide them with multiple copies of this monitoring form. This form asks clients to monitor engagement in valued actions on a daily basis, including the emotions they experienced when they engaged in valued actions and any barriers they encountered that interfered with valued actions. In addition to this monitoring form, clients are once again asked to complete the same version of the self-destructive behaviors monitoring form they've been completing since the session on increasing impulse control (Valued Actions: Outside-of-Session Monitoring Form 3, available for download at http://www.newharbinger.com/53622).

Identifying and Overcoming Barriers to Valued Actions

At the start of the next session on values, it is important to review your client's experiences engaging in valued actions since the previous session, using the Valued Actions: Outside-of-Session Monitoring Form 1 as the basis for this discussion. Check in with your client about what it was like to focus on engaging in valued actions throughout the week. Did they notice more opportunities to engage in valued actions than they expected throughout the day? Did the process of engaging in valued actions help them clarify or identify values? What emotions did they experience after engaging in valued actions? Did they notice any barriers to valued actions? As you discuss your client's experiences completing this outside-of-session exercise, highlight any barriers they identified and acknowledge how common it is to encounter barriers to valued actions.

Next, use Valued Actions: In-Session Handout 1 (Barriers to Valued Actions) to orient your client to the concept of barriers to valued actions. This handout can be found at the end of this chapter and is available for download at http://www.newharbinger.com/53622. It can be helpful to begin by explaining that these barriers can be organized into two categories: external barriers and internal barriers (Orsillo & Roemer, 2011).

External Barriers

External barriers are barriers that exist outside of the individual, such as situational, interpersonal, or environmental factors. It is reasonable to expect that there could be a number of factors external to your client that could interfere with valued actions, including financial limitations, limited time, a friend cancelling a get-together at the last minute, limited access to resources or services, or lack of transportation.

External barriers can be addressed through basic problem-solving skills. The first step is for clients to clearly define the problem or the barrier they are facing. Then, they can move on to brainstorming possible solutions to the problem. These solutions can take a number of different forms. If the barrier is modifiable or if your client has some level of control over the barrier, they may be able to identify other valued actions they could take in service of addressing or overcoming that barrier. For example, if your client finds that a lack of time is interfering with their valued action of connecting with family or friends, they could identify other actions they could take (for example, setting limits at work, organizing their schedule, or delegating responsibilities) that would free up additional time to spend with their family or friends. In so doing, those additional actions would also be considered valued actions, as they are actions in service of their value of connecting with family or friends. This is an important point to emphasize for clients: even if the actions they take to address external barriers to valued actions don't appear on the surface to be actions consistent with that value, they are indeed valued actions because they are in service of moving forward in that valued direction.

Alternatively, your client could brainstorm other ways of giving expression to that value given the barriers they are facing. This approach can be useful if there is not an immediate solution to an external barrier. For example, your client could make a point to send a quick text message or email to a family member during their lunch break. They could also commit to being present and engaged whenever they have the opportunity to connect with family members. Table 13.1 provides example language for discussing strategies for overcoming external barriers with your client.

TABLE 13.1. Example Therapist Language: Addressing External Barriers
One client who received this treatment identified a value of taking care of herself physically and a valued action of eating healthier food by buying fresh organic vegetables. However, she hadn't realized how expensive it would be to purchase these vegetables. Once she saw the cost, she identified this expense as a financial barrier to this valued action. Therefore, in order to problem-solve this barrier, she explored other options that might be available to her. She looked into farmers' markets and other local stores to see if she could find cheaper options. She also looked up recipes that were healthy but didn't rely heavily on expensive ingredients. She also considered other ways in which she could act consistent with this value of taking care of herself physically, such as by exercising more regularly and going to bed earlier. Finally, she decided that by taking an additional babysitting shift one night a week, she could earn extra money that she could put toward buying healthier food. In the end, problem solving how to address this external barrier opened up a number of other opportunities for valued actions that she hadn't thought of previously. Moreover, although she didn't originally think of babysitting as consistent with her value of taking care of herself physically, it became a valued action because it was in service of that value.

Internal Barriers

Often more common and pervasive than external barriers to valued action are internal barriers. Internal barriers refer to the internal experiences (for example, thoughts, emotions, or physical sensations) of a client that may interfere with valued actions. These are the barriers that most clients will encounter as they begin the process of increasing engagement in valued actions, and the primary reason why these actions can be so challenging for clients. Common internal barriers include shame, guilt, anxiety, self-doubt, worry thoughts, hopelessness, and negative self-judgments.

Once you've introduced your client to the concept of internal barriers, it can be helpful to highlight for them that many of the previous sessions of this ERT have focused on strategies for responding effectively to these internal barriers and, thus, can be used to help them navigate these barriers as they work to incorporate more valued actions into their daily life. Specifically, one of the most effective strategies for addressing internal barriers to valued action is willingness (reviewed in chapter 9).

Remind your client that not only are unpleasant thoughts and emotions an inescapable and natural part of being human, they may be elicited by engagement in valued actions, as the things in life that matter the most to people also bring with them the potential for emotional pain. If something doesn't matter to your client, it is far less likely to bring about emotional distress. The possibility of distress is a sign that whatever your client is doing matters to them.

Finally, revisit the benefits of emotional willingness in the context of valued action, reinforcing the information your client learned about this skill previously. Remind them that practicing willingness of thoughts and emotions provides a way to do the things in life that matter to them no matter what internal experiences are present. In this way, painful thoughts and emotions cease to be barriers to valued action as they can choose to engage in these actions *with* whatever thoughts or feelings are present at the time. We recommend posing the following question from ACT (Hayes et al., 1999) to your client in the context of this discussion: "Can you put your emotions and thoughts in your pocket and carry them with you while you engage in valued action?" This is a helpful heuristic for thinking about how willingness facilitates valued action. In fact, many clients who've received this ERT in the past have found it helpful to concretize this practice by writing out their internal barriers on a sheet of paper and putting it in their pocket while they engage in valued actions.

There are two metaphors that can be used in ERT to illustrate how willingness can be used to address internal barriers to valued action. One of these is described in table 13.2, and the other (the "Bubble in the Road" metaphor from ACT; Hayes et al., 1999) is available for download at http://www.newharbinger.com/53622 in the addendum to table 13.2 (Additional Metaphor for Illustrating the Use of Willingness to Address Internal Barriers to Valued Actions).

TABLE 13.2. Metaphor for Illustrating the Use of Willingness to Address Internal Barriers to Valued Actions

Metaphor	Script
Swamp metaphor (Hayes et al., 1999)	Let's say that you find yourself standing at the bank of a disgusting, smelly, foul swamp. On the other side of that swamp is where you want to go. It's the place with everything that matters to you. You look to your left and to your right, but all you see is the swamp. It goes on forever, so there is no way to get around it. The only way to get to the other side is to walk through the swamp. You look down at the swamp and wonder if you can do it. The water is murky and slimy. You see leeches, bugs, and other creepy-looking animals, and yet the water is so dark and murky that you don't know what else might be lurking beneath the surface. Even so, the only way you'll be able to get to the other side and everything that matters to you is to walk through it. So, you take a deep breath and wade in. As soon as you do, you notice that it really isn't as deep as you thought it would be, and although it is disgusting, the bugs and other animals aren't dangerous. You even start to get used to the foul odor the longer you are in it. So, in the end, as much as you'd prefer not to have to go through the swamp, you are able to do it and it's definitely worth it to get to where you want to go.
	It's important to remember that willingness is not about wanting. If there is a bridge that goes over the swamp and to the other side, then by all means, take the bridge! The idea is not to put ourselves into contact with emotional pain just for the sake of doing so. If you can get to where you want to go without coming into contact with those painful experiences, then definitely do so. The dilemma is that more often than not, there is no way to avoid coming into contact with emotional pain if you are pursuing the life you want to live. Doing the things that matter to you almost always opens up the potential for emotional pain. Therefore, in those moments, the question is whether you let that pain keep you from the life you want or whether you jump into the swamp and move forward to build a life that is meaningful.

Skill Consolidation and Generalization

The outside-of-session exercises for this session expand upon the exercises from the previous session and involve identifying and addressing barriers to valued actions. First, clients are asked to complete a worksheet similar to the in-session exercise they completed during the previous session that assists them in identifying specific doable actions they can take consistent with a value over the course of the next week, Valued Actions: Outside-of-Session Exercise 1 (Overcoming Barriers to Valued Actions). However, this worksheet expands upon the worksheet from the previous session by asking clients to identify and address all of the barriers to these valued actions they could encounter. Specifically, clients are instructed to translate the external barriers they identified into new (modified) valued actions and then rate their willingness to experience the internal barriers. This exercise can be found at the end of this chapter and is available for download at http://www.newharbinger.com/53622.

Likewise, the primary outside-of-session monitoring form for this session, Valued Actions: Outside-of-Session Monitoring Form 2 (Monitoring Valued Actions II), expands upon the valued actions monitoring form from the previous session by asking clients to identify any internal or external barriers they encountered, as well as how they overcame those barriers (or plan to address them in the future). As with the previous valued actions monitoring form, clients are asked to complete this monitoring form on a daily basis for any value they are focused on during the week. This monitoring form can be found at the end of this chapter and is available for download at http://www.newharbinger.com/53622. Finally, clients are once again asked to complete the same version of the self-destructive behaviors monitoring form they've been completing since the session on increasing impulse control (Valued Actions: Outside-of-Session Monitoring Form 3, available for download at http://www.newharbinger.com/53622).

Commitment

The final session dedicated to values in this ERT focuses on commitment as a strategy for facilitating valued action. Given that the goal of all of these sessions is to support clients in moving forward in the process of building a meaningful life by increasing engagement in valued actions, it is helpful to start this session by discussing your client's experiences engaging in valued actions since the last session. Focus this discussion around the different types of barriers your client encountered and the strategies they used to address and overcome those barriers, making sure to reinforce any instances of effective problem solving or emotional willingness.

We recommend focusing this discussion on the process versus outcomes, with an emphasis on recognizing and reinforcing the efforts your client made to address barriers to valued actions and the steps they took consistent with the process of moving in valued directions (even if there were times when they did not overcome the barriers to valued actions or didn't engage in valued actions on some days). Remind your client that even if they miss some opportunities to engage in valued actions, there are an infinite number of opportunities to do so starting in the next moment, and there is meaning and benefit in efforts to overcome barriers to valued actions (even if they are not overcome in that moment). Ask your client what they learned from that experience, and whether they are better equipped to address those barriers in the future. It can also be helpful to highlight how the very act of attempting to overcome barriers to valued actions requires recognition that those actions are worth pursuing and may be considered a valued action in its own right.

Following this discussion, introduce your client to the concept of commitment as a helpful strategy for facilitating valued action when internal barriers seem overwhelming and willingness is low.

Defining Commitment

Just as we recommended when introducing the concept of *values* to clients, we recommend beginning the discussion of commitment by asking clients what comes to mind when they hear the term "commitment." Clients commonly bring up words such as "stuck," "promise," "scary," "never ending," or "attached." Thus, it can be helpful to clarify once again that the term *commitment* means something different in this ERT.

Next, give your client the in-session handout on commitment, Valued Actions: In-Session Handout 2 (Commitment to Valued Actions), and use this to guide your discussion of the definition and meaning of commitment within this treatment. This handout can be found at the end of this chapter and is available for download at http://www.newharbinger.com/53622. There are several key points to emphasize during this discussion. First, similar to the emphasis within values on process versus outcome, the concept of commitment within this ERT refers to the act of committing to the process of engaging in valued actions rather than the specific end point of engaging in a particular valued action. As a result, commitment within ERT involves inherent flexibility and provides clients with multiple ways of honoring their commitment. Specifically, in contrast to committing to a particular action or end point, committing to the process of valued actions frees clients up to engage in any number of actions consistent with their values and can help clients get unstuck from the idea that there is one "right" choice. Moreover, by committing to the process of engaging in valued actions, anything they do in service of a valued direction is consistent with that commitment and moves the client forward in building a meaningful life.

Second, committing to an intention to act versus a particular action also means that clients never lose the opportunity to engage in valued actions. Even if they miss one opportunity, they can commit to engaging in valued action in the next moment, and the moment after that, and so on. Third, commitment is not conditional. It is all or nothing. Commitment only works as a strategy because it is not conditional on the presence or absence of particular emotional states. Rather, clients are asked to commit 100 percent to the process of engaging in valued actions regardless of whatever internal experiences are present at the time. Finally, willingness is a necessary component of commitment, as it involves committing to the process of engaging in valued actions with whatever emotions or thoughts are present at the time. A key point to emphasize in this part of the discussion is that it is possible for clients to *feel* unwilling to do something and yet still *act* willing by making the choice to engage in a valued action regardless of the internal experience at the time.

Strategies for Facilitating Commitment

The last half of the in-session handout on commitment reviews concrete strategies for facilitating commitments. As much as committing to the process of engaging in valued actions is a powerful tool, it isn't easy and can require a dramatic change in the way clients approach internal barriers. Therefore, introducing your client to some practical strategies for "committing to commitment" and practicing this skill effectively can be incredibly helpful. Specific strategies for facilitating commitment and key points to emphasize during the discussion of these strategies with your client are summarized in table 13.3.

TABLE 13.3. Strategies for Facilitating Commitment

1. Ensure that clients commit only to actions that are consistent with their personal values. Clients will be more likely to follow through with a commitment to the process of valued action if they feel connected to that process and find it rewarding.

2. Make sure the actions your client chooses are "doable." Valued actions should be well-defined, simple, and realistic. By focusing on small steps that can be taken at any moment in time, your client will be in a better position to implement valued actions throughout their day and across contexts, as well as to identify multiple opportunities for valued action in any moment.

3. Emphasize the importance of focusing on the present moment and actions that can be taken in each moment. In addition to increasing contact with and awareness of opportunities for engaging in valued actions throughout the day, being present while engaging in valued actions increases the likelihood that clients connect with the naturally reinforcing consequences of valued actions.

4. Have your client write down their commitment and post copies of this list in relevant places, such as their home, work, and car. Clients are more likely to follow through on commitments that are in the forefront of their mind.

5. Have your client identify someone from their social support network who can serve as a commitment "buddy." This person can provide support and increase accountability, especially during moments of unwillingness.

6. Have your client share their commitment out loud to someone else they trust. The simple act of saying a commitment out loud can increase connection to and accountability for the commitment.

7. Encourage your client to reward themselves for following through on a commitment. Maintaining commitments can be challenging. Having clients reward themselves for maintaining commitments can increase their motivation to continue to engage in these actions moving forward.

8. Encourage your client to find meaning in their actions and why they chose to make this commitment to begin with. What is this commitment in the service of? How will this help them build the life they want to live? Encourage clients to connect with the fact that every small step they take consistent with a value reflects progress toward building a meaningful life.

Skill Consolidation and Generalization

The outside-of-session exercise for this session, Valued Actions: Outside-of-Session Exercise 2 (Making a Commitment to Valued Actions), is very similar to the exercise clients completed after the previous session. The only difference is that this version of the exercise capitalizes on the power of the commitment skills clients learned in this session by asking them to commit to engaging in the valued actions they identified *with* whatever emotions or thoughts are present at the time. This exercise can be found at the end of this chapter and is available for download at http://www.newharbinger.com/53622. Likewise, both of the outside-of-session monitoring forms for this session, Valued Actions: Outside-of-Session Monitoring Form 2 (Monitoring Valued Actions II) and Valued Actions: Outside-of-Session Monitoring Form 3 (Self-Destructive Behaviors Monitoring Form), are the same forms clients completed following the previous session.

Valued Actions: In-Session Exercise 1

Identifying Valued Actions

Please choose two values to focus on for the next week:

Value 1: _____

Value 2: _____

Next, develop some "doable" actions that you can engage in this week that are consistent with these valued directions in life. Please list at least five actions per value.

Value:	Actions
	1) 2) 3) 4) 5)

Value:	Actions
	1) 2) 3) 4) 5)

Valued Actions: Outside-of-Session Monitoring Form 1

Monitoring Valued Actions I

Please indicate one of the values you have chosen to focus on this week. Next, reflect on the steps you took each day that were consistent with this value by completing the following monitoring form.

On this form, please indicate what you did (if anything) that was consistent with this valued direction.

> ➤ If you did act in a way consistent with this value, please indicate whether you experienced any emotions in response to engaging in this action. For example, some people find that acting consistent with a value can bring up anxiety (which is one of the reasons why people sometimes avoid acting in valued ways). On the other hand, moving in a valued direction can also result in feelings of pride, joy, or excitement.

> ➤ If you did not act in a way consistent with this value, please reflect on what stopped you from doing so. In particular, did some type of emotional response interfere with you acting in a way consistent with this valued direction? For instance, did anxiety about engaging in the behavior cause you to avoid it?

Chosen value: _____

Date	Did you do anything today that was consistent with this value?	**If yes,** what did you do exactly? Did you experience any emotions in response to this action?	**If no,** what got in the way? What were the barriers to acting in a valued direction?
___/___			
___/___			
___/___			
___/___			
___/___			
___/___			
___/___			
___/___			

Increasing Valued Actions

Valued Actions: In-Session Handout 1
Barriers to Valued Actions

What kinds of things interfere with living a valued life?

External Barriers

- Situational or interpersonal factors that interfere with following through with valued actions

- **Solution:** Problem solving
  - Identify other valued actions that may address the barrier
  - Break down the valued action into smaller steps

Internal Barriers

- Negative emotions (for example, fear, anxiety, shame)

- Unwanted or negative thoughts (for example, "I can't do this.")

- **Solution:** Willingness
  - Can you act *with* these feelings and thoughts?
  - Can you carry these internal experiences with you on your journey?
  - Choose to act no matter what you are feeling
  - By choosing to move forward with your emotions and thoughts, they stop being a barrier to building the life you want to live

Valued Actions: Outside-of-Session Exercise 1

Overcoming Barriers to Valued Actions

Please choose a valued direction to focus on for the next week:

Value: _____

Next, choose some "doable" actions that you could take in your life today—this moment — that would be consistent with this valued direction. First, come up with at least five "doable" actions. Remember to think about small, meaningful steps, rather than large goals. For each action, list all of the obstacles or barriers you think you could encounter. Consider both internal (e.g., fear, shame) and external (e.g., money, time) barriers.

Actions	External Barriers	Internal Barriers
1)		
2)		
3)		
4)		
5)		

> - Next, see if you can translate the external barriers into new actions.
> - Rate your willingness to experience the internal barriers you identified.
> - Make a choice to engage in the modified actions, *with whatever feelings and thoughts you have*.

Modified Actions	Internal Barriers	Willingness (0-100)

Increasing Valued Actions

Valued Actions: Outside-of-Session Monitoring Form 2

Monitoring Valued Actions II

Please indicate one of the values you have chosen to focus on this week. Next, reflect on the steps you took each day that were consistent with this value by completing the following monitoring form.

On this form, please indicate what you did (if anything) that was consistent with this valued direction.

- ➤ If you did act in a way consistent with this value, please indicate what you did and if you experienced any emotions in response.
- ➤ Did you encounter any internal or external barriers to valued action? If so, what were the barriers you encountered?
- ➤ Were you able to overcome these barriers?
- ➤ If yes, write down what you did to overcome these barriers. Specify strategies you used to overcome both external and internal barriers.
- ➤ If no, write down what got in the way of overcoming these barriers. Then write down what you could do to address these barriers in the future.

Chosen value: _____

Date	Did you do anything consistent with this value?	If yes, what did you do? Did you experience any emotions in response?	What internal or external barriers did you encounter?	Were you able to overcome these barriers?	If yes, how did you overcome these barriers?	If no, what got in the way? How could you address these barriers in the future?
__/__						
__/__						
__/__						
__/__						
__/__						
__/__						
__/__						
__/__						

Valued Actions: In-Session Handout 2

Commitment to Valued Actions

Commitment helps you act in valued directions

Commit to act no matter what you are feeling

- ➤ Commitment is about moving in a valued direction, acting in a valued way, *with* whatever feelings you have
- ➤ Willingness is a necessary component
  - ➢ You can *feel* unwilling to do something and still *be willing* to move in a valued direction

Commitment is 100%, all or nothing

- ➤ A commitment cannot be conditional or partial

Commitment is a process, not an outcome

- ➤ You can fully commit to moving in a valued direction
  - ➢ You do not commit to the outcome of that process

Strategies for facilitating commitments

- ➤ Commit to actions that are of value to you, not someone else
- ➤ Make the actions "doable"—stay concrete, simple, and realistic
- ➤ Focus on the present moment and actions you can take now
  - ➢ If you wake up late, start then; if you're behind, begin anyway
- ➤ Write down the commitment and put copies everywhere (e.g., car, home, office, etc.)
- ➤ Get someone to help you—have a commitment "buddy"
- ➤ Commit to someone else, not just yourself (tell others about your commitment)
- ➤ Plan a reward for yourself after you follow through on your commitment
- ➤ Find meaning in the action (e.g., repeat over and over again why you are committing to this, why it matters, etc.)

Valued Actions: Outside-of-Session Exercise 2

Making a Commitment to Valued Actions

Please choose a valued direction to focus on for the next week:

Value: _____

Next, make a commitment to some "doable" actions that you could take in your life today—this moment—that would be consistent with this value. First, come up with at least five "doable" actions. Remember to think about small, meaningful steps, rather than large goals. For each action, list all of the obstacles or barriers you think you could encounter. Consider both internal (e.g., fear, shame) and external (e.g., money, time) barriers.

Actions	External Barriers	Internal Barriers
1)		
2)		
3)		
4)		
5)		

> Next, see if you can translate the external barriers into new actions and rate your willingness to experience the internal barriers you identified.

> Then, make a commitment to engage in the modified actions, *with whatever feelings and thoughts you have.*

Modified Actions	Internal Barriers	Willingness (0-100)

CHAPTER 14

Maintaining Treatment Gains and Preventing Relapse

The final sessions of ERT focus on helping clients consolidate and integrate the skills they learned throughout this treatment, as well as learn new strategies to assist them in maintaining the gains they've made in treatment after the treatment ends. Depending on your client's needs and clinical presentation, you can cover the strategies reviewed in this chapter in one to two sessions. Specifically, rather than teaching clients new emotion regulation skills, the goal of these final ERT sessions is to teach clients strategies for preventing relapse and continuing to improve their emotion regulation moving forward. Indeed, although most clients who receive this ERT experience considerable improvements in all aspects of emotion regulation targeted in this treatment (including emotional acceptance, awareness, understanding, willingness, and modulation, as well as impulse control and valued action), it is important to recognize that these improvements and the changes clients have made in long-standing patterns of emotional and behavioral responding are still at an early stage and, as such, may not be fully integrated into their daily lives. Thus, not only will the skills they learned throughout this treatment require continued practice and integration once this ERT ends, clients may also be at risk for slipping back into previous, less effective patterns of behavior, particularly during challenging, stressful, or high-risk times.

There are several strategies for consolidating skills, maintaining treatment gains, and preventing relapse within this ERT. Each of these will be reviewed here. We recommend reviewing these with your client in the final session(s) of this ERT.

Maintaining a Commitment to Valued Actions

As we described previously in chapters 12 and 13, identifying values is a process. In fact, identifying values can be considered a life-long process. At this stage in this ERT, most clients will have identified a handful of values they can focus on to guide their actions and will be in the process of building the life they want to live. However, the expectation is that clients will maintain a commitment to this process and continue to identify and connect with values long after this treatment ends, allowing them to continue the process of building a meaningful life. To ensure that clients leave this treatment with a commitment to the ongoing work of living a valued life, it can be helpful in this session to reintroduce clients to the concept of valuing the process of valuing. Specifically, we recommend reminding clients to approach their life with openness and curiosity to continue to discover what matters to them and to shed light on values they may not have considered before or realized were important to them. Even in the absence of clear values, the process of discovering values can be a meaningful and reinforcing experience.

It can also be helpful during this discussion to remind your client of the importance of balance and flexibility when acting consistent with valued directions. In particular, we recommend reminding clients that there isn't one right way to act in accordance with their values. Thus, even though different choices may take them down different paths, as long as these choices are guided by their values, they will be beneficial. It can also be useful to reemphasize the importance of balance when it comes to valued actions and to encourage clients to regularly take stock of their different valued domains and their specific values within each domain. Specifically, we recommend reminding your client to periodically assess if certain domains or values are being prioritized for certain reasons, and if others are not being attended to despite their importance. The key is to encourage your client to work toward tending to their values within each domain at some point in the course of living, while also installing flexibility when it comes to emphasizing or deemphasizing certain values at certain times.

Addressing Mood Congruent Behaviors

In the previous sessions on valued actions, clients learned how to identify and address internal barriers to valued actions. One of the goals of this session is to introduce clients to a specific type of internal barrier that can interfere with valued actions: *mood congruent behavior*. The idea behind this concept is that people tend to act in ways that are consistent with their current mood. For example, people in the midst of a depressive episode tend to isolate, and those experiencing chronic anxiety tend to avoid. The reason this is relevant to clients maintaining their treatment gains following completion of this ERT is that many of the behaviors tied to mood states that are likely to be quite common among clients in ERT (specifically, mood states characterized by depression or anxiety) can interfere with valued actions, or at least serve as barriers to these actions.

Therefore, it is important to assist clients in proactively identifying mood states they may experience that could interfere with valued actions in the future, as well as specific strategies for overcoming these internal barriers. Relapse Prevention: In-Session Exercise 1 (Identifying and Addressing Mood Congruent Behaviors) can assist with this. This exercise can be found at the end of this chapter and is available for download at http://www.newharbinger.com/53622. To begin, assist your client in identifying the mood states they are most likely to experience in the future that could serve as barriers to valued actions. These may be mood states your client has experienced in the past, or states associated with their particular clinical difficulties or diagnoses (e.g., depression, anxiety, posttraumatic stress disorder, etc.). Next, work with your client to identify ineffective or maladaptive mood congruent behaviors that may stem from the mood states they entered. Finally, help your client identify strategies for combatting these mood congruent behaviors and engaging in valued actions despite their mood.

One helpful strategy to keep in mind when assisting your client with this exercise is to focus on small, doable, momentary behaviors that are consistent with their values. Remind clients that valued actions don't have to take the form of large, complicated, or time-intensive actions. Even small, quick, low-effort actions are meaningful and move clients forward in the process of building a life worth living. Moreover, engaging in small, doable values-consistent actions can prevent a depressed or anxious mood state from getting worse, as well as put clients in contact with positive reinforcement that may ultimately increase their motivation to continue to engage in valued actions and help the negative mood state pass more quickly.

Other skills clients learned earlier in this treatment can also be helpful for combatting mood congruent behaviors and engaging in valued actions despite negative moods, including the skills they learned for responding more adaptively to judgments about emotions (reviewed in chapter 6), overcoming internal barriers to valued actions (reviewed in chapter 13), and increasing emotional willingness (reviewed in chapter 9). Finally, reminding clients to mindfully engage in valued actions will help them connect with the naturally reinforcing qualities of valued actions, increasing their motivation for these actions and the likelihood they will continue to engage in them.

Identifying and Managing High-Risk Situations

A key strategy of relapse prevention is the proactive identification of high-risk situations in which a client may be at greater risk of returning to old (less effective) patterns of behavior, including engaging in self-destructive behaviors or emotional avoidance. For example, during periods of extreme stress or chaos, clients may feel as if they don't have the time or energy to focus on valued actions or engage in effective emotion regulation skills. It may be easier (or more reinforcing in the moment) to instead fall back into old habits of avoiding emotions, including engaging in self-destructive behaviors that provide temporary but immediate relief from emotional distress. Likewise, there are other situations or experiences that may increase a client's vulnerability for emotion dysregulation and a return to ineffective behavior, such as interactions with particular people, specific work stressors, or even physiological factors such as illness or injury. Because many of these high-risk situations are unavoidable to some extent, it is important for clients to plan ahead for how to cope with these situations in an effective way.

Relapse Prevention: In-Session Exercise 2 (Identifying and Managing High-Risk Situations) can assist with this. This exercise can be found at the end of this chapter and is available for download at http://www.newharbinger.com/53622. To begin, assist your client in identifying high-risk situations (either external events or internal experiences) that may make it more challenging for them to use the skills they learned in this treatment, or that may increase urges to engage in emotional avoidance or self-destructive behaviors. Next, work with your client to identify all of the maladaptive or unhealthy behaviors that they are at risk for in these situations/contexts, such as emotional avoidance, self-destructive behaviors, isolation, lashing out, or secondary emotional responses. Finally, assist your client in identifying strategies for responding effectively to these situations using the skills they learned in this treatment. Additional tips for addressing high-risk situations are presented in Relapse Prevention: In-Session Handout 1 (Managing High-Risk Situations). This handout can be found at the end of this chapter and is available for download at http://www.newharbinger.com/53622.

Rule Violation Effect

The rule violation effect is one of the most helpful concepts to introduce to clients in the context of relapse prevention. It can occur whenever someone attempts to change or stop a behavior, and is driven by the hard-and-fast rules people often make for themselves when attempting to make a behavioral change. Specifically, it is common for people to think that setting rules for themselves about behaviors that they either cannot or must engage in will help them enact the desired behavior change or be motivating in some way. The problem, though, is that these types of rules often backfire and interfere with the very behavior changes the individual is trying to make. Specifically, when someone engages in (or fails to engage in) a behavior that is counter to their rule (which is the most likely outcome, due to both the rigidity and inflexibility of rules and nonlinear nature of behavior change), the rule is considered to be broken. And, this violation of the rule (even if the behavior didn't have any significant negative consequences) can lead people to abandon the rule (and their commitment to the behavior change) altogether. Basically, once the rule has been broken, it can seem as if there is no reason to adhere to it any longer, leading to a paradoxical increase in the behavior the individual was trying to stop (or a paradoxical decrease in a desired behavior the individual was trying to increase).

For example, if your client was trying to reduce binge-eating, they might set a rule for themselves that they cannot eat any sweets at all. However, if they then have one bite of cake at an office birthday party, or one sample of a cookie from their local grocery store, this means that the rule has been violated and, therefore, there's no reason to stop engaging in that behavior. Once the rule has been broken, there is nothing keeping your client from continuing to engage in the behavior, increasing the likelihood of a binge-eating episode. According to their rule, there is no difference between one bite of cake and eating an entire cake, or between having one bite of a cookie and eating an entire package of cookies. This means that what could have been an inconsequential behavior or minor lapse can turn into a much more severe and problematic relapse.

The bottom line is that setting all-or-nothing rules around behavior change establishes a standard of perfection that is nearly impossible for clients to achieve, especially as they are learning new skills and working to change long-standing patterns of behavior. Moreover, when they inevitably break these rules, they are likely to experience guilt, shame, frustration, and/or a sense of failure—all of which could further increase motivation for self-destructive or impulsive behaviors. For these reasons, we recommend reviewing the downsides of these rules and the rule violation effect and encouraging clients to commit to reducing these behaviors and replacing them with valued actions. Committing to the process of changing behaviors (rather than developing all-or-nothing rules around behavior change) fosters flexibility and adaptability and decreases the likelihood that minor slips will turn into more severe instances of the behaviors in question.

Distinguishing a Lapse from a Relapse

When discussing the rule violation effect with your client, it can be helpful to distinguish between a lapse and a relapse. Whereas a *lapse* is a momentary slip or minor instance of a behavior (e.g., having one extra glass of wine for someone trying to reduce their drinking, or scratching their arm with their fingernails for someone trying to reduce cutting behavior), a *relapse* is a full-blown return of an old pattern of behavior. We recommend reminding clients that lapses are likely to occur as they learn new skills for managing their emotions and replacing self-destructive and emotionally avoidant behaviors with more adaptive emotion regulation strategies. Changing long-standing patterns of behaviors and learning new ways of responding to their emotions is a process that takes time and is not expected to occur overnight. Therefore, what matters is not if a slip occurs (which is to be expected), but how they respond to that slip.

Encourage clients to approach a slip as a momentary lapse and then recommit to engaging in valued actions and reducing self-destructive behaviors. It can also be helpful to review with clients other skills they learned in this ERT that can be helpful for preventing a lapse from turning into a relapse. For example, if your client experiences feelings of guilt or frustration in response to a lapse, encourage them to approach those emotions with willingness, identify the information being provided by those emotions, and use that information to guide their behaviors and recommit to reducing self-destructive or emotionally avoidant behaviors. Likewise, if your client experiences self-judgments following a lapse, encourage them to apply the skills they learned for responding to judgments about emotions (reviewed in chapter 6) to these self-judgments, including check the facts, mindfulness, and cognitive defusion. Finally, skills such as consequence modification (reviewed in chapter 11) can assist clients in reducing the impact of a slip and getting back on course.

Recognizing Progress

It is common for clients to minimize their progress and the effective choices they are making and, instead, to focus their attention on ineffective behaviors, missed opportunities for valued action, or lapses. Therefore, it is important to spend time during the last sessions of this ERT assisting clients in recognizing and acknowledging the progress they've made and the skills they are implementing in their lives. Remind your client that changing behavior and how they respond to their emotions is not easy and can be incredibly uncomfortable in the moment. Therefore, it's important that they take a moment to recognize their progress on an ongoing basis and mindfully connect with the experience of implementing new skills, resisting urges to engage in self-destructive or ineffective behaviors, and engaging in valued actions.

Additional Recommendations

Depending on their presenting problems and severity at the start of this treatment, clients can be in different places at the end of this ERT. Whereas some will be implementing the skills they learned regularly and with ease and, thus, will likely feel confident to end treatment, others may still be struggling with the skills and have more anxiety about ending treatment. If your client is anxious about ending treatment, we recommend validating this anxiety. Regular contact with a therapist can provide a sense of security and accountability, in addition to assistance in implementing skills. At the same time, it is important to remind clients that they are the ones responsible for the progress they have made and the positive changes they have made in their lives. If your client continues to express anxiety about the end of treatment, it can be helpful to schedule a couple of booster sessions following treatment, or to spread out the final couple of sessions (for example, schedule them two weeks apart) so that clients get some exposure to what it might be like to not be in treatment each week. Finally, we recommend providing your client with additional copies of the monitoring forms and exercises from this ERT so that they can continue to practice the skills they learned in this treatment on an ongoing basis, as well as monitor their progress.

Relapse Prevention: In-Session Handout 1

Managing High-Risk Situations

Keep this sheet handy and try some of the suggestions below when you notice you are avoiding certain emotions or valued actions, or having urges to engage in self-destructive behaviors. These suggestions can help you increase your willingness to engage in valued action and resist urges for unhealthy behaviors.

- Spend some time thinking about why the valued direction you have chosen matters to you. Find a quiet, comfortable place, close your eyes, and imagine yourself acting in ways that are consistent with this value.

- Think about the times that you have tried to avoid activities or limit your life in order to avoid certain thoughts and feelings. Think about what it has cost you when you have chosen avoidance.

- Think about the times you have tried to avoid or control your emotions in the past. Consider whether that approach has been helpful.

- Read over your handouts from this treatment and think about the concepts that we have discussed such as acceptance, willingness, values, and commitment.

- Choose one emotion regulation strategy or impulse control strategy to practice each week. Practice it when you are feeling overwhelmed or having urges to do something that is not healthy for you. Pick a new one every week to keep things fresh.

- Focus on times you have overcome internal barriers and practiced willingness in the service of engaging in a valued action. Think about what this experience was like, and the positive consequences you experienced as a result.

- Practice observing your emotions and noticing the information they are providing. Think of ways to act on this information in ways consistent with your values.

- Practice self-compassion. Be kind to yourself and focus on all of the progress you have made and all of the steps you have taken that are consistent with your values.

Relapse Prevention: In-Session Exercise 1

Identifying and Addressing Mood Congruent Behaviors

High-risk mood state: What are specific mood states that could serve as barriers to valued actions in the future (e.g., depression, anxiety)?	**Ineffective mood congruent behaviors:** What are the specific mood congruent behaviors that may stem from this mood state and interfere with valued actions (e.g., isolation, avoidance)?	**Strategies to combat ineffective mood congruent behaviors:** Please list specific strategies you could use to combat these mood congruent behaviors and maintain a commitment to valued action.

Maintaining Treatment Gains and Preventing Relapse

Relapse Prevention: In-Session Exercise 2

Identifying and Managing High-Risk Situations

High-risk situation	What maladaptive or unhealthy behaviors are you at risk for in this situation (e.g., emotional avoidance, self-destructive behaviors, isolation)?	What specific skills or strategies could you use to cope with this situation and respond effectively?
External events/situations		
Internal experiences		

Acknowledgments

I am incredibly grateful to the mentors and colleagues who have supported my work on this treatment over the years. First, I would like to express my utmost gratitude to Liz Roemer for her thoughtful and gifted mentorship on acceptance-based behavioral therapies and treatment development. I am also incredibly grateful to John Gunderson for supporting me in securing the funding for the first trial of this emotion regulation therapy and helping to set the stage for all of the work that followed. I would also like to gratefully acknowledge the clients who participated in the first trial of emotion regulation group therapy and whose experiences informed the refinement of this treatment and inspired me to continue to share this therapy with others.

None of our work on the Swedish trials of this treatment or its adaptations for adolescents would have been possible without Lars-Gunnar Lundh, who identified emotion regulation group therapy as an efficacious treatment for self-injury and began our collaboration with the National Self-Injury Project of Sweden and an amazing team of researchers from the Karolinska Institute: Johan Bjureberg, Hanna Sahlin, Brjánn Ljótsson, Erik Hedman-Lagerlöf, and Clara Hellner. We are immensely grateful for their support of and enthusiasm for this emotion regulation therapy, their friendship and ongoing collaborations, and their efforts spearheading the adaptations of this therapy for adolescents. I am also incredibly grateful to Jennye Garibaldi at New Harbinger for her support, dedication, and patience throughout this process, and to Brady Kahn for editorial assistance.

I am also grateful to my parents, Linda and Dave, for their steadfast support, love, and validation throughout my life, and to Sadie and Lily for bringing so much love, joy, and peace to our lives. Sadie in particular remains an exceptional writing companion who motivates me to write for hours without a break. Finally, neither this book nor this treatment would have been possible without my amazing co-author and husband, Matt Tull. I am forever grateful to Matt for his support in developing this treatment, his tireless efforts on the trials for this treatment (including delivering this treatment to numerous clients), and his partnership in training others to deliver this treatment (including multiple trips to Sweden). His collaboration and partnership have made this process far more enjoyable and meaningful, and his unwavering emotional, physical, and culinary support make everything possible. I am immensely grateful to have him as a true partner both professionally and personally.

—Kim L. Gratz

I share with Kim my appreciation for the mentoring and support of Lizabeth Roemer. I am grateful for all the time and energy she devoted and has continued to devote to my professional life and personal growth. I would also like to express my gratitude to our colleagues at the Karolinska Institute. I feel incredibly fortunate to have had the experience of working with and learning from them through the National Self-Injury Project of Sweden and other projects. I am even more grateful that, in our pursuit of meaningful endeavors, we were able to develop friendships that I will always hold dear. I would also like to acknowledge all the clients with whom I worked through the years, especially those in the clinical trials for our emotion regulation group therapy. I am deeply touched by their willingness to share their stories with me and provide me with the opportunity to bear witness to their courage, commitment, and perseverance as they worked toward building the life they wanted to live. It was an honor.

I would also like to express my gratitude to my family. Their love and support is constant, and I appreciate the fact that they have always given me the freedom to choose my own path in life. I am also appreciative of my in-laws, David and Linda Gratz, for their love and support. I am also incredibly grateful for Lily and Sadie. They have been an invaluable addition to my life. They bring me into the present moment and help me connect with joy, love, comfort, and peace.

Finally, I consider it a privilege to be able to write this book with my colleague and wife, Kim Gratz. I would have never taken on such an endeavor without her support. Kim, I am continuously amazed by your brilliance and commitment to your work. Thank you for including me in the process of developing and evaluating this treatment, as well as including me in your life and providing never-ending love, support, and patience. You have made me a stronger researcher, clinician, and human being.

—Matthew T. Tull

References

Abela, J. R., & Hankin, B. L. (2011). Rumination as a vulnerability factor to depression during the transition from early to middle adolescence: A multiwave longitudinal study. *Journal of Abnormal Psychology, 120*(2), 259–271.

Akbari, M., Seydavi, M., Hosseini, Z. S., Krafft, J., & Levin, M. E. (2022). Experiential avoidance in depression, anxiety, obsessive-compulsive related, and posttraumatic stress disorders: A comprehensive systematic review and meta-analysis. *Journal of Contextual Behavioral Science, 24,* 65–78.

Aldao, A., Nolen-Hoeksema, S., & Schweizer, S. (2010). Emotion-regulation strategies across psychopathology: A meta-analytic review. *Clinical Psychology Review, 30*(2), 217–237.

Altman, E. G., Hedeker, D., Peterson, J. L., & Davis, J. M. (1997). The Altman Self-Rating Mania Scale. *Biological Psychiatry, 42*(10), 948–955.

Appleton, A. A., Buka, S. L., Loucks, E. B., Gilman, S. E., & Kubzansky, L. D. (2013). Divergent associations of adaptive and maladaptive emotion regulation strategies with inflammation. *Health Psychology, 32*(7), 748–756.

Arnarson, E. Ö., Matos, A. P., Salvador, C., Ribeiro, C., de Sousa, B., & Craighead, W. E. (2016). Longitudinal study of life events, well-being, emotional regulation and depressive symptomatology. *Journal of Psychopathology and Behavioral Assessment, 38,* 159–171.

Babor, T. F., Higgins-Biddle, J. C., Saunders, J. B., & Monteiro, M. G. (2001). *AUDIT: The Alcohol Use Disorders Identification Test: Guidelines for use in primary health care* (No. WHO/MSD/MSB/01.6 a). World Health Organization.

Baker, T. B., Piper, M. E., McCarthy, D. E., Majeskie, M. R., & Fiore, M. C. (2004). Addiction motivation reformulated: An affective processing model of negative reinforcement. *Psychological Review, 111*(1), 33–51.

Berking, M., Neacsiu, A., Comtois, K. A., & Linehan, M. M. (2009). The impact of experiential avoidance on the reduction of depression in treatment for borderline personality disorder. *Behaviour Research and Therapy, 47*(8), 663–70.

Berman, A. H., Bergman, H., Palmstierna, T., & Schlyter, F. (2007). *DUDIT. The Drug Use Disorders Identification Test–E manual.* Stockholm, Sweden: Karolinska Institutet.

Bjureberg, J., Ojala, O., Hesser, H., Häbel, H., Sahlin, H., Gratz, K. L., et al. (2023). Effect of internet-delivered emotion regulation individual therapy for adolescents with nonsuicidal self-injury disorder: A randomized clinical trial. *JAMA Network Open, 6*(7), e2322069.

Bjureberg, J., Sahlin, H., Hedman-Lagerlöf, E., Gratz, K. L., Tull, M. T., Jokinen, J., et al. (2018). Extending research on Emotion Regulation Individual Therapy for Adolescents (ERITA) with nonsuicidal self-injury disorder: Open pilot trial and mediation analysis of a novel online version. *BMC Psychiatry, 18,* 326.

Bjureberg, J., Sahlin, H., Hellner, C., Hedman-Lagerlöf, E., Gratz, K. L., Bjärehed, J., et al. (2017). Emotion regulation individual therapy for adolescents with nonsuicidal self-injury disorder: A feasibility study. *BMC Psychiatry, 17,* 411.

Borkovec, T. D., & Roemer, L. (1995). Perceived functions of worry among generalized anxiety disorder subjects: Distraction from more emotionally distressing topics? *Journal of Behavior Therapy and Experimental Psychiatry, 26*(1), 25–30.

Brockmeyer, T., Bents, H., Holtforth, M. G., Pfeiffer, N., Herzog, W., & Friederich, H. C. (2012). Specific emotion regulation impairments in major depression and anorexia nervosa. *Psychiatry Research, 200*(2–3), 550–553.

Brockmeyer, T., Skunde, M., Wu, M., Bresslein, E., Rudofsky, G., Herzog, W., & Friederich, H. C. (2014). Difficulties in emotion regulation across the spectrum of eating disorders. *Comprehensive Psychiatry*, 55(3), 565–571.

Bryant, F. B., & Smith, B. D. (2001). Refining the architecture of aggression: A measurement model for the Buss–Perry Aggression Questionnaire. *Journal of Research in Personality*, 35(2), 138–167.

Buckholdt, K. E., Parra, G. R., Anestis, M. D., Lavender, J. M., Jobe-Shields, L. E., Tull, M. T., & Gratz, K. L. (2015). Emotion regulation difficulties and maladaptive behaviors: Examination of deliberate self-harm, disordered eating, and substance misuse in two samples. *Cognitive Therapy and Research*, 39(2), 140–152.

Chambless, D. L., & Gracely, E. J. (1989). Fear of fear and the anxiety disorders. *Cognitive Therapy and Research*, 13, 9–20.

Chapman, A. L., Gratz, K. L., & Brown, M. Z. (2006). Solving the puzzle of deliberate self-harm: The experiential avoidance model. *Behaviour Research and Therapy*, 44(3), 371–394.

Cisler, J. M., & Olatunji, B. O. (2012). Emotion regulation and anxiety disorders. *Current Psychiatry Reports*, 14(3), 182–187.

Dodd, A., Lockwood, E., Mansell, W., & Palmier-Claus, J. (2019). Emotion regulation strategies in bipolar disorder: A systematic and critical review. *Journal of Affective Disorders*, 246, 262–284.

Farmer, R. F., & Chapman, A. L. (2008). *Behavioral interventions in cognitive behavior therapy: Practical guidance for putting theory into action.* Washington, DC: American Psychological Association.

Fergus, T. A., & Bardeen, J. R. (2014). Emotion regulation and obsessive–compulsive symptoms: A further examination of associations. *Journal of Obsessive-Compulsive and Related Disorders*, 3(3), 243–248.

Foa, E. B., Huppert, J. D., Leiberg, S., Langner, R., Kichic, R., Hajcak, G., & Salkovskis, P. M. (2002). The Obsessive-Compulsive Inventory: Development and validation of a short version. *Psychological Assessment*, 14(4), 485–496.

Forbush, K. T., Wildes, J. E., Pollack, L. O., Dunbar, D., Luo, J., Patterson, K., et al. (2013). Development and validation of the Eating Pathology Symptoms Inventory (EPSI). *Psychological Assessment*, 25(3), 859–878.

Garke, M. Å., Isacsson, N. H., Sörman, K., Bjureberg, J., Hellner, C., Gratz, K. L., et al. (2021). Emotion dysregulation across levels of substance use. *Psychiatry Research*, 296, 113662.

Garofalo, C., & Velotti, P. (2017). Negative emotionality and aggression in violent offenders: The moderating role of emotion dysregulation. *Journal of Criminal Justice*, 51, 9–16.

Garofalo, C., Velotti, P., & Zavattini, G. C. (2018). Emotion regulation and aggression: The incremental contribution of alexithymia, impulsivity, and emotion dysregulation facets. *Psychology of Violence*, 8(4), 470–483.

Gioia, F., Rega, V., & Boursier, V. (2021). Problematic internet use and emotional dysregulation among young people: A literature review. *Clinical Neuropsychiatry*, 18(1), 41–54.

Goodman, F. R., Brown, B. A., Silva, G. M., Bradford, D. E., Tennen, H., & Kashdan, T. B. (2022). Motives and consequences of alcohol use in people with social anxiety disorder: A daily diary study. *Behavior Therapy*, 53(4), 600–613.

Goodman, F. R., Kashdan, T. B., & İmamoğlu, A. (2021). Valuing emotional control in social anxiety disorder: A multimethod study of emotion beliefs and emotion regulation. *Emotion*, 21(4), 842–855.

Gratz, K. L. (2001). Measurement of deliberate self-harm: Preliminary data on the Deliberate Self-Harm Inventory. *Journal of Psychopathology and Behavioral Assessment*, 23(4), 253–263.

Gratz, K. L. (2003). Risk factors for and functions of deliberate self-harm: An empirical and conceptual review. *Clinical Psychology: Science and Practice*, 10(2), 192–205.

Gratz, K. L. (2007). Targeting emotion dysregulation in the treatment of self-injury. *Journal of Clinical Psychology, 63*(11), 1091–1103.

Gratz, K. L., Bardeen, J. R., Levy, R., Dixon-Gordon, K. L., & Tull, M. T. (2015). Mechanisms of change in an emotion regulation group therapy for deliberate self-harm among women with borderline personality disorder. *Behaviour Research and Therapy, 65*, 29–35.

Gratz, K. L., Dixon-Gordon, K. L., & Tull, M. T. (2014). Predictors of treatment response to an adjunctive emotion regulation group therapy for deliberate self-harm among women with borderline personality disorder. *Personality Disorders: Theory, Research, and Treatment, 5*(1), 97–107.

Gratz, K. L., & Gunderson, J. G. (2006). Preliminary data on an acceptance-based emotion regulation group intervention for deliberate self-harm among women with borderline personality disorder. *Behavior Therapy, 37*(1), 25–35.

Gratz, K. L., Levy, R., & Tull, M. T. (2012). Emotion regulation as a mechanism of change in an acceptance-based emotion regulation group therapy for deliberate self-harm among women with borderline personality pathology. *Journal of Cognitive Psychotherapy, 26*(4), 365–380.

Gratz, K. L., Moore, K. E., & Tull, M. T. (2016). The role of emotion dysregulation in the presence, associated difficulties, and treatment of borderline personality disorder. *Personality Disorders: Theory, Research, and Treatment, 7*(4), 344–353.

Gratz, K. L., & Roemer, L. (2004). Multidimensional assessment of emotion regulation and dysregulation: Development, factor structure, and initial validation of the difficulties in emotion regulation scale. *Journal of Psychopathology and Behavioral Assessment, 26*, 41–54.

Gratz, K. L., & Tull, M. T. (2010). Emotion regulation as a mechanism of change in acceptance- and mindfulness-based treatments. In R. A. Baer (Ed.), *Assessing mindfulness and acceptance: Illuminating the processes of change*. Oakland, CA: New Harbinger Publications.

Gratz, K. L., & Tull, M. T. (2011). Extending research on the utility of an adjunctive emotion regulation group therapy for deliberate self-harm among women with borderline personality pathology. *Personality Disorders: Theory, Research, and Treatment, 2*(4), 316–326.

Gratz, K. L., & Tull, M. T. (2022). A clinically useful conceptualization of emotion regulation grounded in functional contextualism and evolutionary theory. *World Psychiatry, 21*(3), 460.

Gratz, K. L., Tull, M. T., & Levy, R. J. P. M. (2014). Randomized controlled trial and uncontrolled 9-month follow-up of an adjunctive emotion regulation group therapy for deliberate self-harm among women with borderline personality disorder. *Psychological Medicine, 44*(10), 2099–2112.

Gratz, K. L., Weiss, N. H., McDermott, M. J., Dilillo, D., Messman-Moore, T., & Tull, M. T. (2017). Emotion dysregulation mediates the relation between borderline personality disorder symptoms and later physical health symptoms. *Journal of Personality Disorders, 31*(4), 433–448.

Gross, J. J., & Levenson, R. W. (1997). Hiding feelings: The acute effects of inhibiting negative and positive emotion. *Journal of Abnormal Psychology, 106*(1), 95–103.

Hayes, S. C., & King, G. (2024). Acceptance and Commitment Therapy: What the history of ACT and the first 1,000 randomized controlled trials reveal. *Journal of Contextual Behavioral Science, 33*, 100809.

Hayes, S. C., Luoma, J. B., Bond, F. W., Masuda, A., & Lillis, J. (2006). Acceptance and commitment therapy: Model, processes and outcomes. *Behaviour Research and Therapy, 44*(1), 1–25.

Hayes, S. C., Strosahl, K. D., & Wilson. K. G. (1999). *Acceptance and commitment therapy: An experiential approach to behavior change*. New York: Guilford Press.

Helbig-Lang, S., Rusch, S., & Lincoln, T. M. (2015). Emotion regulation difficulties in social anxiety disorder and their specific contributions to anxious responding. *Journal of Clinical Psychology, 71*(3), 241–249.

Hogarth, L., Hardy, L., Mathew, A. R., & Hitsman, B. (2018). Negative mood-induced alcohol-seeking is greater in young adults who report depression symptoms, drinking to cope, and subjective reactivity. *Experimental and Clinical Psychopharmacology, 26*(2), 138–146.

Horowitz, M. J. (1986). Stress-response syndromes: A review of posttraumatic and adjustment disorders. *Psychiatric Services, 37*(3), 241–249.

Kane, N. S., Hoogendoorn, C. J., Tanenbaum, M. L., & Gonzalez, J. S. (2018). Physical symptom complaints, cognitive emotion regulation strategies, self-compassion and diabetes distress among adults with Type 2 diabetes. *Diabetic Medicine, 35*(12), 1671–1677.

Kashdan, T. B., Goodman, F. R., Machell, K. A., Kleiman, E. M., Monfort, S. S., Ciarrochi, J., & Nezlek, J. B. (2014). A contextual approach to experiential avoidance and social anxiety: Evidence from an experimental interaction and daily interactions of people with social anxiety disorder. *Emotion, 14*(4), 769–781.

Kessler, R. C., Chiu, W. T., Demler, O., & Walters, E. E. (2005). Prevalence, severity, and comorbidity of 12-month DSM-IV disorders in the National Comorbidity Survey Replication. *Archives of General Psychiatry, 62*(6), 617–627.

Khantzian, E. J. (1997). The self-medication hypothesis of substance use disorders: A reconsideration and recent applications. *Harvard Review of Psychiatry, 4*(5), 231–244.

Kim, S. W., Grant, J. E., Potenza, M. N., Blanco, C., & Hollander, E. (2009). The Gambling Symptom Assessment Scale (G-SAS): A reliability and validity study. *Psychiatry Research, 166*(1), 76–84.

Kollin, S. R., Gratz, K. L., & Lee, A. A. (2024). The role of emotion dysregulation in self-management behaviors among adults with Type 2 diabetes. *Journal of Behavioral Medicine, 47*(4), 672–681.

Kwon, M., Lee, J. Y., Won, W. Y., Park, J. W., Min, J. A., Hahn, C., et al. (2013). Development and validation of a smartphone addiction scale (SAS). *PLoS ONE, 8*(2), e56936.

Lane, R. D., & Smith, R. (2021). Levels of emotional awareness: Theory and measurement of a socio-emotional skill. *Journal of Intelligence, 9*(3), 42.

Lavender, J. M., Wonderlich, S. A., Peterson, C. B., Crosby, R. D., Engel, S. G., Mitchell, J. E., et al. (2014). Dimensions of emotion dysregulation in bulimia nervosa. *European Eating Disorders Review, 22*(3), 212–216.

Law, K. C., Khazem, L. R., & Anestis, M. D. (2015). The role of emotion dysregulation in suicide as considered through the ideation to action framework. *Current Opinion in Psychology, 3*, 30–35.

Linehan, M. M. (1993a). *Cognitive behavioral treatment of borderline personality disorder*. New York: Guilford Press.

Linehan, M. M. (1993b). *Skills training manual for treating borderline personality disorder*. New York: Guilford Press.

Linehan, M. M. (2015). *DBT skills training manual* (2nd ed.). New York: Guilford Press.

Lovibond, S. H., & Lovibond, P. F. (1995). *Manual for the depression anxiety stress scales*. Sydney, Australia: Psychology Foundation.

Mattick, R. P., & Clarke, J. C. (1998). Development and validation of measures of social phobia scrutiny fear and social interaction anxiety. *Behaviour Research and Therapy, 36*(4), 455–470.

McCoy, K., Fremouw, W., Tyner, E., Clegg, C., Johansson-Love, J., & Strunk, J. (2006). Criminal-thinking styles and illegal behavior among college students: Validation of the PICTS. *Journal of Forensic Sciences, 51*(5), 1174–1177.

Mennin, D. S., Heimberg, R. G., Turk, C. L., & Fresco, D. M. (2002). Applying an emotion regulation framework to integrative approaches to generalized anxiety disorder. *Clinical Psychology: Science and Practice, 9*(1), 85–90.

Messman-Moore, T. L., Walsh, K. L., & DiLillo, D. (2010). Emotion dysregulation and risky sexual behavior in revictimization. *Child Abuse & Neglect, 34*(12), 967–976.

Metalsky, G. I., & Joiner, T. E. (1997). The Hopelessness Depression Symptom Questionnaire. *Cognitive Therapy and Research, 21*(3), 359–384.

Miola, A., Cattarinussi, G., Antiga, G., Caiolo, S., Solmi, M., & Sambataro, F. (2022). Difficulties in emotion regulation in bipolar disorder: A systematic review and meta-analysis. *Journal of Affective Disorders, 302*, 352–360.

Moore, K. E., Clemens, K. S., Gratz, K. L., & Tull, M. T. (2022). Treatment-relevant factors among adults receiving court-mandated substance use treatment: The role of emotion dysregulation. *Psychological Services, 21*(1), 155–165.

Orsillo, S. M., & Roemer, L. (2011). *The mindful way through anxiety: Break free from chronic worry and reclaim your life*. New York: Guilford Press.

Orsillo, S. M., & Roemer, L. (2016). *Worry less, live more: The mindful way through anxiety workbook*. New York: Guilford Press.

Osman, A., Bagge, C. L., Gutierrez, P. M., Konick, L. C., Kopper, B. A., & Barrios, F. X. (2001). The Suicidal Behaviors Questionnaire-Revised (SBQ-R): Validation with clinical and nonclinical samples. *Assessment, 8*(4), 443–454.

Paulus, D. J., Heggeness, L. F., Raines, A. M., & Zvolensky, M. J. (2021). Difficulties regulating positive and negative emotions in relation to coping motives for alcohol use and alcohol problems among hazardous drinkers. *Addictive Behaviors, 115*, 106781.

Pfohl, B., Blum, N., St. John, D., McCormick, B., Allen, J., & Black, D. W. (2009). Reliability and validity of the Borderline Evaluation of Severity Over Time (BEST): A self-rated scale to measure severity and change in persons with borderline personality disorder. *Journal of Personality Disorders, 23*(3), 281–293.

Pontes, H. M., & Griffiths, M. D. (2016). The development and psychometric properties of the Internet Disorder Scale–Short Form (IDS9-SF). *Addicta: The Turkish Journal on Addictions, 3*(2), 1–16.

Prefit, A. B., Candea, D. M., & Szentagotai-Tătar, A. (2019). Emotion regulation across eating pathology: A meta-analysis. *Appetite, 143*, 104438.

Racine, S. E., & Wildes, J. E. (2013). Emotion dysregulation and symptoms of anorexia nervosa: The unique roles of lack of emotional awareness and impulse control difficulties when upset. *International Journal of Eating Disorders, 46*(7), 713–720.

Roemer, L., Salters, K., Raffa, S. D., & Orsillo, S. M. (2005). Fear and avoidance of internal experiences in GAD: Preliminary tests of a conceptual model. *Cognitive Therapy and Research, 29*, 71–88.

Rosenfarb, I. S., Hayes, S. C. & Linehan, M. M. (1989). Instructions and experiential feedback in the treatment of social skills deficits in adults. *Psychotherapy: Theory, Research, and Practice, 26*, 242–251.

Sahlin, H., Bjureberg, J., Gratz, K. L., Tull, M. T., Hedman, E., Bjärehed, J., et al. (2017). Emotion regulation group therapy for deliberate self-harm: A multi-site evaluation in routine care using an uncontrolled open trial design. *BMJ Open, 7*(10), e016220.

Sahlin, H., Bjureberg, J., Gratz, K. L., Tull, M. T., Hedman-Lagerlöf, E., Bjärehed, J., et al. (2019). Predictors of improvement in an open-trial multisite evaluation of emotion regulation group therapy. *Cognitive Behaviour Therapy, 48*(4), 322–336.

Salters-Pedneault, K., Tull, M. T., & Roemer, L. (2004). The role of avoidance of emotional material in the anxiety disorders. *Applied and Preventive Psychology, 11*(2), 95–114.

Shear, M. K., Brown, T. A., Barlow, D. H., Money, R., Sholomskas, D. E., Woods, S. W., et al. (1997). Multicenter collaborative panic disorder severity scale. *American Journal of Psychiatry, 154*(11), 1571–1575.

Sloan, E., Hall, K., Moulding, R., Bryce, S., Mildred, H., & Staiger, P. K. (2017). Emotion regulation as a transdiagnostic treatment construct across anxiety, depression, substance, eating and borderline personality disorders: A systematic review. *Clinical Psychology Review, 57*, 141–163.

Smout, M., Davies, M., Burns, N., & Christie, A. (2014). Development of the Valuing Questionnaire (VQ). *Journal of Contextual Behavioral Science, 3*(3), 164–172.

Spitzen, T. L., Tull, M. T., & Gratz, K. L. (2022). The roles of emotion regulation self-efficacy and emotional avoidance in self-injurious thoughts and behaviors. *Archives of Suicide Research, 26*(2), 595–613.

Spitzer, R. L., Kroenke, K., Williams, J. B., & Löwe, B. (2006). A brief measure for assessing generalized anxiety disorder: The GAD-7. *Archives of Internal Medicine, 166*(10), 1092–1097.

Squires, L. R., Hollett, K. B., Hesson, J., & Harris, N. (2021). Psychological distress, emotion dysregulation, and coping behaviour: A theoretical perspective of problematic smartphone use. *International Journal of Mental Health and Addiction, 19*, 1284–1299.

Stepp, S. D., Scott, L. N., Morse, J. Q., Nolf, K. A., Hallquist, M. N., & Pilkonis, P. A. (2014). Emotion dysregulation as a maintenance factor of borderline personality disorder features. *Comprehensive Psychiatry, 55*(3), 657–666.

Stern, M. R., Nota, J. A., Heimberg, R. G., Holaway, R. M., & Coles, M. E. (2014). An initial examination of emotion regulation and obsessive compulsive symptoms. *Journal of Obsessive-Compulsive and Related Disorders, 3*(2), 109–114.

Tangney, J. P., & Tracy, J. L. (2012). Self-conscious emotions. In M. Leary and J. P. Tangney (Eds.), *Handbook of self and identity* (2nd ed.). New York: Guilford Press.

Tull, M. T., & Gratz, K. L. (2008). Further examination of the relationship between anxiety sensitivity and depression: The mediating role of experiential avoidance and difficulties engaging in goal-directed behavior when distressed. *Journal of Anxiety Disorders, 22*(2), 199–210.

Tull, M. T., Rodman, S. A., & Roemer, L. (2008). An examination of the fear of bodily sensations and body hypervigilance as predictors of emotion regulation difficulties among individuals with a recent history of uncued panic attacks. *Journal of Anxiety Disorders, 22*(4), 750–760.

Tull, M. T., & Roemer, L. (2007). Emotion regulation difficulties associated with the experience of uncued panic attacks: Evidence of experiential avoidance, emotional nonacceptance, and decreased emotional clarity. *Behavior Therapy, 38*(4), 378–391.

Tull, M. T., Vidaña, A. G., & Betts, J. E. (2020). Emotion regulation difficulties in PTSD. In M. T. Tull and N. A. Kimbrel (Eds.), *Emotion in posttraumatic stress disorder: Etiology, assessment, neurobiology, and treatment*. London, UK: Academic Press.

Turchik, J. A., & Garske, J. P. (2009). Measurement of sexual risk taking among college students. *Archives of Sexual Behavior, 38*(6), 936–948.

Twohig, M. P., Levin, M. E., & Ong, C. W. (2021). *ACT in steps: A transdiagnostic manual for learning acceptance and commitment therapy*. New York: Oxford University Press.

Vine, V., & Aldao, A. (2014). Impaired emotional clarity and psychopathology: A transdiagnostic deficit with symptom-specific pathways through emotion regulation. *Journal of Social and Clinical Psychology, 33*(4), 319–342.

Waldrop, A. E., Back, S. E., Verduin, M. L., & Brady, K. T. (2007). Triggers for cocaine and alcohol use in the presence and absence of posttraumatic stress disorder. *Addictive Behaviors, 32*(3), 634–639.

Weathers, F. W., Litz, B. T., Keane, T. M., Palmieri, P. A., Marx, B. P., & Schnurr, P. P. (2013). *The PTSD Checklist for DSM-5 (PCL-5)*. US Department of Veterans Affairs.

Wegner, D. M., Schneider, D. J., Carter, S. R., & White, T. L. (1987). Paradoxical effects of thought suppression. *Journal of Personality and Social Psychology, 53*(1), 5–13.

Weiss, N. H., Sullivan, T. P., & Tull, M. T. (2015). Explicating the role of emotion dysregulation in risky behaviors: A review and synthesis of the literature with directions for future research and clinical practice. *Current Opinion in Psychology, 3*, 22–29.

Wierenga, K. L., Lehto, R. H., & Given, B. (2017). Emotion regulation in chronic disease populations: An integrative review. *Research and Theory for Nursing Practice, 31*(3), 247–271.

Williams, A. D., Grisham, J. R., Erskine, A., & Cassedy, E. (2012). Deficits in emotion regulation associated with pathological gambling. *British Journal of Clinical Psychology, 51*(2), 223–238.

Yuan, Y., Schreiber, K., Flowers, K. M., Edwards, R., Azizoddin, D., Ashcraft, L., et al. (2024). The relationship between emotion regulation and pain catastrophizing in chronic pain patients. *Pain Medicine, 25*(1), 468–477.

Index

A

acceptance. *See* emotional acceptance

acceptance and commitment therapy (ACT), 37; "Million Dollars to Fall in Love" metaphor, 106–107; "Path Up the Mountain" metaphor, 147–148; "Polygraph Test" metaphor, 106–107; "Skiing" metaphor, 146–147; taking step back from negative beliefs, 60; "Tug-of-War with a Monster" metaphor, 109–110

acceptance-based emotion regulation therapy (ERT), 8–15; empirical support for, 11–14; theoretical basis, 8–10; using flexibly in treatment, 14–15

acceptance-based language, modeling in session, 37–38

acceptance-based stance toward emotions, modeling, 32–37

acceptance-based themes, emphasizing throughout treatment, 39–44; avoiding emotions has paradoxical consequences, 39–40; emotional willingness is optional, 41; emotion regulation doesn't mean controlling emotions, 40; emotions are functional, 39; emphasis on process vs. outcome, 41–42

ACT. *See* acceptance and commitment therapy

actions. *See* valued actions

adaptive strategies. *See also* approach strategies; distraction strategies: defined, 9; removing positive consequences of impulsive behaviors, 138

adolescents, ERT for, 10–12

Aggression Questionnaire, 28

Alcohol Use Disorder Identification Test, 28

all-or-nothing rules, 184

Altman Self-Rating Mania Scale, 30

anger: action urges associated with, 58; information provided by, 57, 74; as primary and secondary emotion, 86; prompting events and components, 68; substitute strategies to obtain relief from, 125

"Annoying Joe" metaphor, 111–112

anxiety: Depression Anxiety Stress Scales, 31; disorders related to, 18–19, 21; distinguishing from fear, 72; ending treatment and, 185–186; goals and, 145; information provided by, 73–74; as internal barrier, 168; mood congruent behavior, 182; as primary and secondary emotion, 86; values and, 149, 152, 155

approach strategies. *See also* emotion modulation: avoidance vs., 120; to beliefs about emotions, 61, 63; distraction strategies vs., 122–123; identifying, 123–124; lapse in behavior, 185; replacing avoidance with, 124–125; responding to clear and cloudy emotions, 93; responding to primary and secondary emotions, 85, 87

assessing progress, 26–31; best practices for, 30–31; treatment progress measures, 27–30

avoidance. *See* emotional avoidance

awareness. *See* emotional awareness

B

barriers to valued actions, 166–170; external, 167–168; internal, 168–169; skill consolidation and generalization, 170

behavioral component, of emotions, 67

behavioral substitution, 134

bipolar disorder, 20

blended emotions, 69

Borderline Evaluation of Severity over Time self-report measure, 30

borderline personality disorder, 17–18

C

clarity. *See* emotional clarity

clear emotions: distinguishing from cloudy emotions, 89–99; effective responses to, 92–93

clients: assisting to identify functions of self-destructive behaviors, 48; introducing concept of emotional willingness to, 109–110; orienting to ERT treatment, 50; teaching emotional acceptance skills to, 62–65

clinicians (therapists), 168; addressing external barriers, 168; on constancy of values, 150; guiding discussion on emotional awareness, 71; guiding discussion on emotional willingness, 101; guiding discussion on negative beliefs about emotions, 55; identifying negative beliefs about emotions, 35–37; introducing emotional willingness, 109; modeling acceptance-based approach emotions, 38; teaching consequence modification, 139; using information provided by emotions and values to guide choices, 152

cloudy emotions: adaptive responses to, 93; distinguishing from clear emotions, 89–99; effective responses to, 92–93; factors that cloud emotions, 91–92

cognitive component, of emotions, 67

cognitive defusion, 60–61

commitment, 170–180; defining, 171; maintaining to valued actions, 181–182; skill consolidation and generalization, 173–180; strategies for facilitating, 172

components of emotions: increasing awareness of, 70–72; psychoeducation on, 67

consequence modification, 135–139

control behaviors, 102

controlling emotions. *See* emotional control

C-reactive protein, 21

D

DBT. *See* dialectical behavior therapy

DBT Skills Training Manual, Second Edition (Linehan), 54

decision-making (choices): role of values in, 149–150; using information provided by emotions and values to guide, 152

delay strategies, for impulse control, 132–133

Deliberate Self-Harm Inventory, 28

Depression Anxiety Stress Scales, 29

Depression Symptom Index-Suicide Subscale, 29

DERS (Difficulties in Emotion Regulation Scale), 15, 26–27

diabetes (type 2 diabetes), 21

dialectical behavior therapy (DBT), vii, 37, 53; check the facts, 60; PLEASE skills, 93

differentiated emotions, 69

Difficulties in Emotion Regulation Scale (DERS), 15, 26–27

disgust: action urges associated with, 58; information provided by, 57

disorders: bipolar disorder, 20; borderline personality disorder, 17–18; eating disorders, 20–21; generalized anxiety disorder, 18; major depressive disorder, 19; obsessive-compulsive disorder, 19; panic disorder, 18; posttraumatic stress disorder, 20; social anxiety disorder, 19; substance use disorders, 21; symptoms, 29–30

distraction strategies. *See also* emotion modulation: approach strategies vs., 122–123; avoidance vs., 14, 120–123; goal of, 40; identifying, 123–124; for impulse control, 132–133; replacing avoidance with, 124–125; when to begin teaching, 118

Drug Use Disorder Identification Test, 28

dysregulation. *See* emotion dysregulation

E

eating disorders, 20–21

Eating Pathology Symptoms Inventory, 28

embarrassment, 58

emotional acceptance, 53–65; judgments about emotions, 53–61; negative beliefs about emotions, 53–56; psychoeducation on function and utility of emotions, 56–59; responding to secondary emotions, 85; skill consolidation and generalization, 61–62; teaching clients emotional acceptance skills, 62–65

emotional avoidance: approach strategies vs., 120; consequences of, 39–40, 101–103; difficulty identifying emotions and, 69; disorders and, 18–20; distraction strategies vs., 120–123; identifying avoidance strategies, 124; psychoeducation on reasons for, 103–104; reinforce material from previous sessions, 102; replacing with distraction strategies, 124–125; short-term vs. long-term consequences of, 104, 107–108; subtle and overt attempts, 102

emotional awareness, 66–80; importance of, 14–15; increasing awareness of components of emotions, 70–72; levels of, 67–70; psychoeducation on, 67–70; responding to emotions, effectively, 72–75; skill consolidation and generalization, 76–80 emotional clarity, 89–99; effective responses to clear and cloudy emotions, 92–93; psychoeducation on clear vs. cloudy emotions, 89–91; psychoeducation on factors that may cloud emotions, 91–92; skill consolidation and generalization, 93–94

emotional control: consequences of, 101–103; metaphors for paradoxical consequences of, 106–107; paradoxical consequences of, 105–107; short-term vs. long-term consequences of, 104; "White Bear" exercise, 105

emotional pain, emotional suffering vs., 40, 84

emotional suffering, 40–41

emotional unwillingness: consequences of emotional avoidance/control, 101–103; decreasing, 101–108; learning consolidation, 108; paradoxical consequences of emotional control, 105–107; psychoeducation on reasons for emotional avoidance, 103–104

emotional willingness, 100–117; chosen in any moment, 111; decreasing emotional suffering, 112–113; increasing, 109–117; introducing clients to concept of, 109–110; not about liking or pursuing emotional pain, 111–112; not about resignation or giving up, 111; as optional, 41; positive effect of clinicians' modeling of, 38; psychoeducation on, 110–113; skill generalization and consolidation of increasing, 113–117

emotion dysregulation: anxiety disorders, 18–19; defining, 8; eating disorders, 20–21; identifying target behaviors, 22–25; mood disorders, 19–20; physical health problems, 21; posttraumatic stress disorder, 20; self-destructive and maladaptive behaviors, 16–18; substance use disorders, 21; symptoms and target behaviors driven by, 16–25; tracking target behaviors throughout ERT, 25

emotion modulation, 118–130; framework for conceptualizing strategies, 119–122; identifying effective strategies, 123–124; psychoeducation on role of context in, 122–123; replacing unhealthy with adaptive strategies, 124–125; review of previously used strategies, 119; skill consolidation and generalization, 125–130

emotion regulation: different from controlling emotions, 40; sharing struggles with, 38

emotion regulation group therapy (ERGT). See group ERT

emotions. *See also* emotional clarity; primary emotions; secondary emotions: components of, 67, 70–72; expressing, identifying healthy ways of, 74–75; functions of, 39, 56–59; modeling acceptance-based stance toward, 32–37; negative beliefs about, 53–60; responding effectively to, 72–75; as universal and evolutionarily adaptive, 56

empirical support for ERT, 11–14; empirically-supported versions of ERT, 10–11; mechanism of change, 13–14; predictors of treatment response, 14; treatment outcomes, 11–13

ERGT (emotion regulation group therapy). *See* group ERT

escaping emotions. *See* emotional avoidance

exercises, psychoeducation, 35–36. *See also* in-session exercises; outside-of-session exercises

F

face-to-face treatment, 10, 12–13

failure, feelings of: all-or-nothing rules and, 184; emotional control and, 107–108; "Path Up the Mountain" metaphor, 147–148

fear: action urges associated with, 58; distinguishing from anxiety, 72; information provided by, 57; as primary and secondary emotion, 86; prompting events and components, 68

flexibility: commitment and, 171; individual ERT and, 15; process-focus vs. outcome-focus, 148; relapse prevention and, 184; valued actions and, 165–166; valued directions and, 182

functional analysis, 22–25; consequences of target behavior, 24–25; identifying target behavior, 22–23; preceding factors to target behavior, 23–24; vulnerability factors for target behavior, 24

functions of emotions, 56–59; communicating to others, 59; deepening experience of life, 59; helping respond quickly, 59; preparing for action, 58; providing information about environment, 57–58

future, imagined events, 91

G

Gambling Symptom Assessment Scale, 28

generalized anxiety disorder, 18, 29

goals: emotional control, 103; future-focused nature of, 145; negative consequences of, 145; values vs., 145–146, 154, 159

good behavior, rewarding, 136

Gratz, K. L., 9

group ERT, 1, 15, 121; for adolescents, 10; emotional awareness, 66; emotional clarity, 81; emotional willingness, 100; overview, 10–11; valued actions, 144, 164

guilt: action urges associated with, 58; distinguishing from shame, 72; information provided by, 58; as internal barrier, 168; as primary and secondary emotion, 86; prompting events and components, 68

H

handouts, psychoeducation: emotional acceptance, 53, 56, 64; emotional awareness, 66–67, 70, 73, 76–78; emotional clarity, 82, 85, 89, 91, 95–96; emotional willingness, 103, 107, 111, 114–115; emotion modulation, 119, 123, 126; impulse control, 131–132, 140–141; relapse prevention, 183, 187; target behavior functions, 49, 52; valued actions, 167, 171, 176; valued directions, 145–146, 159

happiness. *See* joy/happiness

helplessness, 145

high-risk situations, 183

hopelessness: emotional unwillingness and, 101; goals and, 145; as internal barrier, 168

I

Illegal Behavior Checklist, 29

immediacy, sense of, 132

impulse control, 131–143; behavioral substitution, 134; consequence modification, 135–139; distraction and delay strategies, 132–133; impulsive behaviors, 132, 134–135; removing, 136; skills consolidation and generalization, 139–143

inadequacy, feelings of, 108

in-session exercises: emotional acceptance, 63; emotional awareness, 70, 79; emotional clarity, 87, 97; emotional willingness, 101, 116; emotion modulation, 123–124, 127–128; impulse control, 132–133, 135, 142–143; relapse prevention, 182–183, 188, 189; target behavior functions, 47–49, 51; valued actions, 166, 174; valued directions, 142–143

internal barriers, to valued actions, 176

Internet Disorder Scale--Short Form, 28

JKL

joy/happiness: action urges associated with, 58; information provided by, 57; as primary and secondary emotion, 86; prompting events and components, 68

judgments about emotions: identifying, 53–56; stepping back from, 59–61

language: addressing external barriers, 168; constancy of values, 150; ERT-consistent therapeutic statements, 42; ERT-inconsistent therapeutic statements, 43–44; identifying information provided by emotions, 73; introducing emotional willingness, 109; nonjudgmental language when discussing emotions, 33–35; using information provided by emotions and values to guide choices, 152

lapse, 184–185

life, quality of, 30

"Lighthouse in a Storm" metaphor, 151

M

major depressive disorder, 19

maladaptive behaviors, 16–18; assessing treatment progress, 27–29; borderline personality disorder, 17–18

mechanism of change, 13–14

metaphors: "Annoying Joe" metaphor, 111–112; "Lighthouse in a Storm" metaphor, 151; "Million Dollars to Fall in Love" metaphor, 106–107; "Path Up the Mountain" metaphor, 147–148; "Polygraph Test" metaphor, 106–107; "Skiing" metaphor, 146–147; "Swamp" metaphor, 169; "Swimming in a Riptide" metaphor, 113; "Tug-of-War with a Monster" metaphor, 109–110

"Million Dollars to Fall in Love" metaphor, 106–107

mindfulness-based language, modeling in session, 37–38

Miola, I., 20

modulation. *See* emotion modulation

monitoring: consequences of target behavior, 50–52; participants, 50–52

mood congruent behaviors, 182–183, 188
mood disorders, 19–20; bipolar disorder, 20; major depressive disorder, 19

N

negative beliefs about emotions, 54–55
normalizing beliefs and emotions, 42, 54, 62, 76, 94, 103

OPQ

obsessive-compulsive disorder, 19
Obsessive Compulsive Inventory-Revised, 29
Orsillo, S. L., 156
outside-of-session exercises, 143; emotional acceptance, 61, 65; emotional awareness, 76, 80; emotional clarity, 88, 93, 98–99; emotional willingness, 108–109, 113, 117; emotion modulation, 125, 129–130; impulse control, 139; target behavior functions, 50; valued actions, 166, 170, 177, 180; valued directions, 156, 160–163; valued domains, 160
pain, emotional, 40, 84
panic disorder, 18
Panic Disorder Severity Scale, 29
"Path Up the Mountain" metaphor, 147–148
perfectionism, 38, 156, 165, 184
physical/bodily component, of emotions, 67
physical health problems, 21
physical health symptoms, 30
PLEASE skills, 93
"Polygraph Test" metaphor, 106–107
posttraumatic stress disorder, 20
precipitants, monitoring, 50–52
predictors of treatment response, 14
pride, 58
primary emotions: adaptive responses to, 87; distinguishing from secondary emotions, 81–89; effectively responding to, 85–87; secondary emotions linked to, 87–88
progress: assessing, 26–31; recognizing, 185–189
psychoeducation. *See also* exercises, psychoeducation; handouts: on clear vs. cloudy emotions, 89–91; on components of emotions, 67; on emotional avoidance, 103–104; on emotion modulation, role of context, 122–123; on factors that cloud emotions, 91–92; on function and utility of emotions, 56–59; on functions of emotions, 56–59; on levels of emotional awareness, 67–70; on paradoxical consequences of emotional control, 107–108; on primary vs. secondary emotions, 82–83; on utility of emotions, 56
psychological disorder symptoms, 29–30
PTSD Checklist for the DSM-5, 30
quality of life, 30

R

randomized controlled trials (RCTs), 11–13
regulation. *See* emotion regulation
relapse, preventing, 181–189; addressing mood congruent behaviors, 182–183; identifying and managing high-risk situations, 183; maintaining commitment to valued actions, 181–182; recognizing progress, 185–189; recommendations, 185–189; rule violation effect, 184–185
rewarding good behavior, 136
Roemer, L., 9, 156
rule-governed behavior, 55
rule violation effect, 184–185
rumination, 19, 20

S

sadness: action urges associated with, 58; information provided by, 57; as primary and secondary emotion, 86; prompting events and components, 68
secondary emotions: adaptive responses to, 87; avoidance and, 102; becoming escalating cycle, 83; distinguishing from primary, 81–89; effectively responding to, 85–87; as emotional responses to primary emotions, 82; identifying, 84–85; increase emotional suffering, 83; linking to primary emotions, 87–88; as not functional, 83; skill consolidation and generalization in identifying, 88; teaching to deal with, 89
self-care, cloudy emotions and, 91
self-destructive behaviors, 16–18; assessing treatment progress, 27–29; borderline personality disorder, 17–18; consequences of, 47–51; identifying functions of, 47–48; psychoeducation on functions of, 49–50
self-doubt, as internal barrier, 168

self-efficacy: avoidance and, 108; defined, 102; emotion modulation and, 118; goals and, 145; values and, 146

self-judgments, 62, 94; avoidance and, 102; lapses in behavior and, 185

self-medication hypothesis, 21

self-punishment, 75, 137–138

self-report measures: psychological disorders, 29–30; self-destructive and other maladaptive behaviors, 28–29

sense of immediacy, 132

Sexual Risk Survey, 28

shame: all-or-nothing rules and, 184; cloudy emotions and, 94; distinguishing from guilt, 72; emotional awareness and, 67; as internal barrier, 168; as primary and secondary emotion, 86–87; unique example of, 75

"Skiing" metaphor, 146–147

Skills Training Manual for Treating Borderline Personality Disorder (Linehan), 53–54

Smartphone Addiction Scale, 28

social anxiety disorder, 19, 21

Social Phobia Scale, 29

substance use disorders, 21

suffering, emotional, 40–41

Suicidal Behaviors Questionnaire—Revised, 29

surprise, 57–58

"Swamp" metaphor, 169

"Swimming in a Riptide" metaphor, 113

T

target behaviors: identifying emotion-regulating function of, 46–52; identifying for ERT, 22–25; identifying functions of self-destructive behaviors, 47–48; monitoring consequences of, 50–52; orienting clients to ERT treatment, 50; psychoeducation on functions of self-destructive behaviors, 49–50; tracking throughout ERT, 25

theoretical basis of ERT, 8–10

therapeutic stance, 32–44; emphasizing acceptance-based themes throughout treatment, 39–44; modeling acceptance-based stance toward emotions, 32–37; modeling mindfulness- and acceptance-based language in session, 37–38; sharing struggles with emotion regulation, 38

treatment: addressing mood congruent behaviors, 182–183; emphasizing acceptance-based themes throughout, 39–44; identifying and managing high-risk situations, 183; maintaining commitment to valued actions, 181–182; maintaining treatment gains, 181–189; outcomes, 11–13; recognizing progress, 185–189; recommendations, 185–189; response predictors, 14; rule violation effect, 184–185; using ERT flexibly, 14–15

"Tug-of-War with a Monster" metaphor, 109–110

U

unprocessed or unacknowledged emotions, 92

unwillingness. *See* emotional unwillingness

V

valued actions, 164–180; barriers to, 166–170; commitment, 170–180; identifying, 164–166; maintaining commitment to, 181–182; purpose of, 165

values: as alternatives to goals, 145–146; clarifying, 154–155; constant, 149–151; and controlling internal experiences, 153; as defined by actions vs. feelings, 151–153; examples of, 155; give life meaning and direction, 153–154; goals vs., 154, 159; as moment-to-moment process, 146–149; obstacles during clarification of, 157–163; as personal, 149; "valuing valuing" concept, 156

vulnerability factors, 24

WXYZ

"White Bear" exercise, 105

willingness. *See* emotional willingness

worry, 168. *See also* anxiety

Kim L. Gratz, PhD, is a senior clinical quality manager and clinical lead of the dialectical behavior therapy (DBT) program at Lyra Health. She also holds an appointment in the department of psychology at the University of Toledo, where she previously served as professor and chair. She has received multiple awards for her research on emotion regulation, personality disorders, and self-injury; and has authored more than 250 peer-reviewed publications and eight books on borderline personality disorder (BPD), self-injury, and DBT.

Matthew T. Tull, PhD, is a clinical quality supervisor at Lyra Health, and also holds an appointment in the department of psychology at the University of Toledo. Tull's research and clinical work emphasize the role of emotion regulation in anxiety disorders; trauma and stressor-related disorders; and high-risk behaviors such as substance use, self-injury, and suicide. His work has been recognized through awards from the Association for Behavioral and Cognitive Therapies, and the International Society for Traumatic Stress Studies.

Foreword writer **Steven C. Hayes, PhD,** is Nevada Foundation Professor in the department of psychology at the University of Nevada, Reno. He has been president of numerous professional organizations, and is author of nearly fifty books and more than 700 articles and book chapters. Hayes is originator and codeveloper of acceptance and commitment therapy (ACT), a powerful therapy method that is useful in a wide variety of areas.

Real change *is* possible

For more than fifty years, New Harbinger has published proven-effective self-help books and pioneering workbooks to help readers of all ages and backgrounds improve mental health and well-being, and achieve lasting personal growth. In addition, our spirituality books offer profound guidance for deepening awareness and cultivating healing, self-discovery, and fulfillment.

Founded by psychologist Matthew McKay and Patrick Fanning, New Harbinger is proud to be an independent, employee-owned company. Our books reflect our core values of integrity, innovation, commitment, sustainability, compassion, and trust. Written by leaders in the field and recommended by therapists worldwide, New Harbinger books are practical, accessible, and provide real tools for real change.

Join the New Harbinger Clinicians Club— Exclusively for Mental Health Professionals

In our ongoing dedication to supporting you and your essential work with clients, we created the **New Harbinger Clinicians Club—** an entirely free membership club for mental health professionals.

Join and receive these exclusive club member benefits:

- A special welcome gift
- 35% off all professional books
- **Free client resources for your practice**—such as worksheets, exercises, and audio downloads
- Free e-books throughout the year
- Access to private sales
- A subscription to our *Quick Tips for Therapists* email program, new book release alerts, and e-newsletter
- Free e-booklets of the most popular *Quick Tips for Therapists*
- Surveys on book topics you'd like to see us publish, and resources you're looking for to better serve your clients

Join the New Harbinger Clinicians Club today at
newharbinger.com/clinicians-club

MORE BOOKS from NEW HARBINGER PUBLICATIONS

INTEGRATING MINDFULNESS INTO PSYCHOTHERAPY FOR TRAUMA

A Clinician's Guide to Using Mindfulness Processes to Facilitate Healing and Reduce Suffering

978-1648484650 / US $64.45

CONTEXT PRESS
An Imprint of New Harbinger Publications

ACT-INFORMED EXPOSURE FOR ANXIETY

Creating Effective, Innovative, and Values-Based Exposures Using Acceptance and Commitment Therapy

978-1648480812 / US $64.95

CONTEXT PRESS
An Imprint of New Harbinger Publications

GETTING UNSTUCK IN ACT

A Clinician's Guide to Overcoming Common Obstacles in Acceptance and Commitment Therapy

978-1608828050 / US $34.95

TRAUMA-FOCUSED ACT

A Practitioner's Guide to Working with Mind, Body, and Emotion Using Acceptance and Commitment Therapy

978-1684038213 / US $64.95

CONTEXT PRESS
An Imprint of New Harbinger Publications

THE EMOTIONALLY FOCUSED THERAPY WORKBOOK FOR ADDICTION

How to Heal the Loneliness and Shame That Trigger Addictive Behaviors

978-1648482403 / US $25.95

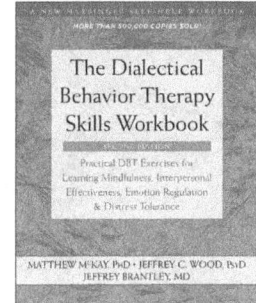

THE DIALECTICAL BEHAVIOR THERAPY SKILLS WORKBOOK, SECOND EDITION

Practical DBT Exercises for Learning Mindfulness, Interpersonal Effectiveness, Emotion Regulation, and Distress Tolerance

978-1684034581 / US $24.95

newharbingerpublications
1-800-748-6273 / newharbinger.com

(VISA, MC, AMEX / prices subject to change without notice)

Follow Us

QUICK TIPS for THERAPISTS

Written by leading clinicians, Quick Tips for Therapists are free e-mails, sent twice a month, to help enhance your client sessions.

Visit **newharbinger.com/quicktips** to sign up today!

Did you know there are **free tools** you can download for this book?

Free tools are things like **worksheets**, **guided meditation exercises**, and **more** that will help you get the most out of your book.

You can download free tools for this book—whether you bought or borrowed it, in any format, from any source—from the New Harbinger website. All you need is a NewHarbinger.com account. Just use the URL provided in this book to view the free tools that are available for it. Then, click on the "download" button for the free tool you want, and follow the prompts that appear to log in to your NewHarbinger.com account and download the material.

You can also save the free tools for this book to your **Free Tools Library** so you can access them again anytime, just by logging in to your account! Just look for this button on the book's free tools page.

+ Save this to my free tools library

If you need help accessing or downloading free tools, visit **newharbinger.com/faq** or contact us at **customerservice@newharbinger.com**.